Blackness and La Francophonie:

Anti-Black Racism, Linguicism
and the Construction and Negotiation
of Multiple Minority Identities

T0345301

AMAL MADIBBO

Blackness and La Francophonie:

Anti-Black Racism, Linguicism and the Construction and Negotiation of Multiple Minority Identities

Presses de l'Université Laval

Financé par le gouvernement du Canada
Funded by the Government of Canada

Nous remercions le Conseil des arts du Canada de son soutien.
We acknowledge the support of the Canada Council for the Arts.

Conseil des arts   Canada Council
du Canada   for the Arts

Les Presses de l'Université Laval reçoivent chaque année de la Société de développement des entreprises culturelles du Québec une aide financière pour l'ensemble de leur programme de publication.

SODEC
Québec

Révision linguistique : Linda Arui

Mise en pages : Diane Trottier

Maquette de couverture : Laurie Patry

Dépôt légal 4ᵉ trimestre 2021

ISBN : 978-2-7637-5577-9
ISBN PDF : 9782763755786

Les Presses de l'Université Laval
www.pulaval.com

To Mathieu Da Costa, the icon of French/
Canadian nationhood, and to the Black Pioneers
of Alberta who echoed his courage, paving the way
for my generation and many others.

TABLE DES MATIÈRES

ACKNOWLEDGEMENTS

The research participants exemplified "experiential knowledge," for they provided narratives that teach us how to construct and negotiate identities in inclusive ways. The research assistants did more than "assist," since they helped me reconceptualize my own thinking. Anne Robineau and Éric Forgues, the editors of Les Presses de l'Université Laval's Collection Langues officielles et sociétés, volunteered their expertise and time to provide constructive and competent feedback that improved the manuscript. Great thinkers and souls of our time, Professors James Frideres, Kenise Kilbride and Daniel Béland provide me with unequivocal intellectual and human support. My aunt/mother Safia Tawfiq Salih Gibreil, who left on May 19 2019, offered me the wisdom to navigate diasporas. The Black Francophones and Sudanese help me capture the intricacies of being Black and Francophone in Canada.

FOREWORD

by Professor Afua Cooper

Killam Professor of Black Canadian History and the African Diaspora
Director: A Black People's History of Canada Research Project
Dalhousie University

W hat does Blackness in Canada mean? What is its make-up? What are its dimensions and textures? What are the lived experiences of Blackness? Does Blackness have a specific geography? a particular language? Is Blackness a blessing or a curse?

Dr. Amal Madibbo has taken us on a journey of multiple Blacknesses in this ground-breaking and judicious monograph *Blacks and La Francophonie: Anti-Black Racism, Linguicism, and the Negotiation of Multiple Minority Identities*. Viewed through the lens of historical sociology, critical race theory, and critical ethnography, she documents how particular inter-sectionalities work to disadvantage, and also empower Black people, in this case, Black Albertans who also share a Francophone identity. Thus, she provides insightful answers to the questions posed.

This work contributes to our knowledge and understanding of Black Canadian history and sociology. It buttresses other works that lay out the facts and trajectories of the 400-year plus experience of Black Canadians. Usually, our study and research of Black history follows a particular direction. It usually begins in Nova Scotia around 1604, followed by the period of enslavement, then by the narratives of Black Loyalists, the Jamaican Maroons, and the refugees of the War of 1812. Quebec is then covered, but solely during the period of enslavement, the first phase of which ended in 1760 at the Conquest, and the second phase which lasted until 1834, when slavery was officially abolished. Ontario is then studied, with the period of the Underground Railroad (1818 to 1861) covered extensively. The researcher then moves on to British Columbia, and trains their lens on the Black community from California who arrived in Victoria in 1858. The focus then jumps back east, this time to Alberta (perhaps Saskatchewan and Manitoba), and the Black collective dubbed the "Black Pioneers" who arrived in the first two decades of the 20th century is given attention. Some discussion may also be given to Black cowboys, John Ware in particular, who arrived in the declining decades of the 19th century.

Most of these historical inquiries rarely address the middle and latter decades of the 20th century, and most are placed in the linguistic frame of English. In other words, most of the Black Canadians written about are English speakers, whether they immigrated to Canada or lived there for several generations. Therefore, studies of English-speaking Blacks have dominated Black Canadian historiography and research.

Dr. Amal Madibbo has resisted that impulse by placing Black African Francophones under her scholarly lens, and then temporally privileging the last half of the 20th century and the early decades of the 21st century. As a result, she has squarely and firmly placed Black Francophones as a significant group in the mainstream of Black Canadian scholarship.

History, to which I will return later, is consistently deployed in this work. And it is with this instrument that Madibbo begins her work. She documents that, historically, Francophones, in this case Whites, who originally came from the province of Quebec and Europe, were the first Europeans to enter and settle in what is now Alberta. They arrived, settled and worked there during the 18th and 19th centuries. They went from having a majority European settler status, where their language and religion were recognized, to a minority identity status, a situation which was solidified by the 1920s, in which the French language and the Catholic religion were marginalized. For example, French was excluded from the province's official language framework, and Catholicism bore the brunt of discrimination, especially from the Orange Order. For all intents and purposes, Francophones suffered linguistic and religious discrimination.

However, they eventually deployed what the author calls "strategic nationalism." They organized themselves politically, and demanded and won certain rights, especially language rights and the right to educate themselves and their progeny in the French language. In so doing, Madibbo argues, they created a "Francophone space" within the province. Thus, by 1990, Francophones in Alberta could be said to have achieved certain key rights.

Strategic nationalism was bolstered by the civil rights movement of the 1950s and 1960s, the decolonization movement in the Global South, the nationalist uprising in Quebec in the 1960s and 1970s, and the change in Canada's immigration policy in 1962, a policy which disavowed Canada's sole preference for those of White heritage to include racialized peoples from the Caribbean, Africa, and Asia, who had been deemed undesirable for immigration to Canada. The agitation of Francophones in Alberta was further aided by the passing by the federal government of the *Official Languages Act* in 1969. This Act gave French equal status with English as an official language of Canada.

It is argued and shown that race played a huge role in Alberta's Francophones gaining acceptance and winning the rights that had been denied them. For one, in the colonial discourse, the French are conceptualized as one of the founding peoples of Canada. Though, as Anglos gained dominance in the Canadian political and economic space, especially after the Conquest in 1760, and certainly by 1840, Francophones were relegated to a secondary tier in the pyramidical structure of Canadian identity. But their role and status as a founding people could not be refuted. Secondly, as the province of Alberta, carved out of the Northwest Territory, became increasingly hostile to Black migration, in fact to all migration of racialized peoples, and subjugated Indigenous nations through warfare and other pernicious measures and marginalized their communities, Whiteness became a measure. Though Ukrainians and other Central and Southern Europeans were not seen as "top" Whites, their Whiteness and European heritage gave them a favoured spot in the Canadian racial hierarchy. They could be assimilated into Anglo cultures, a situation that the rulers of society felt could not happen for Black people because of their skin colour and African heritage. Thus, disabilities Central and Southern Europeans may have suffered at the beginning of their migration and settlement eventually disappeared as they gained acceptance in the dominant Albertan culture, which was White and Anglo.

Race then became a salient factor in determining Canadian identity, and how that identity has been articulated. The case of Black Francophones in Alberta is instructive.

Black people have been living in Alberta and the Prairies as a whole from the era of the fur trade during the 18th and 19th centuries. Many of these early Blacks were men who travelled with White French men from Quebec in the pursuit of this particular economic endeavour. Not a few were enslaved. A concerted Black migratory effort began in the latter part of the 19th and early part of the 20th centuries by African Americans from Texas, Oklahoma, Kansas, and other American plain states. Some were cowboys like John Ware, others were farmer-emigrants like the collective led by Rev. Henry Sneed, who journeyed from Oklahoma. By 1912, at least 1,500 African Americans had crossed the border into Alberta intent on making new lives for themselves.

But this move was quickly quashed by local individual White Albertans, organizations, women's groups, and the federal government itself, which eventually passed legislation to stop the immigration of Black people (from anywhere in the world) to Alberta. Blacks were seen as undesirable, and unassimilable. Added to that was the eugenic discourse popular at the time, in which Blacks were theorized as biologically inferior. It was not until 1962, with the liberalization of Canada's immigration policy, that a steady migration of Black people to Alberta began in earnest.

Two points stand out in all of this. White Francophones in towns like Morinville joined other Whites in opposing Black migration, and in implementing racist practices against Black immigrants, as Madibbo points out. In the half century after 1962, Blacks arrived from other parts of the French-speaking world, especially Africa, claiming a Francophone identity.

Black Francophones stepped into a space in which they experienced anti-Black racism on two counts: within the English-dominated public space and within the Francophone space. Their Francophone status did not shield them from racism, even as they experienced discrimination from the wider society as Blacks and as Francophones. Because of anti-Black racism, Black Francophones in Alberta and elsewhere were prevented from leveraging their Francophone status to gain certain rights and privileges accorded to their White counterparts. This was/is because, in Alberta and elsewhere, La Francophonie has been defined as White. Blacks and other racialized Francophones are therefore excluded from this definition. The irony is this: it is the migration of French-speaking Blacks that enlarged the Francophone space in Alberta—the Francophone community has grown and continues to grow because of Black migration.

The racism Black Francophones experience in Alberta ties in with the wider experience of Black people all across Canada. In the Blackness in Canada Project, carried out by York University professor Lorne Foster, 70% of Blacks, the highest among racialized groups, reported facing racism on a regular basis. Furthermore, Statistics Canada's police-reported hate crime report for 2019 informs us that Black people were the "most targeted group overall" for that year. In other words, Blacks endured the most police-reported hate crime in Canada.

The two reports just mentioned hint that, in some quarters, Black people are not seen as belonging to Canada, and that they suffer gross alienation. The experience of Black Albertan Francophones, documented by Dr. Madibbo, corroborates these findings.

Madibbo is hopeful, however. She pins her hope on the fact that Black Francophones are resisting and challenging anti-Black racism and the alienation they suffer in both the Anglophone and Francophone contexts. Every demographic sector in the Black Francophone community is organizing itself, within and outside the White-dominated Francophone space. The challenge by Black Francophones to Whites with respect to Black History Month bears this out.

The author documents that Black Francophones themselves use history as a tool of resistance to fight and challenge the racial discrimination they suffer. This discrimination results in feelings of unbelonging, which is a form of alienation. One way that history is deployed is by celebrating and commemorating Black History Month. This event by the way was denied by the mainstream Alberta Francophone organization as not being of importance to La Francophonie, since La Francophonie is defined in a way that excludes Blacks and other racialized Francophones.

Not only do Black Albertan Francophones memorialize Black History Month, they recall African history, Black liberation movements, and Black intellectuals—Francophones and others—in their struggle. The writings, voices, and theories of intellectual Frantz Fanon provide inspiration and impetus for Black Francophones. Madibbo herself is a child of Fanon, deeming his work, especially *Black Skin, White Masks,* central to critical race theory and in trying to make sense of what is happening to Black Francophones in Alberta. Her discussion about the objectification of Black people by Whites, and the ensuing alienation that Blacks suffered and endured, owes much to Fanon's work.

But back to history. Fanon posits, and Madibbo agrees, that it is through history that oppressed people can counter alienation and objectification and bring themselves into a conscious and empowered selfhood. And Black Francophones in Alberta are doing just that. "We have been here for a long time; we have contributed to this country and province; and we belong here too; this is our place," declares the Black Francophonie.

Dr. Madibbo's dual dedication is a deployment of history as an instrument of resistance and defiance. The work is dedicated to Mathieu Da Costa and the Black Pioneers of Alberta. Da Costa looms large in Black Canadian history and in the Black imaginary as a founding Black Canadian ancestor. Documents point to his presence here in 1608, as a translator/linguist for the French. Da Costa was an African who lived at numerous intersections. Described as a Portuguese African, he also spoke French—in fact, he was contracted to work for the French during the early colonial period as a linguist, translator and cultural broker with the Mi'kmaq nation. Yes, he also spoke Mi'kmaq. And Dutch. He was either kidnapped or pressured by the Dutch at one point to work for them in Canada.

So here we have an early progenitor of Blackness right from the very point that the land space we now call Canada was coming into being. This is certainly problematic if one thinks that Da Costa was helping the colonial project. At the same time, the last we heard of him was that he was jailed in Amsterdam for "insubordination" to his White employers. Thus, even as Da Costa walked in "colonial company," his subordinate status as a Black African was used against him.

Nonetheless, Madibbo challenges the notion of a White Francophonie by stating that it was a Black man who from the early beginnings of Canada was among those who initiated the building of a Francophone space. How ironic then that this space has evolved as White. This insight is significant.

The Black Pioneers of Alberta are also acknowledged as Black Canadian forebears. Their lives in Alberta are a study in racism and Black resistance. Their presence in the province fuelled White supremacists from the government to the lowliest yeoman in a successful campaign to ban Black immigrants and remove those who arrived. Yet the few hundred who did manage to make it into the province built institutions to serve the needs of the community. They also created organizations that challenged White supremacy and anti-Black racism through lawsuits, petitions, and other means. As a foundational Black group in the province of Alberta, the Black Pioneers remain iconic and inspiring.

Black Francophones are creating new communities of resistance in Alberta. They have redefined what it means to be Francophone, and they are also writing and shaping Black history. While White people have seen Blackness as a curse, Blacks themselves have seen it as a beautiful blessing. In putting Black Francophones under her scholarly lens and centring their voices, Madibbo gives visibility to this community by documenting the saliency of their struggles and victories.

This is a cogent meditation on Blackness in Canada. One that is multilayered, textured, imaginative, fresh, and bold. By steering away from the usual Anglo-dominated narratives of Blackness, Madibbo has broken the silence of this particular form of alienation. *Blackness and La Francophonie* is a manifesto of empowerment.

CHAPTER 1
INTRODUCTION

"[C]reate a new kind of nation, and a new kind of national story. A story that accommodates all of us" (Adrian Harewood 2004).

CONTEXT

A central feature of identity is that it is constructed and negotiated in order to express its meaning and determine the place that identity groups occupy in society. Identity construction is the "creation, formulation, and expression of . . . identities" (Rummens 2003, 22) and encompasses the social, political, and cultural interpretations that describe it. While identity negotiation is "the political nature of . . . identification . . . between or among, and by or within groups" (Rummens 2003, 22) and encapsulates discursive and practical strategies that enhance or refute identity construction, these dynamics are not neutral, since they are imbued with relations of power in the form of dominance and resilience (Kenny 2004). They reveal the extremes of the two main approaches to conceptualizing identity, the primordial and constructivist perspectives on identity (Isajiw 1993). The primordial perspective considers identity in an essentialist manner, as being fixed, permanent, and a matter of genealogical inheritance (Korostelina 2007), while the constructivist approach considers identity a socially constructed category that is changing and evolving. In the process, complementary, dichotomous, or even conflicting perceptions of identity surface, as social actors define their belongingness and negotiate it to find a place for themselves in society. Dominant groups construct identities by assigning differential meanings to establish who is part of the

1

nation and who is not, construing positive perceptions about themselves and imposing negative connotations on marginalized groups to exclude them from the realm of belongingness. Dominant groups negotiate identities through the inclusion of some groups in the social fabric and the marginalization of others. Marginalized groups construct identities by redefining their meaning in positive ways, and negotiate them by taking social and political action to ensure the equitable distribution of social resources. Therefore, access to societal resources, or lack thereof, is a crucial facet of identity because, as Stuart Hall (2000) puts it, "identity has determinate conditions of existence including the material and symbolic resources required to sustain it" (17). Societal resources serve to maintain the privilege and power of the dominant groups, while disadvantaging minority groups.

In this book, I delve into the complexity of identity by analyzing three identities that first-generation Black-African[1] Francophone[2] immigrants from Sub-Saharan Africa residing in the province of Alberta, Canada, constructed and negotiated. These are Canadian, Francophone, and Black-African affiliations, which I explore through the meanings the research participants ascribed to them, and juxtaposed these meanings with the dominant perceptions associated with these identities. In addition, I explore how these meanings are negotiated and how they impact the lives of the Black-African Francophones. In so doing, I shed light on the role that identity attributes, namely race and language, and to some extent ethnicity and religion, play in the construction and negotiation of the three identities. I draw on the criterial tradition, critical race theory (Gillborn 2006), critical multiculturalism (May & Sleeter 2010), and critical ethnography (Madison 2012) to investigate the topic. A critical reading of the literature on immigration and La Francophonie allowed me to put forth the racism and linguicism that Black-African Francophones are subjected to. Two qualitative research methods (Berg & Lune 2012), semi-structured interviews and document gathering, and the interpretation of the data through the

---

1.   I use the signifier "Black-African" because the research participants utilized it to identify themselves in order to associate Blackness with African-ness.
2.   The mainstream Francophone discourse uses two terms to identify French speakers in Canada: Francophone and French Canadian. The term Francophone alludes to all French-speaking people regardless of their background, while the identifier French Canadian refers to white French-speaking people of French origin. I employ the term Francophone because it is more inclusive than French Canadian. I only utilize this latter notion in contexts where I specifically allude to white French-speaking people.
      I use the term "white" in lower case letters as an act of resistance to refute white privilege embedded in this socially constructed racial category.

use of content analysis (Denzin & Lincoln 2011) allowed me to analyze the narratives of the research participants and draw on their perspectives to suggest ways to enhance the inclusion of Black-African Francophones in La Francophonie and Canadian society as a whole.

In regard to Canadian identity, on the one hand, its construction and negotiation revolve around dominance that privileges some groups while excluding others. On the other hand, these aspects of identity corroborate marginalized identity groups' protest against identity exclusion. Biles, Burstein, and Frideres (2008) state that Canadian identity has evolved throughout history in response to key events, which marginalized groups took advantage of to advocate for justice and the Canadian state used to accommodate their demands. One dominant construction of Canadian identity associates it with being white, Protestant, and of British origin. I argue that this perception is rooted in the colonial imaginary that projects the British as the conquerors of Canada whose racial, cultural, and civilizational superiority founded Canada. This identity construct is negotiated in a subtle manner, since it is entrenched in the stratified structure of Canadian society. It is also demonstrated overtly in volatile extremist discourse and praxis that white supremacists (Baergen 2000) embrace to reserve the Canadian identity for the Aryan race. In so doing, white supremacists consider immigrants, and especially racialized immigrants, polluters of the "racial purity" that they believe defines Canadian-ness. The construction of Canadian identity as white and Protestant was challenged in "the late 1960s and early 1970s, as the Canadian state grappled to find a way to forge a new national identity in reaction to the challenges and concerns associated with, among other developments... Quebec nationalism, and growing immigration diversity" (Christopher & Black 2008, 45).

Francophones,[3] immigrants, and Indigenous peoples[4] (Coburn 2015) sought to redefine Canadian identity in inclusive ways in order to strengthen their inclusion in the Canadian polity. Francophones were not placed on the same footing as British Canadians because the dominant perception about the Canadian identity did not consider them equal citizens (Carlson Berg 2014, Denis 2008. Hébert 2003). The construction and negotiation

---

3.   Francophones, including French Canadians, *are* immigrants to Canada. I treat them separately from other immigrants, in this case first-generation Black-African Francophones, because French Canadians are assigned a special status, that of a "founding people" of Canada.

4.   Indigenous issues are crucial to any analysis about Canada, but I only refer to them briefly in this book because they extend beyond the scope of the study.

of the Francophone identity has historically been centred on Francophones' marginalization in Canadian society on the one hand, and the long struggle they embarked on to counter discrimination, on the other. Porter (1965) best exemplified the plight of Francophones in *The Vertical Mosaic*, stressing that they were placed second to British Canadians in Canada's stratified social order. Ethnic hierarchies within the category of white Canadians led British Canadians to exert linguicism ("the ideologies, structures, and practices which are used to legitimate, effectuate, and reproduce an unequal division of power and resources between groups which are defined on the basis of language" (Phillipson 1992, 47)) on Francophones. In the Canadian context, linguicism towards Francophones includes discrimination based on their language, French, and the social aspects expressed in this language: religion (Catholicism) and the Francophone culture. Consequently, Francophones were excluded in Canadian society; they were economically disadvantaged and lacked political power and representation at the highest levels of decision making, since these arenas were largely dominated by white British Canadians. This domination contributed to the linguistic and cultural assimilation of Francophones into the larger, predominantly English-speaking society, a quandary that resulted in the decline of the French language and culture.

To improve their status in society, Francophones engaged in a long struggle in which they resorted to "strategic nationalism" (Breton 2005), which consisted of four crucial facets. First, they claimed nationhood, the status of a "founding people" of Canada. Francophones contended that they were entitled to this status because they participated in the historical formation of Canada, the settlement of many regions in the country, and the evolution and development of Canadian society. In the process, they denounced their identification as "mainstream Canadians who happen to speak French but live in Québec [and the rest of Canada]" (Fleras & Elliott 2007a, 215) or "just another ethnic minority" or "immigrants." To Franco-phones, being a "founding people" meant acquiring rights and power. Second, they aimed to use these resources to promote bilingualism in Canada. They sought to strengthen both institutional bilingualism, the use of French in government institutions and the provision of services in French, and societal bilingualism, fostering bilingualism in Canada from coast to coast to coast. Francophones are keen on bilingualism because it allows them to maintain the French language and culture, counter assimi-lation, and enhance Canada's image as a bilingual country where French has a key status. Third, they planned to achieve "the project of the Francophone Space" in Canada (Thériault et al. 2008, 21), a goal that encompassed both the ideological and physical notions of space. The project meant establishing autonomous institutions and organizations that function in French and are governed by Francophones. Fourth, Francophones aimed to participate at two institutional levels: in Canada-wide institutions in order to secure "control of the means required for society building in its economic, cultural, and linguistic dimensions" (Breton 2005, 298), and in the Francophone space in order to control their autonomous, French-language institutions and organizations and use them to enhance their power, organize to claim additional rights and resources, and impact policy. Thus, they used strategic nationalism to consolidate their status in the Canadian federation and society to prove that they are genuine Canadians.

The Canadian state conceded to the demands of Francophones, endorsing key constitutional provisions to grant them a better place in society. They were recognized as one of Canada's two "founding peoples," the other being the British Canadians, and the Canadian government adopted the *Official Languages Act* (OLA) in 1969, which guarantees measures and resources to benefit Francophones. In addition, it granted the province of Quebec autonomy over its internal affairs and considered Francophones outside Quebec official language minority communities. This status also came with resources to enhance their prosperity and development. Furthermore, Canada enacted the *Canadian Charter of Rights and Freedoms* (the Charter), which gave Francophones outside Quebec the right to education in French. These provisions meant that the dominant construction of Canadian identity shifted from its focus entirely on British Canadian Protestants to include Francophones. Meanwhile, Canada needed more people to sustain its demographic and economic growth, which led it to take in white Western, then Eastern European immigrants, including Germans and Ukrainians. These new groups raised concerns that the provisions for Francophones ignored their place in Canadian society because they projected Canada as a bilingual and bicultural society based on the languages and customs of the British and the French. For this reason, these immigrants advocated recognition of the contributions they made to Canadian society.

To accommodate these immigrants, Canada embraced multiculturalism. In this regard, Fleras and Elliott (2002) remind us that multiculturalism has four meanings: it is a fact, an ideology, a policy, and a practice. Multiculturalism as a fact refers to the racial, ethnic, cultural, linguistic, and religious diversity of a society, while the ideology of multiculturalism encompasses ideals that promote this fact—diversity—and theorize how to accommodate it. There are in general two multiculturalism ideologies, which are liberal multiculturalism and critical multiculturalism. As a policy, multiculturalism contains a set of government rules and programs that apply the multiculturalism ideology to ensure that diversity is respected and reflected in institutions and in the social, political, economic, and cultural facets of society. The practice of multiculturalism encompasses the ways in which the state applies multiculturalism policies, and in which social groups use multiculturalism to advance their interests. I suggest that the four meanings of multiculturalism are interconnected insofar as each of them complements the other to help achieve inclusion. We[5] will see that all four interpretations of multiculturalism are mirrored in Canada. In this context, Canada adopted its Multiculturalism Policy (the Policy) in 1971, which meant that the Canadian identity was extended again to embrace another group, in this case, white European immigrants. The scholarship on immigrants (James 2010) reveals that the number of those immigrants was not sufficient to sustain Canada's development, which led Canada to open its doors to additional groups, resulting in the arrival of racial and visible minority immigrants in Canada.

Neither the notion of "founding people" or the multicultural perception about Canada had accommodated racialized immigrants. This is because the perception about the founding of Canada is a racialized misconception. As Razack (2007) aptly puts it, the story of Canada's building "is manifestly a racial story" predicated upon the "disavowal of conquest, genocide, slavery, and the exploitation of the labour of people of color" (74). The narrative about Canada's nation building is mistakenly constructed as exclusively white European, an image that overlooks the Indigenous peoples and racialized communities. It is evident that Canada could not have been built without the input of these people, whether through their presence in Canada preceding or coinciding with the arrival of European colonialists in Canada, their intellectual and social contributions, the exploitation they suffered in the course of slavery, or their cheap labour that fueled the railways, mines, and factories. The image of the "two founding peoples" of Canada is a colonial master narrative (Shohat & Stam 2013) that glorifies British Canadians and French Canadians, while distancing racialized groups. No racialized minority is considered part of the "founding peoples," whether they are English-speaking, French-speaking, Arabic-speaking, Christian, or Muslim. The racialized were not

---

5. I use the pronoun "we" to allude to myself, the participants, the readers, and social justice supporters more generally.

considered genuine citizens within the Canadian identity that embraced multiculturalism. This is because, in that climate, white immigrants became increasingly included in society, but incorporation proved to be tenuous for racialized groups, who experienced numerous types of racism (Galabuzi 2006). Since the former were white European and Christian, their integration was easier because of the similarity between their skin colour, religion, and culture and that of the white Canadians. The differential treatment of white and racialized immigrants was obvious in Canada's immigration system, which was racialized at the onset (Satzewich & Liodakis 2013). That system exhibited a preference for whites over racial and ethnic immigrants and for Europe (and the US) over the developing world. Thus, Canada took white Europeans' concerns about exclusion in society more seriously than those of racialized immigrants. As a result, multiculturalism assisted the former group of immigrants more than the latter.

The multiculturalism policy in Canada evolved in three phases[6] (Fleras & Elliott 2002). The first, ethnic multiculturalism, was the initial phase that was implemented to accommodate white Europeans. When racialized groups realized that that phase did not allow them to advance in society, they claimed the need to address and redress the racism that they were subjected to. That was an identity negotiation whose aim was to be considered genuine Canadians. Canada made changes to the multiculturalism policy to improve the incorporation of racialized minorities in society, and it is in that context that the multiculturalism policy shifted to its second phase, equity multiculturalism. We consider that action another change in the construction of Canadian identity that attempted to include the racialized in the—Canadian—spaces of belongingness. However, that move was symbolic more than actual, since, although equity multiculturalism helped to alleviate the marginalized status of some racialized minorities, such as Asian groups, they still came after white immigrants in Canada's racialized order. In addition, other racialized communities, especially Blacks, remained largely excluded from society. Equity multiculturalism could have accommodated all racialized peoples, had it been applied properly and for a longer period of time, but it was cut short before it achieved that goal. Canada moved on to the third phase of multiculturalism, civic multiculturalism, when concerns were raised that equity multiculturalism ghettoized immigrants and ethnic minorities. It was argued that those dynamics jeopardized racialized groups' sense of

---

6.   I address the three phases in greater detail in a subsequent section.

belonging to Canada, and therefore threatened Canadian unity. This is yet another shift in the construction of the Canadian identity, a civic identity that stresses shared citizenship and social cohesion among citizens (Knefelkamp 2008). However, this change did not improve the plight of some marginalized minorities either, again, notably Black Canadians who remained largely marginalized in all facets of society (Dei 2008; Massaquoi & Wane, 2007; Mensah & Williams 2015). Thus, the master narratives about Canada established whiteness as the normative, normal, acceptable, desirable, and rewarded form of belongingness. Canadian identity was broadened to include Francophones, but it privileged the whites among them. It was expanded to embrace immigrants, but it prioritized the whites among them as well.

While white privilege determines Canadian identity, it also shapes the Francophone identity. As in the case of the Canadian society in general, the Francophone population was never solely white/European (Huot 2017; Mianda 2020; Veronis, 2012). The very presence of the Métis speaks to that reality. Black Francophones have had a long-established history in Canada for, as early as the turn of the 17th century, Mathieu Da Costa played a key role in the establishment of French Canada, and others followed suit. Canada's Francophonie is becoming increasingly diverse, as many—racialized—immigrants relocate from various continents and regions, including Africa and the Caribbean. Various generations of these immigrants contributed to the transformation of La Francophonie, creating spaces that are vibrant with cultural fusion and pluralism. Nevertheless, the dominant image of Francophone identity remains racialized, entrenched in white privilege. It continues to construe a "true" Francophone as being white, of French European origin, and Catholic (Carlson Berg 2012). It constructs the dominant Francophone identity in opposition to that of "ethnics" and "immigrants," and negotiates it through the marginalization of Black-African Francophones.[7] Black-Africans are excluded in the mainstream organizations and institutions that constitute the Francophone space (Madibbo 2016; Moke Ngala 2005). By far, they are less prosperous than white Francophones, despite a high level of education that in some cases surpasses that of white Francophones. Thus, the racialized assumptions about the founding of Canada serve to establish a Eurocentric society structured around deep-rooted racism that undergirds

---

7.   Though Black-African Francophones are the largest group among racialized Francophones in Alberta, there are other Blacks and racialized groups. I do not mention the other racialized groups because this book focuses on the issues of Black-African Francophones.

the ensuing racialized societal constitutional order. La Francophonie replicates inequitable power that confined the Francophone affiliation to whites. That identity exclusion extends to the Black-African identity to which the participants adhered.

To comprehend the construction and negotiation of the Black-African identity, we need to take a look at anti-Black racism (Das Gupta 1996a; Mwaniki 2014), which plagues the participants and inhibits their identities. Anti-Black racism goes beyond Canada, since the prejudice, negative stereotypes, and behaviour that target Black people are rooted in the global imperialism that infected Blacks with slavery and colonialism (Garvey 2005) and the ensuing racism. It instilled "the belief that there's something wrong with [B]lack people," (Coates, in Washington 2013). Toni Morrison (1992) teaches us that this belief encompasses "assumptions, readings, and misreadings that accompany Eurocentric learning about [Blacks]" (7). These are the connotations that equate Blackness with pejorative images, such as violence, criminality, evil, backwardness, and laziness (Foster 2007). It is important to emphasize that anti-Black racism is deeply rooted in Canada, for it is entrenched in the enslavement and colonialism that Blacks endured in this country. Contemporary anti-Black racism is a continuation of that colonial legacy and infects the Black identity. In the realm of identity, Frantz Fanon (1967) theorizes that anti-Black racism annihilates the Black identity through two processes, which are the objectification of the Black subject and the denial of the existence of a Black history specifically. The omission of the Black identity translates to the exclusion of Blacks from resources. Fanon (1967) also theorizes that Blacks negotiate this marginalization by subverting the objectification into subjectivity and redefining the Black identity. In addition, he drew on Negritude (Césaire 1939; Damas 1937; Senghor 1945) to stress that identity imposition is refuted by re-establishing the terrain of Black history. In this regard, Black Canadians have suffered and fought this identity exclusion throughout history. For example, the Maroons organized in Eastern Canada in the early 17th century (Bristow 1994; Cooper 2006), and Blacks in Nova Scotia established Africville in Halifax in the early 1800s to solidify their decolonizing efforts. Blacks drew on these enterprises to reconstruct Black identity in a positive manner and affirm the longevity of Black history in Canada.

Thus, Black Canadians have been afflicted by and subjected to marginalization. In contemporary Canada, this exclusion is negotiated in the continuing exclusion of Black Canadians who experience racism in the labour market (Baffoe 2009-2010), the education system (Zaami 2017), housing (Creese 2011), and the criminal "justice" system (Fanjoy 2015;

Henry & Tator 2006; Wane 2013), as well as in other societal and institutional arenas. Among Blacks, continental Africans are severely marginalized (Mensah 2010), although they are among the most highly educated and skilled groups in Canada (Reitz & Banerjee 2009; Tettey & Puplampu 2005). Black Francophones are equally highly educated, yet more disenfranchized. They are exposed to multiple jeopardy because they are caught up in the interface of anti-Black racism and linguicism, especially racialized linguicism. In addition to exclusion from the dominant perception of Canadian identity and the pejorative construction of Black identity, they are excluded from Francophone identity. Nevertheless, contemporary Black Canadians also engage in a struggle to redefine Black identity in positive ways and extend the meanings of Canadian (Cooper 2006) and Francophone (Madibbo 2014, 2006) identities to find a place for themselves in society. However, the analysis of these experiences remains inconclusive as a result of scant scholarships for the study of Black Canadians. While Black Canadians are one of the most understudied groups in Canada (Mensah & Williams 2015), Black-African Francophones are even less explored. Therefore, this book fills gaps in the scholarship concerning Black Canadians by focusing on Black-African Francophones. I analyze the multiple identities that they embrace—Canadian, Francophone, and Black-African—to demonstrate that their oppression is rooted in Canada's colonial, Eurocentric foundational principles. These processes continue to permeate Canadian society and La Francophonie. Happily, the uplifting narratives of Black-African Francophones reveal a resilience that echoes Harewood's statement at the beginning of this chapter, alluding to the need to redefine belongingness in Canada to instill justice. This is because the participants invite us to reconstruct and renegotiate identities in an inclusive manner that speaks to the changing demographics of the 21st century. I make recommendations to improve policy and expand research in order to achieve inclusion. This endeavour requires a framework of critical thinking that captures the seriousness of the issues at hand, which is why I opted for the critical tradition in terms of theory and methodology. These are critical race theory and critical multiculturalism and a qualitative research methodology guided by critical ethnography as a philosophical underpinning. Although they are interwoven in the analysis, a brief description will allow us to better decipher how they enabled the analysis in this book.

THEORETICAL FRAMEWORK

Critical Race Theory

The term "critical" refers to an ideology and an activity (Madison 2012). With regard to ideology, it signifies anti-oppression and anti-subordination knowledge that seeks to achieve human liberation. In term of activity, it encapsulates actions that aim to accomplish social justice, and these actions range from thinking modest thoughts or making suggestions to political activism (Ladson-Billings & Tate 1995). Critical race theory (CRT) embraces the critical approach inasmuch as it merges anti-oppressive theory with praxis to pursue social justice (Martinez 2014). Scholars of colour, mostly Blacks, developed CRT in American law schools in the late 1980s, contending that the law should be improved because it serves to maintain racism. Such transformation is needed to effect positive change in the lives of racialized people. The theory then extended to numerous disciplines and has been used to analyze various social problems in many regions and countries.

> [CRT] combines social activism with a critique of the fundamental role played by White racism in shaping contemporary societies.... [It] has its roots in the centuries-old diasporic experiences and struggles of people of color, especially enslaved Africans and their descendants in the US. The perspective builds on this tradition in numerous ways, including the central role it devotes to political struggle, its concern for storytelling, and the significant position accorded to key Black intellectual figures of the nineteenth and twentieth centuries such as Frederick Douglass and W. E. B. Du Bois (Gillborn & Ladson-Billings 2010, 40-41).

> Critical race theorists believe ... [that] racism is ordinary, not aberrational ... color-blindness ... can thus remedy only the most blatant forms of discrimination.... [The] 'social construction' thesis holds that race and races are products of social thought and relations (Delgado & Stefancic 2017, 20-21).

These statements inform us that, though CRT officially organized itself as an intellectual and activist movement in the 1980s in the US, its origins date back to a much earlier era. It is rooted in the aforementioned diasporic experiences of Blacks, such as the legacy of slavery and colonialism. It is also inspired by Black people's resistance, such as the anti-slavery movements, the anti-colonial struggle on the African continent, and the civil rights movement in the US. The above quotes[8] suggest the central tenets of CRT, which are of the utmost relevance to this book: social constructivism, the centrality of race and racism, the anti-racist struggle, the critique of liberalism, experiential knowledge, contradiction-closing cases, differential racialization, and the use of the intellectual and political thought of peoples of African descent—in this case, Blacks. I drew on the CRT's latter emphasis to incorporate works that specifically analyze Black identity: the theorizing of Frantz Fanon (1967) and Negritude (Senghor 1945). I view CRT's tenets as being interconnected and complementary, which is why I present them in relation to one another instead of defining them as separate concepts as they are laid out in the existing literature.

Social constructivism, which is demonstrated in the above quotes through the excerpts of "products of social thought," is a sociological approach that views phenomena as socially constructed (Dixon & Rousseau 2005). It favours subjectivity to uncover how people interpret social phenomena according to their experiences and worldviews. As such, CRT projects race as a social construct, which is illustrated in the quotes about CRT such as "race and races are products of social thought." By regarding race as a social construct, CRT opposes the primordial, objective approach to race that has historically interpreted it through the lens of biological determinism. This perspective was prominent in Europe from the 15th to the 20th century, and extended to North America with the expansion of colonialism. Race was considered genetic and thereby fixed and inherent (Banton 1987). In particular, respected German and French thinkers of the late 17th and early 18th centuries differentiated between racial groups, contending that they belonged to distinct species. The idea of race further crystallized in the 19th century when the Enlightenment era witnessed the development of degeneracy and polygenetic theories. In that context, biological and genetic sciences resorted to "scientific" procedures to confirm the existence of different races. Skin colour and somatic features, including skull size, nose shape, facial angles, and hair texture, were considered "scientific" standards that differentiated between the races. That classification was used to rank the races hierarchically, since it associated biology with culture and cognition. It deemed some racial groups superior and others inferior, a dichotomy that was validated by European philosophers, notably Arthur de Gobineau, who in *The Inequality of Human Races* (1915) maintained that:

---

8.   I will hereafter refer to these quotes as "the quotes about CRT."

The negroid variety is the lowest, and stands at the foot of the ladder. The animal character, that appears in the shape of the pelvis, is stamped on the negro from birth, and overshadows his destiny . . . the strength of his sensations is the most striking proof of his inferiority . . . . The yellow race . . . [T]he yellow man has little physical energy, and is inclined to apathy; he commits none of the strange excesses so common among negroes . . . He tends to mediocrity in everything; he understands easily enough anything not too deep or sublime . . . . [t]he white peoples. These are gifted with reflective energy, or rather with an energetic intelligence. They have a feeling for utility, but in a sense far wider and higher, more courageous and ideal, than the yellow races; a perseverance that takes account of obstacles and ultimately finds a means of overcoming them; a greater physical power, an extraordinary instinct for order, not merely as a guarantee of peace and tranquility, but as an indispensable means of self-preservation. At the same time, they have a remarkable, and even extreme, love of liberty, and are openly hostile to the formalism under which the Chinese are glad to vegetate, as well as to the strict despotism which is the only way of governing the negro (205-207).

De Gobineau developed the theory of "the Aryan master race," in which he claimed the intellectual, civilizational, and moral superiority of the European/Aryan race and the inferiority of the "yellow" race—Asians, Orientals, Indigenous peoples, and Blacks. Darwinism accentuated this binary typology, juxtaposing the European/Aryan race as the bearer of high culture and racialized groups as backward, rendering those racist ideologies more prevalent. These perceptions generated prejudice and stereotypes that legitimized white privilege while injuring the racialized. A "set of prejudgments both irrational and unfounded on grounds of existing or compelling evidence" (Fleras 2014, 99) was established that inculcated prejudice and stereotypes about people without taking into account individual differences (Boyko 1998; Wright & Taylor 2009). As Palmer (1982) states, prejudice and stereotypes are preconceived ideas, feelings, and behaviours that can be racial and generate racism; religious and culminate in religion-based discrimination such as Islamophobia; or ethnocultural and lead to ethnocentrism, such as Eurocentrism (Bar-Tal & Teichman 2005). I emphasize that both race-based prejudice and stereo-types set the framework for the subjugation of racialized groups inasmuch as they projected the Aryan race as advanced and racialized groups as unrefined. Racist prejudice and stereotypes did not end with the classifi-cation of racial groups, they created hierarchies within both whites and racialized people, which still benefited whiteness. De Gobineau's contentions reveal a racial scale that placed whites on the top of the ladder, Asians—the Chinese—after them, and the Blacks at the bottom. De Gobineau (1915) ascertained other racist ideas that dehumanized Blacks, stressing "extreme similarities between the Black and apes." The stereotypes about the racial inferiority of Blacks were imported across the ocean to North America, where they were well received. For example, US writers compiled volumes about the inferiority of Blacks, affirming:

> the close relation between [B]lacks and apes . . . . Negroes are deficient in morality . . . a term used to include thought and knowledge, political and religious ideas . . . that [B]lacks intelligence is less active because of "the narrowness of cerebral organs." For the same reason the heads of their infants are smaller, which accounts for the case with which savage women give birth . . . it is not only their color but the whole bodily structure that governs their capacities, dispositions and temperament. Thus in the Negroes the part of the head concerned with the mastication of food, i.e., jaw, muscles and bones, and teeth, are much bigger and stronger than those of Europeans. Their heads are larger but the brain is smaller and the nerves coarser (Jahoda 2007, 26-27).

In this case, "scientific" measurements meant pejorative prejudice and stereotypes that epitomized Blacks' lack of abilities and adaptability and the backwardness of their cultures and societies, which set the stage for the aforementioned anti-Black racism. Racial divisions among racialized minorities favoured some groups over others, for example Asians over Blacks, but never equated any racialized community with whites. Whites, too, were categorized. Essentially, the British were at the top of the racial scale of whiteness. In particular, the British constructed themselves as superior to the French, a long-established hierarchy that extends back to earlier epochs. These encompass the Hundred Years' War (1337-1453) between the House of Plantagenet, the rulers of the Kingdom of England, and the House of Valois, the rulers of the Kingdom of France. The conflict between the British and the French grew when the British broke with the Roman Catholic Church in the 16th century, which paved the way for animosity between British Protestants and French Catholics. Nevertheless, the idea of the superiority of the British was expanded to include Anglo-Saxons. The Nordic people—the Germanic and Scandinavian people—were classified either as second or equal to the Anglo-Saxons. Then the notion of the superiority of the Anglo-Saxons was further broadened to envelop the Aryan races, and the French and Nordic people were included in this category. Eastern Europeans were first considered inferior to the Aryan races, but were eventually considered part of them. Thus, whiteness became the centre of racial superiority, and white privilege became the norm of social status. While racial divisions between racialized groups did not benefit all of them, the demarcation between whites did not impede any of them. Whites succeeded in making whiteness a signifier of unity to mitigate their conflicts and protect their shared interests, especially imperialism and the associated oppression of racialized groups. For example, whites worked together against Blacks in the course of transatlantic slavery and colonialism and benefited from these atrocities. Similarly, British Canadians and French Canadians were involved in a conflict in Canada, but also cooperated to dehumanize Blacks. For example, the enslavement of Blacks in Canada benefited both groups, since they took advantage of their labour. This analysis reveals the intricacies of racist ideologies: whites can be enemies but also allies when it comes to shared colonial gains.

CRT's tenet of "race as a social construct" disputed biological determinism, contending that genetics do not correspond to cultural and civilizational attributes. This assertion aligns with the intellectual trend that surfaced in the 1950s when scientists and social scientists established that race has no scientific basis and therefore biology does not allow for distinctions among the world's populations. In that context, the generalization about race as a genetic factor was substituted by perceptions of it as a social construct. For critical race theorists, race is socially constructed because it was given social and cultural meanings to advantage whites and disadvantage the racialized. It reproduces an asymmetric racial order that intensifies the power and privilege of whites while entrenching the subordination of the racialized. This marginalization is racism, which CRT conveys through its tenet of "the centrality of racism." This tenet is alluded to in the quotes about CRT through the phrases "white racism" and "racism is ordinary, not aberrational," which indicate that racism is normalized, endemic, and omnipresent because it is entrenched in white supremacy. In this regard, it is important to elaborate on CRT's conceptualization of white supremacy, which it perceives as the belief in the superiority of the Aryan race. This notion is illustrated in two ways, one of which is the "obvious and extreme fascistic posturing" (Gillborn 2005, 485) of the aforementioned white supremacist organizations. These groups seek to isolate, eliminate, separate, or subjugate racialized people in order to preserve the "racial purity" of the Aryan race. The other one is subtle, disguised in mundane behavior that seems neutral and "ordinary." For bell hooks (1989), subtle white supremacy:

is the ... movement away from the perpetuation of overtly racist discrimination, exploitation and oppression of [B]lack people which often masks how all-pervasive white supremacy is in this society [the US, and I would add Canada], both as ideology and as behavior.... [White supremacy means] upholding and maintaining racial hierarchies that do not involve force (i.e. slavery, apartheid)... [it refers to] actions [that] support and affirm the very structure of racist domination and oppression (192-93).

Thus, white supremacy normalized both whiteness and white privilege because these are so ingrained that they appear natural and "ordinary," taken for granted. White racism became a pervasive facet of social life (Crenshaw 2011), and it therefore permeates the macro, meso, and micro levels of society. Consequently, whites hold the most power in the legal, economic, political, social, residential, and educational spheres of society at the expense of targeted racialized groups. Based on these perspectives, critical race theorists perceive racism as discriminatory ideologies and practices that marginalize racialized groups. The theory identifies varied but interrelated types of racism, the most prominent of which are : classical racism, systemic, institutional, cultural, and diplomatic types of racism, as well as racism of extermination and racism of elimination. Classical racism, also labelled biological or scientific racism, is associated with the above-mentioned era of biological determinism and racial classification. Systemic racism is embedded in the foundation of the social system because it guides society's structures, institutions, practices, and social relations (Dei 1996). It means that society is rooted in a racist formation (Omi & Winant 2014) that pervades its history and contemporary structures. Therefore, systemic racism accounts for the other types of racial oppression, such as institutional racism, which involves ideas, policies, practices, and procedures that disadvantage racialized groups within societal institutions (Das Gupta 1996b). Cultural racism, which is also labelled new racism, refers to situations where race is substituted with cultural attributes, such as religion and immigration status (Balibar 1988). Racism of elimination entails the inclusion of minorities but only at subordinate ranks, whereas racism of extermination signifies the total extirpation and destruction of specific racial groups (Baber 2004). Because these types of racism are perpetrated by numerous actors, there is reference to individual, public, official, and state patterns of racism (Henry & Tator 2009). These respectively involve individuals, social groups, officials representing governments, and entire governments that embrace thoughts, attitudes, and actions that perpetuate racism. Furthermore, scholars pinpoint diplomatic racism (Shepard 1983) to connote a subtle form of institutional racism that occurs when govern-ments make overt actions and policies that propagate racial injustice. Anti-Black racism encompasses all these types of racial oppression when they are directed at Blacks. Thus, racism is multidimensional and overlap-ping; it is overt but increasingly subtle and covert. However, in all events it has real material impacts on people, since it benefits the dominant racial groups while it vilifies the marginalized.

Racism gave rise to debates surrounding how to treat the concept of race in the social sciences, whether or not race should be used as an analytical and explanatory concept. Some scholars opine that the social sciences must discard the term race because it was discredited as a biological attribute. Thus, using the term race only perpetuates the racist hierarchies and classifications that created racism in the first place (Banton 1987). They went on to stress that "racism can be studied and condemned without believing in race [and using it]" (Satzewich 1999, 320). This is because the notion of race can be substituted with "neutral" attributes that connote racial oppression, such as "ethnic group," "genogroup," or "cultural community" (Miles & Torres 2007). Critical race theorists disagree; they hold that abasing the biological validity of race did not terminate its differential impacts on people, that "race matters" (West 1994) and continues to be an important factor in social life today. The biological parameters of race shifted to socioeconomic, cultural, and political concep-tions. Perceived physical differences are still exploited to privilege whites and enhance racism against the racialized (Essed 2002). In Omi's and Winant's (1993) words, race is also important because it shapes belonging-ness inasmuch as "race is an ... indissoluble part of our identities" (5). It assigns, as well as denies, identities because racial affiliations are constructed and negotiated differentially, which extends or restrains people's life chances. For Omi and Winant (1993), delegitimizing the concept of race perpetuates the prevalence of racism because there is a close relationship between the concept of race and the reality of racism. While scholars such as Satzewich (1999) posited the possibility of studying racism without engaging with race, critical race theorists asserted the impossibility of interrogating the materiality and reality of racism without using the concept of race (Dei 2003). Therefore, for Mensah (2010) "[a]s long as race continues to have significant social connotations and consequences, it deserves our attention as social scientists" (16). Because racist ideologies generated racism in the first place, the use of race makes it possible to capture how racism functions and how to rectify it. Thus, CRT insists on using race as an analytical concept.

How does CRT counter racism? The quotes about CRT are a blueprint to dismantle racism, which starts with challenging the subtle inconsistencies of liberalism. The notion of "colour-blindness" in the quotes about CRT corroborates the theory's tenet of the "critique of liberalism." Liberalism as a political philosophy encompasses a wide array of values, but this analysis draws on its ethos about equality among citizens, liberty, and freedom of speech (Kymlicka 2011). Liberalism's component of liberal democracy, dubbed Western democracy, is also relevant because its form of governance that supports secular governments and representative democracy is the precept that guides the political systems of Western countries, including Canada. CRT problematizes the basic liberal assumption about equality because it replicates rather than dismantles racism. The liberal principle of equality espouses two interrelated precepts that are believed to guarantee fairness, and these are "colour-blindness" and "meritocracy." As a sociological term, colour-blindness signals that race no longer limits people's opportunities because the contemporary world has entered a new, post-racial era where "race does not matter" (Ladson-Billings 2006). By contrast, meritocracy is based on the assumption that citizens gain access to societal opportunities because of their qualifications, not because of their identity characteristics. Thus, equality means treating everyone the same regardless of their race (or gender, etc.) and calls for implementing race-neutral policies that follow meritocracy in order to ensure fairness. Critical race theorists disagree, arguing that equality and the associated colour-blindness and meritocracy do not guarantee fairness because, as it stands, society is stratified along racial, gender, and class lines, among other divisions. The persistence of racism reveals that citizens were not initially offered equal opportunities to prepare them to have equal access to resources, such as higher education, and compete for opportunities, such as employment. Neither the distribution of resources or the outcomes are fair. In Western societies, liberalism propagates racial oppression because it produces "the denial of racism."

According to CRT, the denial of racism is perpetuated through equality discourses that insist on avoiding race-related policies, and the aforementioned arguments that seek to abandon the use of the term race. It is also illustrated in the silence about racism, which occurs when people do not name racism, confront it, or identify the actors and institutions that perpetrate it. These processes enable racists to escape the accountability and responsibility of their deeds. The denial of racism is also depicted in "denial discourses" (Van Dijk 1992) such as the above contentions, which surmise that the contemporary world is post-racial, or others that justify racism, or even "blame the victims" of racism. For these reasons, CRT opposes the principle of equality and instead endorses the principle of equity, which indicates that the distribution of societal resources must take into consideration identity attributes, such as race, language, and gender. Since people are marginalized—or privileged—by virtue of their identities, society must equip disenfranchised groups with the skills that allow them to compete and achieve desired outcomes. Equity necessitates acknowledging oppression; it recognizes racism by naming it explicitly and examining it in its historical, contemporary, social, economic, and political contexts (Brown 2004). For this reason, CRT stresses racism as a theoretical concept and a social fact that has material consequences for people. The recognition of racism translates into policies that accommodate racial identities, such as affirmative action provisions that are aimed at enhancing the inclusion of targeted marginalized groups.

To better fight racism, CRT also adopts the tenet of "experiential knowledge," which is alluded to in the quotes about CRT in the words "storytelling" and "the centuries-old diasporic experiences and struggles of people of color, especially enslaved Africans." CRT grants a special significance to the lived experiences of racialized groups, especially those of people of African ancestry. It emphasizes that these people have faced injustices, such as slavery, colonialism, and the ensuing racism, which offer them a unique, insider understanding of these systems of oppression. Because CRT believes in the power of the narrative of the marginalized, it brings to the fore the narratives of Black people. Their long-established tradition of "storytelling" and oral history serve as counter-narratives to racist ideologies and practices. Similarly, CRT appreciates the knowledge and expertise embedded in Black intellectual and political thought, which is referred to in the quotes about CRT through the phrase "the significant position accorded to key Black intellectual figures." According to CRT, these "figures" provide a valid alternative to the Eurocentric viewpoints, and their work further consolidates antiracism. For these reasons, CRT capitalizes on Blacks' experiences and intellectualism to recommend their "political struggle" as a viable anti-racist strategy. For critical race theorists, "political struggle" connotes "activity" in the way that the term "critical" depicts it. It is political and social activism—ideas, discourses, protests, alliances and coalition building—that simultaneously influence civil society and grassroots organizations and, I would add, societal institutions and structures. The amalgam of the political struggle becomes a force and defined lobby aimed at achieving racial emancipation

(Tomlinson 2008), which encompasses reconstructing and renegotiating identities in inclusive ways.

CRT cautions us that, when antiracist struggles culminate in positive outcomes, we should examine these achievements critically. Therefore, CRT accentuates the tenet of "contradiction-closing cases," which is depicted in the quotes about CRT in the statement: "remedy only the most blatant forms of discrimination." Some achievements seem as though they are milestones in the antiracist struggle, but they could be superficial. For example, laws and policies may look good on paper but do not result in meaningful outcomes. The danger that the "contradiction-closing cases" pose is that:

> [They] are a little like the thermo-stat in your home or office. They assure that there is just the right amount of racism. Too much would be destabilizing—the victims would rebel. Too little would forfeit important pecuniary and psychic advantages for those in power (Delgado 1995, 80).

Thus, when we think that there is sufficient antiracism, the reality could be that there is ample racism. Institutions may apply equity and affirmative action policies, but not effectively. They may hire some minorities, but that could be tokenism if it is confined to a handful of minorities or if the hired minorities are treated unfairly in the workplace, that is, if they are harassed, denied promotion, and so on. Such measures could eliminate some types of racism, especially overt racial discrimination, but disguise other forms of racism, notably the subtle ones. Accordingly, we must continue to pursue the antiracist struggle, the "political struggle" in CRT's terms, recognizing that some achievements are part of a process of change rather than an end in their own right. Therefore, CRT specifically urges us to focus on the continuity of legal reforms, examine existing laws and policies critically, and advocate their proper implementation. Such reforms seek to transform the relationship between the law, race, and power, so as to ensure that the application of the law is not elusive, but accurate and timely (Crenshaw 2002). In the process, CRT's precept about "differential racialization," which is underscored in the tenet of CRT in the juxtaposition made between "people of color" and "Africans and their descendants," is of utmost benefit. This tenet accentuates the aforementioned racial ideologies that have instilled hierarchies within racialized groups. Racist stereotypes view racialized people differently and differentially; for example, Asians such as Chinese and Japanese are more favourably projected than Blacks. Thus, Blacks face more racism—again, anti-Black racism—than these groups, which allows these groups to be more included in society than Blacks are. CRT cautions us that even equity policies could reproduce differential racialization when they are not thorough enough or applied effectively. For example, Canada took an equity measure by naming four designated groups, which are 1) Aboriginal peoples, 2) women, 3) visible minorities, and 4) persons with disabilities. Although the rationale behind these equity policies is to ensure the inclusion of all the designated groups, in reality they may not leverage all the racialized groups. Designating a category of visible minorities that lumps all racialized people in one group may not improve the status of all of them. This is a result of the persistence of the aforementioned racist hierarchies that privilege Asians over Blacks. Again, CRT reminds us to examine such measures with caution and seek additional—legal—reforms if they create inconsistencies. In short, antiracism must be all-encompassing because racism is ubiquitous. It necessitates a critical understanding of both racism and antiracism and should be accompanied by structural and institutional transformation. Canadian scholars better epitomize these ideas by stating that:

> antiracism [is] an action-oriented [political] strategy for institutional systemic change that addresses racism.... It is a critical discourse of race and racism in society that challenges the continuance of racializing social groups for differential and unequal treatment.... Critical antiracism moves... to the examination of the ways that racist ideas... actions are entrenched, linked... supported in institutional and societal structures (Dei 1996, 252-53).

> Anything less than a comprehensive framework creates a level of effectiveness that is tantamount to applying a cotton swab.... [F]raming racisms as multidimensional in form, process, and outcome calls forth an inclusive anti-racism program incorporating the individual-institutional-ideological-infrastructural nexus (Fleras 2014, 224).

Thus, CRT draws on "social constructivism" to envisage "race" as a social construct that generates "racism." Racism is multilayered and omnipresent, which is why the antiracism struggle requires an exhaustive framework. This encapsulates the "critique of liberalism" to redress the "denial of racism" and "differential racialization." Put together, the "experiential knowledge," "diasporic experiences" and thought of "key Black intellectual figures," and their "political struggle" complement the "critique of liberalism" because they bring to light equity policies and reforms. Not only do they make it possible to understand racism in its "historical and contemporary contexts," they provide insights about the pursuit of racial justice.

They inform how to eradicate racism at its root and examine the successes achieved in a manner that makes it possible to avoid "contradiction-closing cases." For these reasons, CRT is most adequate for the analysis of the polymorphous identities that Black-African Francophones adhered to—Canadian, Francophone, and Black-African affiliations. CRT is pertinent to the analysis of the multiple marginalizations that envelop the construction and negotiation of these identities and the "political struggle" that they engage in to dismantle oppression. Because CRT is grounded in the "experiential knowledge" of Black peoples, I draw on it to make the Black-African Francophone discourse the centre of the analysis. The theory's emphasis on the "centrality of race and racism" led me to use race as both a social construct and an analytical and explanatory category that deciphers racism. I shed light on the racism that surfaced in Canadian society at large and in La Francophonie in its overt forms, such as white supremacy, as well as subtle manifestations. I apply the tenet of "differential racialization" both to whites—Anglophones and Francophones—and within La Francophonie. That enables me to analyze the intricate relationship between the two white groups—white Anglophones and white Francophones—that serves to improve the status of white Francophones at the expense of Black-African Francophones. I combine this tenet—differential racialization—with the precept of legal reform to stress the persistence of anti-Black racism in spite of existing equity policies and legislations. This perspective leads me to suggest legal reforms to help overcome racism. Furthermore, I apply the notion of the "critique of liberalism" to denounce the "denial of racism" that is particularly prominent in La Francophonie. I inspire by the tenet of "contradiction-closing cases" to highlight shortcomings in Canadian legislations, especially the ones that pertain to this analysis, which are the policies of multiculturalism and official languages, and to some extent, the *Canadian Charter of Rights and Freedoms* and employment equity. Explaining that these provisions did not leverage Black-African Francophones, I suggest additional equity provisions and reforms to strengthen their inclusion.

Because all these dynamics impacted the participants while they navigated their identities, CRT's approach to identity is key to this analysis. CRT considers identity as being subjective, evolving, and entrenched in power relations. The work of "key intellectual Black figures"—Frantz Fanon (1967) and philosophers of Negritude (Senghor 1964, 1045)—allowed me to pinpoint the subjugation that afflicts the Black-African identity and the social mechanisms that the participants opted for to give dignity to this affiliation. While CRT resonates with my analysis in a number of ways, like any theory, it is not comprehensive enough to cover all the aspects of the analysis. This leads me to incorporate a complementary theory that also seeks to dismantle oppression and instill justice: critical multiculturalism.

Critical Multiculturalism

Critical multiculturalism (CM) is an intervention on Eurocentrism, a vigorous response to the cultural imperialism that has accompanied the history of Western colonialism (May & Sleeter 2010). As a critical approach, CM aims to strengthen critical consciousness and develop educational and societal practices to disrupt the hegemonic narratives and conditions that Eurocentrism has established. Among the basic tenets of CM, four are directly related to this analysis. They revolve around its 1) rejection of the hegemonic master narratives of Eurocentrism as they pertain to nation building, 2) conceptualization of identity, 3) approach to language, and 4) critique of liberalism and liberal multicultural education. Again, I consider these tenets as interrelated and complementary, not as distinct as they are presented in the literature. With regard to the master narratives, CM posits that the founding of the Western white settler societies, such as Canada, is perceived from a Eurocentric viewpoint. They project the white Western/Europeans as the builders of the modern states while depicting racialized minorities as outsiders who enjoy—and abuse—the welfare of these states (Razack 2007). These narratives create differential identity myths and ingrain them deeply in the public psyche. They construct normative identities and replicate them in the social system, reproducing inequitable power structures. Since CM draws a correlation between the master narratives and identity, examining its stance on identity allows us to better capture these nuances. Like CRT, CM perceives identity as being dynamic and evolving. For CM, identities are products of "an ongoing fluid negotiation of racial group membership" (Kubota 2010, 104). CM adds to CRT's perceptions of identity the multiplicity of identities, stressing that in multicultural societies such as Canada, social actors develop multiple affiliations. In this respect, CM builds on the cosmopolitan and postmodern conceptions of the multiplicity of identities (Nussbaum 1997) and hybridity (Bhabha 1994). However, CM refutes the assertion that all people have an equal opportunity to pick and choose freely from a set of identities readily available to them. CM reminds us that, because identification is regulated by power relations (McLaren 1997), the dominant groups have identity options that they themselves validate in the social system. For them, identity is a choice, which we can apply in the Canadian context by positing that a white person can self-identify as Canadian and/or Francophone and will enjoy the privilege and material benefits that come with whiteness. They may not even need to self-identify or claim a specific—dominant—identity because their skin colour automatically ascribes a privileged identity to them. In addition, if a white person expresses multiple allegiances that include a minority identity, such as French Canadian or Irish Canadian adherence, this identification does not take away their white privilege. On the contrary, it brings them additional recognition and resources, the ones that are granted to white Canadians and those that are reserved for white minorities—i.e. Francophones.

For whites, multiple identities equate to multiple privileges, but the opposite is true for racialized groups such as Blacks. If a Black person embraces a dominant identity, such as a Canadian or Francophone affiliation, they do not receive the material benefits that these identities offer, since these affiliations are predetermined to exclude racialized minorities. Furthermore, if a Black person claims a Black racial identity, this stance does not bring them inclusion because, as we stated previously, Blackness is steeped in a negative identity imposition that dehumanizes the Black subject. Black identity does not ensure profit, nor does a hybrid or multiple identity that encapsulates Blackness, such as being Black Canadian, Black Francophone, or Black, Francophone, and Canadian. For Blacks, multiple identities signal multiple marginalization. Why? Shohat and Stam illuminate our understanding of these intricacies. In *Unthinking Eurocentrism: Multiculturalism and the Media* (2013), they aptly attest that these problematics are rooted in Eurocentrism, because during colonialism Eurocentrism was constituted by a narrow conception of identity that forged the self/other binary. The self and "the Other" are dichotomous, for in order for the self to thrive it must alienate "the Other," if not eliminate them. Thus, identity is seen through the lens of primordialism as being fixed and static. Affiliations such as collective or national identity represent the self and are confined to specific racial groups. Identities do not change or extend to accommodate "the Other"—racialized groups. "The Other" is not compatible with the self; they are the alterity of the self. "The Other" can never "become" Canadian or Francophone, because identity is not a process of becoming in the first place. It is a fixed "being," which means that "the Other" will never become the self. What is worse is that this perspective insists that "the Other" cannot even co-exist with the self. They are not as good as the self, they are inferior. Thus, identity is dichotomous because the self and "the Other" are separate, if not segregated. "The Other" is powerless and should therefore be denied the power that the self holds.

For critical multiculturalists, these inequities are exacerbated by the dominant approach to language. Theorists consider language a cultural aspect which, like all cultural components, is shaped by relations of power and domination (Fairclough 2014). CM acknowledges linguicism (Phillipson 1992), but ascertains that linguistic discrimination is highly racialized (Mianda 2014). It creates linguistic categories that determine who is a "native speaker" of a language and who is not, based on their perceived racial background. For example, English and French are viewed as synonymous with whiteness, which classifies racialized people as non-native or illegitimate speakers of these languages. Their accent is racialized (Gillborn 2006), since they suffer marginalization when it differs from the normative pronunciation of the dominant group. Nevertheless, they are also picked on even when they speak the standard variety of the dominant language. Conversely, whites whose accent does not match the dominant one are not generally victims of linguicism. In fact, their accent may be considered different in a good way, for example as being "cool," such as the case of the dominant Australian or British accents in the Canadian context. Thus, although language is in general a prestigious cultural capital (Bourdieu 1991), it is given a colour that matches stereotypes about the racial characteristics of the language speakers. White privilege disguises negative perceptions about language when it comes to whites; their language difference is invisible, but becomes visible when it comes to racialized minorities regardless of how well they speak the language and with which accent. I use the term "racialized linguicism" to refer to linguicism that collides with racism. This differentiation serves to include some linguistic groups in society while excluding others. While CM discerns language as a means of oppression, it also projects it as a tool of resistance. For Gal (1995) language is an "art of resistance," and for Habashi (2008) it is "a method of political resistance, resilience and reworking" (269). This is because language meaning and language usage allow us to uncover authoritative regimes of knowledge and refute oppression. Language is a discursive space in which vocabulary, grammar, syntax, and rhyme are political acts of resistance. Colonial languages are oppressive, but people's agency can turn them into decolonial instruments of defiance (Madibbo 2007). English is not the property of white/Western people; it is the language of all its speakers. Conversely, French is not only the language of white French Canadians, it is the language of La Francophonie, and thus of all French speakers worldwide. Furthermore, in the same way that we argued that CM associates master narratives with identity, we emphasize that it makes a connection between language and identity. While the master narratives about Canada elect whiteness as the norm of identity, the dominant perceptions about language establish the white speakers of language as the legitimate citizens. However, I draw on CM's conception of language as a tool of resistance to emphasize that the relationship between language and identity can also be one of resistance that allows the marginalized to claim identities because they speak the language that is associated with a specific identity, regardless of their skin colour or background.

Critical multiculturalists are concerned that these inequities prevail in societal structures, especially in the education system. CM has reservations about liberal multiculturalism, which it argues are extended to the education system. It problematizes liberal multiculturalism's treatment of diversity. We recall that liberal multiculturalism is the multiculturalism ideology that guides the Western liberal democracies' approach to diversity. It emphasizes group-specific rights, such as religious and linguistic rights, for minority groups so that they will not be disadvantaged as a result of their culture and cultural status (Kymlicka 1995; Taylor 1994). Like liberalism, liberal multiculturalism seeks the inclusion of minorities through cultural recognition, and in so doing attempts to reconcile cultural specificity with the aforementioned liberal principle of universal equality. However, critical multiculturalists stress that, although cultural recognition is an equity mechanism that could enhance inclusion, liberal multiculturalism fails to merge cultural particularism with equity. CM renounces liberal multiculturalism's perception of culture and the associated cultural diversity, contending that this viewpoint reifies culture (Kubota 2004). This is because liberal multiculturalism considers culture a "thing," an object of knowledge to be discovered, observed, and evaluated. This perspective essentializes culture, depoliticizes it and dissociates it from the structural and inequitable power relationships that diminish the status of racialized cultural groups in society (Haque 2012). Accordingly, liberal multiculturalism interprets the cultural recognition of minority groups as a "celebration of cultural diversity" that promotes the objective cultural characteristics of "ethnic others"—their food, clothes, rituals, and so on. For these reasons, CM insists that liberal multiculturalism is deracialized and therefore lacks the ability to tackle structural inequities, such as the material ramifications of racism and the ensuing poverty, seriously and systematically (May 1999). In the end, liberal multiculturalism enhances the aforementioned master narratives because it projects the cultures that pertain to the racialized communities as a difference against a Eurocentric frame of reference.

Critical multiculturalists refute the application of these principles in the education system, which they argue is done through multicultural education (also labelled liberal multicultural education). They are concerned that multicultural education aims to enhance educational success by making the education system egalitarian, promoting the values of democracy, and guaranteeing all students the equality of opportunities in education without being subjected to racial, ethnic, or gender discrimination (Banks & Banks 2010). To achieve this goal, multicultural education proposes raising awareness about diversity so that students, teachers, and administrators can familiarize themselves with different cultures. Hence, cultural difference is at the core of multicultural education, because it seeks inclusion by building school programs and activities that support the celebration of difference. These activities connote multicultural events that are intended to bring diversity—food and ethnic dress—to the classroom. Such enterprises are also thought to encourage interactions among individuals from different backgrounds, and promote cultural respect and engagement among students, teachers, and administrators. CM opposes multicultural education because it ignores the structural barriers that reproduce inequitable power relations in the education system. CM stresses that, like liberalism, liberal multicultural education sees culture as a "thing," a characteristic of individuals, and that it views conflict as a misunderstanding of differences among individuals, not a result of the dominant norms of whiteness. According to CM, multicultural education's engagement with institutional change is minimal, because this education is attitudinal. Since multicultural education focuses on individual sensitivity and understanding of cultural differences, it disconnects ethnic cultures from the power inequities that marginalize racialized students and teachers at all levels of education.

How does CM correct these shortcomings? Central to CM is the analysis of culture in relation to institutionalized inequities, and linking cultural diversity—linguistic, religious, etc.—to power dynamics (Sharma 2010). Thus, CM is against the imposition of master narratives as the norm of identities, in this case the Canadian and Francophone identities. Instead, it calls for reconstructing and renegotiating identities in order to ensure the inclusion of "the underrepresented, the marginalized, and the oppressed" (Shohat & Stam, in Lugones 2014, 78). Like critical race theory, CM advocates equity, but stresses it particularly in the education system. CM emphasizes that, since educational institutions play a key role in social transformation, equity should be the primary focus of the education system. CM substitutes multicultural education with critical multicultural education (CME). The purpose of CME is to name, actively challenge, and eliminate structural power, such as racism, sexism, and classicism (Vavrus 2010). It questions the master narratives that reproduce Eurocentric knowledge in the education system, along with inequitable educational processes and outcomes. Educational reforms are the way out, because they involve transforming the curriculum and restructuring the educational institutional hierarchy (Gabryś et al. 2011). Thus, teaching materials and pedagogies must be remodelled, and practices in the classroom and at the administrative and institutional levels must be renewed. For the proponents of CME, such reforms boost the educational success, belongingness, and inclusion of racialized students and teachers, which in turn facilitates their incorporation into the larger society.

Thus, CM complemented CRT to channel the analysis because it allows me to deconstruct the colonial master narratives underlying Canada's nation building, which serve to structurally reproduce xenophobic assumptions that make whiteness the normative identity, while silencing racialized minorities and relegating them to a lower status. CM's conceptualization of identity is pertinent to my analysis because I utilize the perspective of the multiplicity of identities to analyze the multiple affiliations that the research participants have embraced. Its perception of the self/other identity binary allows me to explain that this dichotomy caused the participants multiple identity marginalization. In addition, I draw on CM to explore language as a cultural aspect that created inequitable power relations for the research participants, making them a linguistic minority in multiple ways. They suffered linguicism because they are French speaking, and endured racialized linguicism in relation to the English language because they were discriminated against because of their English accent. CM's approach to language as a means of resistance allows me to interpret the resilience with which the participants claimed the Francophone identity because they are speakers of the associated language—French. CM's precept about critical multicultural education is also relevant to the analysis because I employ it to shed light on the participants' perceptions and experiences with the French-language education system. The theory's insistence on educational reforms offers me the opportunity to bring to light an important educational program[9] that Black-African Francophones

---

9.   It is La Caravane contre le racisme et la discrimination (The Caravan against Racism and Discrimination), which will be analyzed in a subsequent chapter.

implemented in the French-language schools to fight the structural inequities that permeate this system. In short, CRT and CM complete one another, which enables me to reveal the anti-Black racism and linguicism that subjugate Black-African Francophones and their struggle in the pursuit of justice. Luckily, the methodology that I employ also proved to be pertinent to my success in this endeavour.

METHODOLOGICAL CONSIDERATIONS

Critical ethnography was relevant to the analysis of the construction and negotiation of the identities that Black-African Francophones embrace because it:

> begins with an ethnical responsibility to address processes of unfairness or injustice ... [and] a compelling sense of duty and commitment.... [The critical] researcher feels an ethical obligation to make a contribution toward ... equity. The critical ethnographer also takes us beneath surface appearance, disrupts the status quo, and unsettles both neutrality and taken-for-granted assumptions .... Because the critical ethnographer is committed to the art and draft of fieldwork, empirical methodologies become the foundation for inquiry ... [to] challenge institutions, regimes of knowledge, and social practices that limit choices, constrain meaning, and denigrate identities and communities. (Madison, 2012, 5-6).

As a critical ethnographer, my commitment to social justice oblige me to examine those identities in order to redress oppression. Critical ethnography speaks to me because it emphasizes that, in order for research to affect positive social change, it must allow us to overcome social oppression. The research must produce emancipatory knowledge that challenges the dominant order, and identify and counter the power inequities that influence social relations (Reinharz & Davidman 1992). In addition, critical ethnography asks the researcher to take a clear position against hegemonic ideas and practices to instill social justice. Critical ethnography's emphasis on the significance of fieldwork research and "empirical methodologies" allows me to utilize the qualitative research methodology because of its capacity to generate culturally specific (van den Hoonaard 2015) and, I would add racially specific, meanings, and strengthen social justice. Both critical ethnography and qualitative research methodology follow the social constructivism tradition, considering "reality" a socially constructed phenomenon, which makes peoples' experiences and perspectives the centre of the analysis. Thus, qualitative methodology echoes the critical tradition inasmuch as it melds emancipatory ideology into social and political activism. Within this methodology, the researcher does not hide behind the positivistic assumptions that require them to apply "objectivity," "neutrality," and "detachment" (Tuohy et al. 2013). Rather, the researcher renounces objectivity and the fragmentation that it requires in favour of subjectivity; they expose the material effects of exclusion, intervene, and offer alternatives (Thomas 1993). The researchers clarify their positionality—i.e., identity—and politics in order to take responsibility vis-à-vis research participants and take a clear stance regarding domination and privilege. The ultimate goal is to give voice to the voiceless and consolidate human agency and resilience.

In line with critical ethnography and the qualitative tradition, I state that my scholarly project is political, since I denounce the hegemony of Eurocentrism that continues to shape Canada, and advocate social justice against the backdrop of the anti-Black racism and racialized linguicism that plague Black-African Francophones. My positionality impacts the research process and analysis. Being a first-generation Black-African immigrant woman who is involved with La Francophonie, I identify with the research participants who are undergoing marginalization with which I am familiar. My lived experiences in Canada expose me to racism in Canadian society, and my career as a university professor offers me a first-hand experience of institutional racism, especially anti-Black racism. Not only does this approach allow me to document the uplifting stories of the research participants, it leads me to make recommendations to help bring about justice.

The research data were gathered through the use of two qualitative research methods: semi-structured interviews and document collection. The data were collected in two phases, first between 2008 and 2011, then from 2012 to 2016. During the first fieldwork, we[10] used a snowball sampling technique to recruit participants. I invited key Black-African Francophone actors to participate in the research, and they then referred additional participants to us. We conducted semi-structured individual interviews in French, which I translated into English. The interviews were guided by a list of open-ended questions, and each interview used an identical base set of questions to ensure that differences in response were not a result of the question's structure (Denzin & Lincoln 2011). We posed questions about participants' self-identification, the reasons that led them to choose their

---

10.   The research team (2008-2011) consisted of myself and three research assistants—Raheela Manji, Josée Couture, and Ali Kamal.

affiliations, and the meanings they associated with these identities. We also asked whether and how the participants experienced racism and racialized linguicism, as well as the practices they used to negotiate their identities. When we reached saturation, we had interviewed 42 participants (see Table 1) who resided in Calgary, Edmonton, and Brooks. The participants mirrored the diversity of Black-African Francophones, since they originated from many Sub-Saharan African countries, including the Democratic Republic of the Congo (DRC), Cameroon, Senegal, Rwanda, Burundi, and Chad. Participants were between the ages of 22 and 54, with a majority in the age ratio of 28 to 40. The sample ensured representation of gender, age, national origin, length of settlement in Canada, and migration patterns. Their migration trajectories echoed the current trends of global migration in that a majority of them first relocated to France before moving to Canada, while others first settled in eastern Canada, and then moved to Alberta. Very few arrived in Alberta directly from their sending countries.[11] In terms of the time since arrival in Canada, a few were children when they moved to Canada, and therefore grew up and were schooled in Canada. A majority had been in Canada for more than 12 years, while others settled in this country about 5 years ago. There are striking similarities in their education and employment, which reflected the general characteristics of Black-African Francophones in Canada. As stated earlier, this community is one of the most educated groups in Canada, yet one of the most marginalized. The research participants were all highly educated, but underemployed.[12] All of them attended post-secondary institutions except for one person who dropped out of high school in Canada. Their degrees ranged from college diplomas to post-graduate degrees and were obtained in Africa, France, another European country and/or Canada. Some obtained two or three degrees, while one participant had four. Participants had commensurate employment in Africa but were underemployed or unemployed in France and Canada (See Appendix A, The Research Participants).

This book analyzes the similar—collective—experiences of the participants, which makes it possible to understand similar structural barriers that Black-African Francophones encounter. This approach uncovers the systemic feature of oppression that targets them all without distinction.

---

11. I use the term "sending country" instead of "home country" because I do not wish to imply that Canada is not the participants' home.

12. Greater detail about participants' education and employment status is provided in subsequent sections.

We collected documents[13] during the fieldwork, and I gathered additional ones between 2012 and 2016, and interviewed the participants in 2016 informally to gain information about their employment status at the time. I extended the data collection to 2016 because that period of time encompassed major events and discourses that influenced Black-African Francophone identities. For example, during the interviews we conducted in 2008-2011, we noted that employment was central to the participants' self-identification, so much so that obtaining good employment made them feel included in society, while underemployment made them feel alienated. In addition, that epoch included an economic recession that began in Alberta in 2015. Given the significance that the participants accorded to employment, I sought to learn about the developments in their employment status both during the economic boom and during the economic downturn. Furthermore, that period of time enveloped events related to white supremacist organizations, which were visible in Alberta during the fieldwork, and the participants referred to them as a factor that jeopardized their sense of belongingness. White supremacist groups surfaced in 2005, then waned in 2013, only to reappear in 2015. I sought to examine connections between the various waves of white supremacy to better capture their functioning and suggest strategies to eradicate them. Put together, those dynamics provided a longitudinal perspective that facilitated an in-depth understanding of the construction and negotiation of Black-African Francophone identities.

The interviews opened a door to the participants' subjectivities and identities, and the documents revealed official discourses along with cultural knowledge of marginalized communities. Between 2008 and 2016, we consulted hundreds of documents but retained 120 sources for the purpose of this analysis. The documents consisted of Alberta's weekly mainstream Francophone newspaper, *Le Franco*, and a wide range of public documents, including press releases, community newsletters and websites, and reports that explored topics concerning Francophones in Alberta, such as immigration and identity, and organizational initiatives. They also included records about federal policies, namely multiculturalism, official bilingualism, the Charter, immigration, and employment equity legislation. In addition, there were internal documents that the research participants shared with me. Consequently, the research data were analyzed using qualitative content analysis, which is "a careful, detailed, systematic examination and interpretation of a particular body of material in an effort to

---

13.   I translated all the cited French documents into English.

identify patterns, themes, biases, and meanings" (Berg & Lune 2012, 349). To do this, I first developed thematic categories, both "sociological constructs" and "in vivo codes" (Strauss 1990). The sociological constructs, which I took from theory and the existing literature, included themes such as "master narratives," "racist ideology," and "the Black subject." In vivo codes, terms that the participants themselves use, consisted of themes such as "identity exclusion" and "Black History Month celebrations." The detailed nature of content analysis enabled me to discern both the "manifest content," the overall impression and immediately evident aspects that the data convey, and the "latent content," the deep social and structural meanings and belief systems that underlay the participants' discourse. I sorted data chunks into these categories to answer the research questions, then placed them in the context of theory—CRT and CM—and the relevant literature—the scholarship on immigration and La Francophonie. The ensuing analysis illuminates the interpretation of the participants' identities.

CONTENTS OF THE BOOK

This book is divided into six chapters. The first chapter, the introduction, offers an overview of the topic being examined and the theory and methodology utilized, and sums-up the contents of the succeeding chapters. The second chapter provides the sociohistorical and contemporary contexts of the two collectives whose trajectories have influenced the participants, and these are Francophones and Blacks in Alberta. In the absence of a single volume that presents an all-encompassing chronology of the social history of these two groups, this chapter compiles the history of the two collectives from their early settlement in Alberta to the present. It lays out the events and discourses that shaped the identity construction and negotiation of the two groups. In the case of Francophones, these revolve around the linguicism they have faced, and their struggle through strategic nationalism to protect their language rights. In addition, the chapter brings to light more recent developments in La Francophonie that build on that history and influence identity. These include the creation of the institutions and organizations that constitute the Francophone space and how they allowed Francophones to negotiate their identity. With regard to Blacks, the chapter documents the anti-Black racism they were subjected to from the outset, and tantiracist resistance they engaged with to find a place for themselves in society. The chapter also teases out events that led to the immigration of Black-African Francophones to Alberta, along with the contemporary profile of this population, which offers insights about their identities.

The succeeding chapters analyze the identity discourses of the research participants. The third chapter spells out Canadian identity. It demonstrates that anti-Black racism and racialized linguicism hinder the participants' sense of belonging to Canada, and exhibits white supremacist organizations as a case study that illustrates an exclusionary approach to Canadian identity. The chapter then posits that the participants reconstruct Canadian identity in inclusive ways to overcome marginalization and achieve their migration goal, which is to build a rich social and economic life and contribute to the social, political, and economic growth of society. The fourth chapter underscores Francophone identity. It stresses that anti-Black racism makes Black-Africans feel that they are not considered genuine Francophones, and they therefore reconstruct the Francophone identity to make it relevant to the reality of the 21st century. The chapter displays an educational program, the Caravane contre le racisme et la discrimin-ation, as a case study that depicts Black-African Francophone efforts to make La Francophonie more inclusive. The fifth chapter is devoted to Black-African identity. It reveals the objectification of Blackness and the denial of Black history that serves to negate Black identity. These dynamics are rooted in white supremacy and the European colonial project, which has historically used anti-Black racism to dehumanize the Black subject. This racist ideology legitimized transatlantic slavery, colonialism, and the ensuing racism that annihilated the Black identity. The chapter reveals that Black-African Francophones negotiate Black identity by subverting objecti-fication into subjectivity, redefining it in positive ways, and restoring Black history. Black-African Francophones' celebrations of Black History Month represent a case study that demonstrates these enterprises. The sixth and last chapter is devoted to the conclusion; it synthesizes the means by which multiple minority identities are constructed and negotiated and the contri-butions the book makes to knowledge, and makes policy recommendations to help make La Francophonie and Canada the true multicultural society that we long for.

CHAPTER 2
SOCIOHISTORICAL BACKGROUND AND CONTEMPORARY CONTEXT

"I learned a good deal, at an early age . . .
the importance of history" (Cheryl Foggo 1990).

FRANCOPHONES IN ALBERTA

The Francophone heritage in Alberta dates back to the earliest days of the fur trade in the 18th century, when the French voyageurs arrived in the Northwest region of Canada in search of business opportunities. Then, migrants from Quebec and immigrants from New England and Europe—France and Belgium—joined them. At that time, Alberta was a part of the Northwest Territories, which included the Yukon Territory, the provinces of Alberta and Saskatchewan, and parts of Manitoba. French was the first European language spoken in what eventually became Alberta. It occupied an important official status in NT, since section 110 of the *Northwest Territories Act* "made the use of French and English mandatory in the writing and publication of statutes and other parliamentary documents, and elective in debates of the Legislature, pleadings, and court proceedings in the Northwest Territories" (SLMC n.d.). That provision made both French and English the official languages of the Northwest Territories. It entered Canadian Confederation in 1870, and the respect of the linguistic rights of the French-speaking people was a condition for that decision. When Alberta became a province in 1905, section 110 of the *Northwest Territories Act* remained in effect, and French and English became the official languages of the Legislative Assembly and the courts of Alberta. From the moment Alberta became a province, the negotiation and construction of Francophone identity echoed the two aforementioned dynamics that influenced this identity; the linguicism that has historically marginalized Francophones, and these actors' struggles through strategic nationalism[1] to gain and protect their rights. In the case of Alberta, the hostility towards Francophones was triggered by the conservatism that surfaced in its formative years. Religious and racial prejudice permeated the province as a result of the increase in the numbers of Anglo-Saxon immigrants, which also meant a rise of the number of Protestants. Among the Anglo-Saxons were followers of the Orange Order, who were extremely anti-Catholic—and anti-"foreign," i.e., anti-immigrant—and their presence boosted social and religious conservatism in Alberta (Baergen 2000). The Bible Belt, an appellation that refers to the region between Calgary and Edmonton, meant the expansion of religious—Protestant—conservatism.

Those developments also made Alberta fertile for white supremacists. In *Patterns of Prejudice: A History of Nativism in Alberta*, Howard Palmer (1982) asserts that Alberta's long-established anti-Catholic tradition—and, I would add, racism—paved the way for the Ku Klux Klan (KKK), which had a fanatical hatred for all things Roman Catholic—and embraced racism, establishing a strong base in Alberta. Put together, these forces mirrored the aforementioned classical racism and xenophobia, inasmuch as they constructed the Anglo-Saxon as the superior race, and Protestantism as the privileged doctrine. In that context, being Albertan meant being white, Anglo-Saxon, and Protestant. To negotiate this identity, the Anglo-Saxons embraced religious bigotry to discriminate against the Catholics (and, as we will see in a subsequent section, espoused the "racial purity" ideology to marginalize Blacks). The zeal against Catholicism meant that Francophones were a primary target, for as (Palmer 1982) put it:

> Anti-Catholicism was complicated in Canada by the largest single groups of Catholics in the country being French-speaking[,] that Catholics and Protestants were locked in a battle over the control of Canada and that

---

1.   Outside Québec, where Francophones are official language minority communities, in this case in Alberta, strategic nationalism is adapted to refer to the building of a Francophone space, strengthening bilingualism, and participating in Canadian and Francophone institutions. It also implies a distinction between Francophones on the one hand, and immigrants and ethnic minorities on the other. Though it is not directly associated with a nation or a founding people, it disguises a certain assumed superiority of white Francophones over their racialized counterparts. Strategic nationalism is not inclusive to racialized Francophones in public discourse or institutional practices within La Francophonie.

the Catholics with their monolithic organization and overwhelming political base in Quebec were gaining the upper hand (186-7).

[Canadian-ness equated] Protestantism . . . one national public [English] schools . . . and one language—English (103).

Anti-Catholicism in Alberta coincided with similar discrimination in the rest of Canada. At the national level, anti-Catholicism infiltrated political and public spaces to combat the power of the Catholic Church and the use of the French language across Canada. At the provincial level in Alberta, the combination of Anglo-Saxon nativism and anti-Catholicism culminated in a strong pro-British sentiment that worked to eradicate the French language and culture. A powerful lobby group pushed to make English the only official language of Alberta. Consequently, in 1924, the courts announced that French had been abolished. Since that time, it has been commonly believed that English is the only official language of Alberta. However, in reality, section 110 of the *Northwest Territories Act* has never been repealed, which is why Francophones continue to argue that the Act is still in effect, which means that French continues to be an official language in Alberta. Francophones in Alberta have been fighting to have section 110 formally reinstated so as to maintain the official status of French. Nevertheless, the omission of French as an official language in 1924 generated a loss of institutional and educational resources in French, which culminated in the assimilation of Francophones into Alberta's predominantly Anglophone society. To counter their marginalization, Francophones in Alberta built a Francophone space. They created the Association canadienne-française de l'Alberta (ACFA),[2] which "has been the representative of the [F]rancophone community in Alberta since 1926. Its role is to promote the interests of this community and ensure its overall development" (ACFA 2016). The ACFA championed the Francophone struggle, advocating linguistic rights and promoting the French language and Francophone culture throughout the province. Two years later, in 1928, The ACFA inaugurated *Le Franco*, Alberta's only French-language newspaper. As a weekly platform, *Le Franco* plays a key community building role; it covers issues of interest to Francophones and connects the Francophone population, since it is distributed across the province.

These enterprises resulted in additional successes. For example, Saint-Jean, a Juniorate of the Oblate Order, which was founded in 1908 for young men who wished to join the Oblate religious order, was expanded

---

2.   The French-Canadian Association of Alberta.

into a classical college for the education of Francophone students in Western Canada. Then, major developments occurred in the 1960s, making positive changes in the lives of Francophones in Alberta and across Canada. The liberatory movements that unfolded in the world in the aftermath of World War II, such as the independence movements in Africa and the Civil Rights Movement in the USA, raised awareness about justice and human rights worldwide. Canada embraced that climate and sought to become a model of inclusion for the world, and to that end aimed to fight existing inequalities in Canadian society. Among other things, it sought to improve the condition of Francophones. It is in that context that Canada responded to Francophone advocacy for the recognition of linguistic rights, and passed the aforementioned *Official Languages Act* (OLA) in 1969. The OLA made English and French the official languages of Canada in order to:

(a) ensure respect for English and French as the official languages of Canada and ensure equality of status and equal rights and privileges as to their use in all federal institutions, in particular with respect to their use in parliamentary proceedings, in legislative and other instruments, in the administration of justice, in communicating with or providing services to the public and in carrying out the work of federal institutions;

(b) support the development of English and French linguistic minority communities and generally advance the equality of status and use of the English and French languages within Canadian society; and

(c) set out the powers, duties and functions of federal institutions with respect to the official languages of Canada (Government of Canada 1985a).

The OLA confirmed Canada's commitment to the flourishing of Francophones through financing and other means. The federal government made all its departments bilingual, giving Francophones more opportunities as civil servants. All federal government institutions were obliged to deliver services in both languages, and all documents are published in both languages. The federal government implemented additional provisions to ensure the full implementation of the OLA. For example, a federal minister, usually the Minister of Canadian Heritage,[3] oversees the implementation of the OLA and fosters development within the Francophone space.

---

3.   It was called the Secretary of State for Canada until 1996 when Canadian Heritage was created following administrative reforms.

Furthermore, the Parliament of Canada created the Special Joint Committee on Official Languages in 1980 to examine the progress made since the inception of the OLA in 1969. In 1984, the Standing Joint Committee on Official Languages Policies and Programs was established, then changed its name to the Standing Joint Committee on Official Languages in 1986. It consisted of senators and members of Parliament, but the senators dissociated themselves from the committee in 2002 and struck their own committee, the Canadian Senate Standing Committee on Official Languages (CSSCOL) (Sénat du Canada n.d.). In so doing, the Senate aimed to focus more thoroughly on official language issues and ensure that the OLA promotes English and French and the vitality of English and French language minority communities in Canadian society. The CSSCOL is also responsible for examining matters pertaining to Canada's official languages generally, such as bills, petitions, and inquiries, and makes recommendations to the federal government accordingly. Moreover, the government created the position of the Commissioner of Official Languages in 1970, an agent of Parliament who acts as Canada's official languages ombudsperson to protect the language rights of Canadians and promote linguistic duality across Canada. In addition, the Commissioner receives complaints about the breach of language rights, and resolves disputes. Aside from these initiatives, the Government of Canada developed the Official Languages Action Plan (OLAP), which it implemented in 2003. As a policy statement that provides financial resources to achieve the goals of the OLA, the OLAP is renewed every five years, and its budget continues to increase. For example, the current Plan, which covers the 2018-2023 period, offered the largest amount to date, $2.2 billion (Canadian Heritage 2017).

The Canadian government granted Francophones additional provisions, notably the Charter, which was incorporated into the Canadian Constitution in 1982. Section 23 of the Charter, which is under the heading "Minority Language Educational Rights," stipulates that Francophones "have the right to have their children receive primary and secondary school instruction in that language [French]" (Government of Canada 2016). The Charter asserts that Francophones will be provided "public funds of minority language instruction" (Government of Canada 2016) to establish schools and obtain educational resources. The Charter was a historic victory for Francophones in Canada because it achieved their most cherished goal since early settlement: to secure their children's schooling in French. As Welch (1993) maintains:

> From the beginning of colonization, French-Canadian families chose to construct French-language ... institutions, especially schooling.... The French-Canadian schools, with their own teachers, curriculum, and textbooks helped to maintain French-Canadian cultural stability and prevented assimilation (322).

Francophones stressed the saliency of schooling in French as a "Creator of Community Identity" (Welch 1993, 322). In general, their standpoint echoes the key role that school plays in the formation of identity inasmuch as it shapes how students see themselves. In particular, it ascertains the critical task of schools in a minority situation. For Francophones, school preserves and transmits the French language and Francophone culture. While the OLA and the Charter afforded Francophones many rights, some Canadian provinces were quicker to implement these provisions than others. Alberta made improvements at the level of institutional bilingualism, creating bilingual employment in federal departments and offering services in both official languages. However, this was not the case for education in French, since Francophones did not obtain sufficient funding to run French-language schools, which forced some schools to close. Francophones resorted to strategic nationalism to protest the abuse of their rights. Three citizens submitted a proposal to the Minister of Education at that time, requesting a new French-language elementary school to be administered by an autonomous French-language school board. The minister rejected the demand, contending that the province had a policy that prohibited the creation of a French school jurisdiction. Instead, the minister advised them to work through the Edmonton Public School Board or the Edmonton Roman Catholic Separate School Board. Both boards refused the initiative. In response, the three citizens brought an action before the Supreme Court of Canada (SCC) against the government of Alberta for violating Francophones' right to obtain autonomous school boards run by them, a right granted under section 23 of the Charter. That action became collective, since it was taken on in the name of all Francophones in Alberta, and received support from many Francophone organizations. The case was brought before the courts in 1983, and in 1990 the SCC made a unanimous decision in favour of Francophones:

> The Supreme Court of Canada ruling in the ... case recognizes the right of parents belonging to the linguistic minority to manage their own educational institutions.

> The Court stipulates that section 23 of the Canadian Charter of Rights and Freedoms was "designed to correct, on a national scale, the

progressive erosion of minority official language groups" and to "remedy past injustices" (Office of the Commissioner of Official Languages n.d.).

Following this ruling, the number of French-language schools in Alberta grew, and Francophones controlled the schools' governance. Nevertheless, the Alberta government violated the French language rights again in a manner that sparked another controversy. This is especially exemplified in the notable "Piquette Affair" that began in 1987. Leo Piquette, then Member of the Legislative Assembly (MLA) of Alberta for the New Democratic Party, rose in the Legislative Assembly during question period and started to ask a question in French about French-language education rights in Alberta. He held that section 23 of the Charter, which confirms the right of Francophones to education in French was still not applied properly. Speaker David Carter interrupted Piquette, ruling that English was the only language permitted in the legislature. He prevented Piquette from speaking in French and asked him to pose the question in English. Piquette held that it was "the right of each and every member of this Assembly to conduct their business in this Assembly at any point in the Assembly's proceedings in either official language" (Woolfrey 1987). He asked the Speaker to reconsider his ruling, which the Speaker refused to do. In response, Piquette appeared before a special hearing of the legislature and argued that it was the legislature's duty to permit members to speak in both English and French. Again, Piquette relied on section 110 of the *Northwest Territories Act*, which stated that members of the Northwest Territories legislature could use both English and French in debates. Piquette reasoned that the Act was still in effect and therefore both French and English remained official languages of the Legislative Assembly and the courts. Francophones across Alberta supported Piquette's action and made it a collective public issue. They held rallies at the legislature in support of the French-language rights and the case, and publicized it in the media. In particular, the ACFA sponsored the case in its capacity as the voice of Francophones in Alberta, providing financial and political support. The case was brought before the SCC, which issued a decision in February 1988 in support of Piquette. The SCC ruled that section 110 of the *Northwest Territories Act* was still in force in Alberta. However, it also stated that the Legislature of Alberta could unilaterally modify its language policy. The Legislature responded to the SCC's ruling by allowing members to speak French, but only if they provided the Speaker with a written translation of their comments in advance. Shortly afterwards, in late 1988, in an attempt to put an end to the thorny question of French-language rights, the Government of Alberta dealt a blow to Francophones, endorsing the *Languages Act*, which made Alberta a unilingual English province. At the same time, it affirmed that Alberta would continue to recognize constitutional obligations, particularly the right to education in French and school governance.

In spite of these setbacks, by that time—the late 1980s and early 1990s—anti-Catholicism had waned, which reduced hostility towards Francophones. In addition, the rights and resources that the federal government guaranteed to Francophones allowed them to strategize better. The Francophone space in Alberta had grown in a manner that further strengthened the Francophone struggle. An important new phenomenon consolidated that process: the migration and immigration of Black-African Francophones to Alberta. Alberta's booming economy attracted substantial numbers of immigrants, and the influx of Black-African Francophones added many assets to La Francophonie in Alberta. It boosted the number of Francophones and helped to strengthen La Francophonie against the backdrop of assimilation and the low birth rate of the French-speaking population. The 2011 census indicated that Alberta's Francophone population[4] grew faster than any French-speaking population in Canada (Statistics Canada 2018), increasing by approximately 18% over 2006. Similarly, the number of the bilingual residents in Alberta rose steadily. In 2011, 238,770 Albertans were bilingual, compared with 178,505 in 1996, an increase of 34% (Government of Alberta 2017a). These demographic changes allowed Francophones to claim—and obtain—additional resources and institutions to accommodate the growing population. They also added to the diversity of La Francophonie, as Black-Africans particularly settled in Alberta's two largest cities, Calgary and Edmonton, as well as in Brooks. Their presence fostered multiculturalism within La Francophonie, making it more heterogeneous and vibrant. They got involved in the Francophone space, and created organizations and associations that added to the existing Francophone platforms. Significantly, they joined the Francophone struggle, strengthening it and making it increasingly collective.

The Francophone space expanded to encompass institutions and organizations in the various fields of social life. There are French-language institutions in the fields of health, sports, and recreation, and at all the educational levels—the aforementioned Collège St. Jean became a full-fledged faculty of the University of Alberta. Additional cultural outlets

---

4.   There is no record of the specific number of Black-African Francophones. The Fédération des communautés francophones et acadiennes du Canada (2009) estimated the number of all Africans at 2,880. But this number largely underestimated their actual weight.

were created, as a radio and TV stations were added to *Le Franco*. French-language churches and mainstream organizations were founded to focus on specific groups, such as seniors, women, and youth and children. Furthermore, Francophones created centres that offer new immigrants settlement and integration services. With respect to the political lobby, the ACFA did not cease to become powerful, establishing 14 branches across the province. At the economic level, Francophones founded the Chambre économique de l'Alberta[5] and the Conseil de développement économique de l'Alberta (CDEA)[6] in 1997. These institutions became "Canadian [F]rancophone economic space[s]" (CDEA 2010) aimed at ensuring that Francophones benefit from Alberta's thriving economy. That goal was materialized insofar as Francophones became an economic force in the province. They participate actively in both Alberta's overall and Francophone labour market. Francophones are well represented in the public service sector, in public administration, education, health, and social services. They also partake in agriculture, mining, construction, and the oil and gas industry. Within La Francophonie, existing autonomous French-language institutions and organizations created employment for Francophones, and the business and entrepreneurship sector was prosperous to the extent that, as early as 2004, "in Alberta… 7,000 francophones [owned] their own business, representing 16.3 percent of the [F]rancophone work force. A large number of them [employed] other people, stimulating the provincial economy" (Fédération des communautés francophones et acadienne du Canada 2009, 6).

These businesses had grown since 2004. These achievements mean that Francophones have effectively benefited from Alberta's booming economy and also contributed to its growth. Put together, the accomplishments that were made in the various sectors helped to promote bilingualism in Alberta. At present, five municipalities—Beaumont, Legal, Falher, Plamondon, and Grande Prairie—are officially bilingual, while other municipalities, such as Edmonton and Calgary, publish brochures in French, and others have bilingual signs. Moreover, new French-language services were implemented across Alberta. With the expansion of institutional and societal bilingualism in Alberta, Francophones are becoming increasingly visible. French language and culture are not only better maintained and promoted within the Francophone space, they are present in the larger Alberta society as well. The Francophone space became a society

---

5.   Alberta Chambers of Commerce.
6.   The Economic Development Council of Alberta.

in its own right, and empowered Francophones to lobby more, which resulted in additional gains. A milestone was reached in 1999 when the Government of Alberta created the Francophone Secretariat (the Secretariat), which acts as a liaison between the government and Francophones. That step was a significant recognition of Francophones because, in the government's words, the Secretariat:

> represents the needs of the Francophone community in Alberta and supports initiatives promoting French language and culture ... and aim[s] to:
>
> Acknowledge and increase awareness of the long-standing and continuing contribution of Alberta's Francophone community to the social, cultural and economic development of Alberta.
>
> Support Francophone organizations, communities and individuals in the development of their capacity to participate in, and contribute to, government sponsored initiatives promoting French language and cultures.
>
> Raise awareness and understanding of current Government of Alberta initiatives providing services to the Francophone community in a number of priority areas.
>
> ... [It] clarifies and represents the needs of the Francophone community within government, with various ministries and agencies.
>
> Represents Francophone Albertans and Alberta in organizations such as conferences of ministers responsible for Francophone affairs.
>
> Participates in the negotiation and implementation of federal or provincial agreements relating to French language, culture and education programs (Government of Alberta 2017b).

These statements resonate with Francophone strategic nationalism because they portray Francophones as a "founding people" of Alberta. Like the previously stated provisions put in place to ensure the proper implementation of the OLA, the creation of the Secretariat secured measures to foster the flourishing of Francophones in Alberta. The Secretariat manages the Canada-Alberta agreement on French-language services and administers the distribution of provincial government funding to Francophones. It also identifies and supports the province's priorities regarding Francophones, which means that it plays a major development and political role in La Francophonie. The Secretariat strengthens the Francophone space; it supports education and the offer of services in French, and promotes bilingualism. Such provisions and resources further empowered

Francophones in Alberta, as they extended their lobby and mobilization across the province. Using strategic nationalism, Francophones in Alberta identified themselves publicly as "full citizens of Canada" whose "historical language rights are not recognized" (ACFA 2015). The ACFA requests additional rights and resources from the Alberta government, and at the same time works with mainstream national Francophone associations, especially the Fédération des communautés francophones et acadienne du Canada,[7] to claim resources for Francophones across Canada, which advantages their counterparts in Alberta as well. These enterprises allowed Francophones to further defend their rights, especially with regard to the status of French in Alberta. As stated earlier, the Government of Alberta made English the only official language in the province, which diminished the status of French. Francophones did not cease to mobilize to improve that status, as they asked that Alberta endorse a French-language policy. It is noteworthy that until 2015 all Canadian provinces but two—Alberta and British Columbia—had French-language policies. The purpose of these policies is to engage provincial governments in the issues of their respective Francophone populations. The policies are crucial because they provide additional financial resources and tools to foster community development. They serve to deliver services in French, and improve the representation of Francophones in institutions, curricula, and so on. Francophones in Alberta found a good ear in the New Democratic Party (NDP) government (2015-2019), which adopted a French-language policy in spring 2016. This initiative is a milestone for Francophones in Alberta because the government stressed that:

> French is one of Canada's two official languages . . . . The Government of Alberta acknowledges the past, present and continued social, cultural and economic contributions of the province's significant and diverse French-speaking population. Through meaningful engagement, dialogue, and collaboration, the government is committed to enhancing services in French to support the vitality of the Francophonie in Alberta in a targeted and sustainable manner (Government of Alberta n.d., 2).

Again, the Government of Alberta backs the strategic nationalism of Francophones, since in this case it acknowledged French as one of Canada's two official languages, which is a recognition of the status of Francophones as a "founding people" of Canada. The French-language policy expands the role and resources of the Secretariat, which strengthens the Francophone

---

7.   The Federation of Francophone and Acadian Communities of Canada.

space and further promotes bilingualism. While a previous government halted the advancement of French, a succeeding government gave it a new—better—status. Thus, if we relate this historical snapshot to critical multiculturalism, we realize that language shaped the construction and negotiation of the Francophone identity in Alberta, since it was used to discriminate against Francophones. If we look at the scholarship on La Francophonie, we note that Francophones have largely achieved the goals of their strategic nationalism. They lobby at both the provincial and national levels. They resort to legality, proclaim legislative recognition, and focus on education and services in the French language, which are key to their prosperity. Their struggle is collective; even when individuals—like Piquette—take action, the collective stands behind them. Their political spokesperson, the ACFA, leads such initiatives, which broadens the scope of the claims and gives them more legitimacy. They participate in both Canada-wide and autonomous French-language institutions and build a Francophone space, which makes it possible to promote bilingualism in Alberta. In the end, Francophones made strides worthy of a "founding people." Although linguicism against them continues, they were given support that placed them in a strong position to lobby for additional rights and resources. For the most part, both Canada's federal and provincial—in this case Alberta's—governments accommodate the claims of Francophones, which means that they receive resources from both levels of government. Francophone identity was largely moved from the margins toward the centre. As Breton (2005) put it, Francophones succeeded in making a shift "from social and institutional isolation, to economic and social participation to the acquisition of power" (297). They became partners in Canada's governance and active participants in decision making and law making, which allows them to impact policy to their benefit. It is therefore evident that Francophone strategic nationalism has been efficient. In this regard, a question that I investigate in this book is whether that strategizing has been successful because it is accurate and whether any marginalized group that requests recognition as a "founding people" of Canada will acquire it if it adopts similar mobilization. I will specifically explore these questions through the experiential knowledge—to use critical race theory's wording—of Black-African Francophones. These actors identify as Francophones, which is why it is important to assess where they stand with respect to the aforementioned Francophone rights that are claimed through the use of strategic nationalism: the status of Francophones as a "founding people" of Canada, the rights and resources allocated to Francophones, and the Francophone space.

If we look at the literature on immigration, we note that interprovincial and international migration has always been the backbone of La Francophonie in Alberta. Immigration maximized the building of the Francophone space. Whether it is the French who moved from France to Alberta, the explorers and settlers, the white French-speaking people from the US and Europe, or racialized immigrants from around the world, these diverse groups made La Francophonie the strong space that it is today. However, when we bring CRT's tenet concerning the saliency of race to this discussion, we note that white French-speaking immigrants did not experience a backlash associated with their immigration status. We stated earlier that Francophones faced hostility, but because of their language and religion, not because of their immigration status. In fact, white Francophone immigrants were welcomed because they were needed to enhance the early Francophone settlement in Alberta. This factor stresses Foggo's (1990) quote at the beginning of this chapter, because it clearly displays that whites and Blacks are treated differentially. Most, if not all, of those white immigrants are no longer considered immigrants: they were included in the "founding people" category, and they themselves reproduced master narratives about the founding of Canada in a manner that allowed them to flourish and thrive. When they immigrated to Alberta, they were given fertile farmland and economic opportunities that allowed them to survive in difficult times, such as the Great Depression of the 1930s, and enjoy economic prosperity up to the present. A later section will reveal that immigration has not been fruitful for Black-African Francophones the way it has been for white Francophone immigrants. To facilitate this analysis, we need to understand the historical roots of Black lives in Alberta to decipher the origins and development of anti-Black racism and relations between Francophones and Blacks in Alberta.

BLACKS IN ALBERTA

The patterns of the construction and negotiation of Black identity—anti-Black racism and Blacks' resistance to it—can be seen throughout the social history of Blacks in Alberta. Blacks reached Alberta in the mid-1800s, when it was part of the Northwest Territories. Given the complexity of that history and the magnitude of the political and social forces that discriminated against Blacks in Alberta, I divide Black history in this province into three major periods: 1) the early settlement in the Northwest Territories, 2) the settlement in Alberta from the early 19th century to WWII, and 3) Black lives from the 1960s to the present. Black history in

Alberta during the two first periods coincided with the aforementioned classical racism that was shaped by biological determinism. The early settlement consisted of fur traders who arrived first in Alberta, followed by cowboys, Black American farmers, and independent businesspeople. They were joined by porters and their families who left the US in search of freedom and prosperity (Alberta's Black Pioneer Heritage n.d.a). The 1901 census counted 27 Blacks in the territory that eventually became Alberta. In spite of the small number of Blacks, white Albertans discriminated against them from the outset, resorting to classical racism to pronounce Blacks an inferior race. In Palmer and Palmer's (1985) words: "Blacks [in Alberta] were thought to be different and exceptional, and were automatically expected to play certain roles . . . . [S]tereotypes abounded and prejudice was undeniable" (368). For example, anti-Black racism was demonstrated when the notable cowboy John Ware came to Calgary for the first time in 1884. He was questioned by the North West Mounted Police for horse theft, which indicated that the colour of his skin immediately made him a suspect. The arrival of Blacks in Alberta coincided with the early settlement of Francophones in the province. However, that was not the first time that the trajectories of Blacks and Francophones collided. Long before then, they met in the processes of transatlantic slavery and colonialism, when the French were slave traders and colonial masters. They enslaved Blacks and colonized them, and that oppression was also replicated in Canada. The French reached Canada through conquest and colonization, and Blacks entered Canada through the channels of enslavement and forced migration. French Canadians participated in the enslavement of Black Canadians and the ensuing colonialism and racism. These patterns of domination were reproduced in Alberta as white Francophones socially distanced themselves from Blacks during the early years of settlement. Francophone hostility towards Blacks only increased as it became particularly overt during the second period of Black settlement.

The second phase of Black settlement in Alberta encompassed the immigration of Blacks from Oklahoma to Alberta—and Saskatchewan— between 1908 and 1911 (Winks 1971). Their movement was compelled by events that occurred both in Oklahoma and Canada in the late 1800s and early 1900s. In the US, upon the creation of the state of Oklahoma in 1907, racial discriminatory legislation was enacted, mandating segregated schools and railroads. It also restricted Blacks' civil and political rights, including the right to vote, and prevented them from buying farms. These events echoed the global pervasiveness of anti-Black racism at the time, in this case in the US. They pushed Blacks to leave Oklahoma, and many considered moving to Canada, thinking that it would be a land of freedom and safety. Meanwhile, in Canada, then Minister of the Interior Clifford Sifton, who was responsible for immigration policy, actively promoted American immigration to Western Canada between 1897 and 1911. Though the government of Canada was only interested in attracting white farmers, immigration agents in Oklahoma circulated the advertisements in community newspapers without ensuring that they would not reach the unintended audience—Blacks. The advertisements encouraged Blacks to move northward to Canada, and it is in that context that between 1,000 and 1,500 Blacks from Oklahoma relocated to Alberta and Saskatchewan.

At the turn of the 20th century, Blacks from Oklahoma established four rural and two urban settlements in Alberta. The rural settlements consisted of Amber Valley, which was the largest and most prosperous Black settlement, Keystone (later Breton), Junkins (later Wildwood), and Campsie (Foggo 1990). The urban settlements were concentrated in Edmonton and Calgary. The rural settlements were isolated from established white communities, and were bush-covered areas where farmland was marginal and the climate was severely cold and damp. In addition, there were no roads to nearby Edmonton or Athabasca, so travelling to these cities for supplies took a few days in dry weather and up to a month in poor weather. This also meant that Black pioneers did not have easy access to hospitals and professional medical help. Furthermore, economic opportunity was very limited. A poignant question that arises is : why did Black pioneers end up in these isolated areas? Some scholars maintain that Blacks may have been directed to these areas by immigration officials who were aware of the apprehension that their arrival had aroused among the whites (Shepard 1983). Others opine that the pioneers deliberately chose isolated areas to avoid white racism. In either case, racism contributed to their settlement in these marginalized areas. In addition, racism resulted in the exclusion of Black children from schools in neighbouring regions. For example, in Campsie, English and Scottish teachers prevented Black children from attending the local school. The pioneers were also not allowed to attend social functions or obtain accommodation in nearby Athabasca.

Black pioneers in the rural settlements mobilized against the backdrop of racism. They resorted to community building, creating a physical infrastructure including institutions such as churches and schools, as well as organizations and associations. They used these infrastructures to create an active social life, organizing debates and sporting and cultural activities. In particular, the famous annual Amber Valley picnic, a two-day event, drew people from other regions, and helped to strengthen relations within and between the settlements. Because social services were not readily available, the pioneers became self-sustaining. They grew their own food and relied on midwives and home remedies. However, the predominantly white Alberta society continued to see them as foreigners to be exterminated. The forces of domination against Black pioneers in the rural settlements were omnipresent, which is why the settlements did not expand. On the contrary, they dwindled. The pioneers experienced difficulties getting bank credit and good land and, as we will see, Black immigration was curtailed to prevent the arrival of more Blacks in Alberta. Unlike white Francophone settlers who, as we stated earlier, were given fertile farmland in favourable locations and economic opportunities that allowed them to survive the Great Depression of the early 1930s, Black pioneers suffered a lack of resources. They did not do well during the Great Depression, which contributed to the stagnation and decline of their settlements. Consequently, only a few Black families remain in the rural settlements today.

When it comes to the urban Black pioneers, by 1911 the census reported 208 Blacks in Edmonton and 72 in Calgary. Again, in spite of the small number of Blacks in these cities, they faced extreme racial hostility (Shepard 1997). Classical racism in reaction to Black immigration was omnipresent both in Edmonton and Calgary. Interlocking systemic, structural, institutional, official, public, individual, and diplomatic types of racism, racism of elimination, and racism of extermination surfaced. For example, institutional racism was echoed in the media through racial slurs, such as the *Edmonton Journal*'s contention: "We want no dark spots in Alberta" (Alberta's Black Pioneer Heritage n.d.a). Other media fabricated stories about crimes committed by Blacks in Alberta. The media's racism exacerbated xenophobia towards Blacks, which ignited public protests and campaigns opposing the arrival of Blacks in Edmonton and Calgary. Institutional racism was also illustrated in the discourse and practices of many organizations. For example, the Edmonton Board of Trade and the Edmonton Trades and Labour Council tried to stop Black immigration by requesting that a head tax of $1,000 be levied on each Black living in Edmonton. That request gained broader approval when similar organizations in Strathcona, Fort Saskatchewan, Calgary, and the French-speaking city Morinville supported it. Other organizations also targeted Blacks; for example, the Alberta branch of the Imperial Order of Daughters of the Empire (IODE) demanded the segregation of Blacks in Edmonton so that they would not live in proximity to white women. IODE proclaimed: "We do not wish that the fair fame of Western Canada should be sullied with the shadow of Lynch Law, but we have no guarantee that our women will be safer in their scattered homesteads than white women in other countries with a Negro population" (Palmer 1982, 36).

The Canadian chapters of the IODE were extensions of the British umbrella organization, which was the largest white women's patriotic organization. Therefore, these statements displayed Alberta white women's agreement with the classical racism of the time, expanding the imperial and colonial myth about the racial superiority of the Anglo-Saxons over Blacks. Not only did the prejudice and stereotypes of the IODE associate Blacks with dishonesty, evil, and lawlessness, they correlated Black men with sexual aggressiveness that threatened white women. The institutional racism of these organizations and the media intensified public racism towards Blacks as Albertans pushed to eradicate Black immigration. To achieve that goal, these forces worked together to halt Black immigration at its source, Oklahoma. Organizations, including the IODE and the Edmonton Board of Trade, as well as businesses—banks and hotels in Edmonton, municipalities, and Albertan citizens, filed a petition to then Prime Minister Wilfred Laurier asking him to stop the immigration of Blacks to Alberta. The petition, which was dated April 18, 1911, embedded blatant racism, whose scope and breadth require a long citation to decipher:

> We, the undersigned residents of the city of Edmonton, respectfully urge upon your attention and upon that of the Government of which you are the head, the serious menace to the future welfare of a large portion of ·Western Canada, by reason of the alarming influx of negro settlers. This influx commenced about four years ago in a very small way, only four or five families coming in the first season, followed by thirty or forty families the next year. Last year several hundred negroes arrived in Edmonton and settled in surrounding territory. Already this season nearly three hundred have arrived; and the statement is made, both to these arrivals and by press dispatches, that these are but the advent of such negroes as are now here was most unfortunate for the country, and that further arrivals in large numbers would be disastrous. We cannot admit as any factors the argument that these people may be good farmers or good citizens. It is a matter of common knowledge that it has been proved in the United States that negroes and whites cannot live in proximity without the occurrence of revolting lawlessness and the development of bitter race hatred, and that the most serious question facing the United States today is the negro problem. We are anxious that such a problem should not be introduced into this lawlessness as have developed in all sections

in the United States where there is any considerable negro element. There is not reason to believe that we have here a higher order of civilization, or that the introduction of a negro problem here would have different results. We therefore respectfully urge that such steps immediately be taken by the Government of Canada as will prevent any further immigration of negroes into western Canada. And your petitioners, as in duty bound, will ever pray (Alberta, Land of Opportunity 2001).

By calling racism in the US "a Negro problem," not "an American problem," white Albertans blamed Blacks for the marginalization that disenfranchised them in the first place. They did not hold the rest of American society, especially whites, accountable for the racism that permeated US society. Neither did Albertans embrace antiracist initiatives to welcome Blacks, which reveals that racism is native to Canada, not an imported phenomenon—especially from the US—as many Canadians like to believe. Again, Albertans followed pre-existing fixed racist perceptions about Blacks. Localities outside Edmonton followed suit to maximize the pressure on the Government of Canada to ban Black immigration. Again, the French-speaking village Morinville endorsed the petition, which displays anti-Black racism on the part of white Francophones. In that climate, public racism against Blacks only increased as more organizations and people joined the protests. The Athabasca Landing Board of Trade submitted a separate petition to the Minister of Interior in 1911 declaring that: "Canada is the last country open to the white race, Are we going to preserve it for the white race, or are we going to permit the Blacks free use of large portions of it?" (Abu-Laban & Gabriel 2002, 39). Such proclamations demarcated racial boundaries between whites and Blacks with the purpose of isolating Blacks as a distinct—inferior—racial category to facilitate imposing racial hatred upon them. How did the Government of Canada respond to the conspiracy against Blacks? It exhibited state racism by supporting the campaign. On August 12, 1911, the Government of Canada, then under the leadership of Sir Wilfrid Laurier, drafted the "deemed unsuitable" Order-in-Council which stated: "For a period of one year from and after the date here of the landing in Canada shall be [sic] and the same is prohibited of any immigrants belonging to the Negro race, which race is *deemed unsuitable* to the climate and requirements of Canada" (Emphasis added) (CanadianContent 2000-2019).

The Government of Canada refused the petition on October 5, 1911, not in support of human rights but rather for political reasons. As Troper (1972) points out, Canadian politicians were reluctant to openly ban Black immigration to avoid alienating Black voters in Ontario and Nova Scotia.

The Government of Canada replaced the overt racism that was entrenched in the order-in-council with a more covert type of discrimination that Shepard (1983) termed diplomatic racism. The government opted for informal procedures to halt Black immigration, including sending immigration agents to Oklahoma to discourage Blacks from moving to Alberta. The agents spread tales of starvation, extreme cold, poor soil, and deadly exposure to the elements. In addition, the Canadian government instructed Canadian immigration officers in the US to deter Black migration into Canada. Furthermore, the "Canadian railway companies were apparently also enlisted to ask American railways to discourage [B]lack migration to Canada" (Alberta's Black Pioneer Heritage n.d.b). Multilayered and multidimensional racism produced virulent anti-Black racism in reaction to a relatively small number of Black immigrants. That racism succeeded in halting Black immigration to Alberta, since by 1912 Black Americans living in Oklahoma lost any interest in immigrating to Alberta or Canada. By 1914, the wave of migration to Canada had virtually stopped, and some Black pioneers even returned from Alberta to the US because of the racial hostility that they suffered in Alberta (Alberta's Black Pioneer Heritage n.d.b). The racial oppression that haunted Black pioneers also epitomized the racism of extermination, albeit figuratively. Immigration policy purposely prevented Blacks from entering Alberta, which resulted in the decline and disappearance of the Black population. Blacks were extinguished, in the sense that these measures prevented the arrival of more Blacks into Alberta. Had it not been for that, there would have been more Blacks in Alberta, as is the case with other groups.

Unfortunately, anti-Black racism was not confined to Alberta because, as the scholarship on immigration posits, that racism echoed nationwide xenophobia, which was entrenched in Canada's immigration policy and practices. We stated earlier that, according to Satzewich and Liodakis (2013), Canada's immigration system operated along the lines of the "racialized hierarchy of desirability" (RHD). The authors identify three scales on that hierarchy: the top, the bottom, and the in-between levels. The top of the hierarchy was reserved for the most desirable future citizens, and these were white British, Americans, and Western Europeans. The bottom of the hierarchy was confined to the groups that were not desirable, and these were non-European non-whites, such as Blacks and Asians. The in-between level targeted people who might cause problems in Canada but could be allowed in as a last resort, for example, if the number of desirable immigrants was not sufficient. The in-between groups were Eastern and Southern Europeans. The hierarchical racist ideologies were stated overtly in Canada's *Immigration Act* of 1910, which instructed immigration officials to "prohibit or limit... permanently" entry into Canada to people:

> of any nationality or race... *deemed unsuitable* to the climatic, industrial, social '...' educational, labour... because such immigrants are deemed undesirable owing to their peculiar customs, habits, modes of life... and because of their probable inability to become readily assimilated or to assume the duties and responsibilities of citizenship (emphasis added) (Canadian Museum of Immigration 2017).

The proximity of this quote, on one hand, between the date of the clause (1910) and that of the aforementioned "deemed unsuitable" order-in-council (1911) and, on the other hand, between the discourses of both clauses—"the deemed unsuitable" contention—was not coincidental. Both the federal government and white Alberta worked together to dehumanize Blacks. Their immigration policies and discourses denoted classical racism, since they exemplified the primordial racist ideologies about the superiority and inferiority of racial groups. They also demonstrated what critical multiculturalism considers a Eurocentric treatment of identity (Shohat & Stam 2013), which perceives identity as fixed and genetic, a matter of "being" rather than "becoming." Although at that time Canada embraced assimilation approaches that required incoming immigrants to meld into the existing Eurocentric culture, that tendency targeted white European and American immigrants. The racialized, including Blacks, were not welcomed immigrants because it was believed that they do not "become"; they cannot assimilate because their genes do not change to accommodate the weather and culture. These processes generated double standards through which Alberta welcomed the immigration of white Americans while denouncing that of their Black counterparts, and the federal government backed that discrimination. In the case of Alberta, Palmer (1982) stated that over half a million white Americans immigrated to the Prairie provinces, including Alberta, between 1898 and 1914 and, by 1911, 22% of Alberta's population was American-born. This period of time coincided with the immigration of Oklahoman Blacks to Alberta. As we stated, nearly every section of Alberta's population vehemently opposed that immigration. It bears noting that nearly every section of the Alberta population, including journalists, government officials, businesspeople, and farmers welcomed the influx of white Americans. Keep in mind that both white and Black Americans often lived under the same weather in the US, yet white Americans were believed to be suitable for Alberta's weather while Blacks were not. Biological determinism asserted white privilege, giving white Americans legitimacy to consider themselves and be considered Canadian and allowing them to support the virulent racism that targeted their fellow citizens—Black Americans. It bears noting that the correspondence between the federal and provincial racist approaches to immigration meant that the number of Blacks did not decline only in Alberta, but at the national level as well. The overall number of Blacks in Canada dropped from 21,500 in 1871 to 18,300 in 1921 (Milan & Tran 2004) and decreased to 18,000 in 1951. This period of time also coincided with the epoch during which the numbers of Blacks in Alberta diminished, as it declined consistently from 1911 to the 1960s. For example, it dropped from 1,048 in 1921 to 702 in 1951. These facts indicate that Black immigration was banned not only in Alberta but in Canada as a whole.

After Black immigration to Alberta stopped and the rural settlements declined, a small Black population remained in the urban regions, especially in Edmonton and Calgary. They were subjected to horrific racism on the part of the white supremacist groups that surfaced in Alberta in the early 1930s (Palmer 1982). This factor will be explored in a subsequent section but, at this juncture, we stress that prejudice and stereotypes led white Albertans to believe that Blacks were meant only to serve, which is why almost all urban Blacks were in the service occupations prior to 1950. In Edmonton and Calgary, the largest number of Black men worked as railway porters, and the women as domestics. That displayed racism of elimination because Blacks were "included" in the lower levels of society but did not get better opportunities. Furthermore, Blacks faced restrictions in housing, jobs, and public facilities. Hospitals refused to admit Blacks into nurse training programs, while the public ridiculed Blacks, showing white actors in blackface (Palmer & Palmer 1985). Racial segregation occurred in public facilities as swimming pools and dance halls disallowed Blacks to use their premises. Furthermore, public demands for segregation were made in both Calgary and Edmonton. In Calgary in 1920, about 500 residents of the Victoria Park district, representing three fifths of its households, signed a petition and submitted it to the City Council. The petition stated: "We request that they [Blacks] be restrained from purchasing any property in the said district and any who may now be residing there will be compelled to move into some other locality" (Foggo 2015). Anti-Black racism took its toll when the City Council did not reject the petition right away and instead wrote to 16 Canadian cities inquiring whether those cities segregated Blacks or prevented them from residing within their jurisdiction. These attempts revealed tendencies of racism of extermination because they aimed to wipe out Blacks from the public spaces that they inhabited. In that context, Calgary's City Council turned the petition down only after those cities confirmed that there was no such precedent. While the City Council did not endorse the petition, the Mayor of Calgary advised Victoria district residents that "an aroused public opinion on such actions would accomplish more than any move the city authorities could make" (Foggo 2015). The Mayor showed diplomatic racism, since, while he did not formally approve the petition, he encouraged Victoria's residents to target the real estate agents who sold properties to prevent them from selling properties to Blacks. That measure could have been as effective as any overt racist policy.

Similar attempts at segregation occurred in Edmonton in 1924 when a city commissioner asked that Blacks be banned from all public parks and swimming pools. Although the city refused the request, it did not take firm action to prohibit racism. Thus, it displayed what critical race theory considers the denial of racism, which was harmful because it propagated racial discrimination. Although in the end Alberta did not endorse any formal segregation legislation, officials were complicit in the residential segregation of Blacks because this segregation disparaging Blacks was still practised. Unfortunately, the racial bigotry towards Blacks did not end there, it only doubled because it was compounded by the extremes of hostility in the form of racial hatred and racial violence when white soldiers attacked Blacks in Calgary in 1940.

Again, classical racism towards Blacks did not end with the 1940 event, continuing to plague them until the 1950s, while during that time xenophobia against other groups lessened. For example, the in-between groups, Eastern and Southern Europeans, were welcomed into Canada as a "last resort" when Canada needed more people to sustain its growth. White privilege leveraged them to the status of desirable immigrants, and hostility towards them diminished. In addition, Canada's approach to assimilation shifted to accommodate them. Palmer (1982) explains that it was then believed that these groups could assimilate, and the question was what needed to be done to allow them to assimilate. While debate about the assimilation of Blacks and Asians remained unchanged, it was still assumed that it was impossible for these people to meld into the white culture. Though there is no evidence to suggest that Eastern and Southern European immigrants reproduced racism towards Blacks, there is no proof that they defended Blacks either. This allows us to argue that these immigrants exerted anti-Black racism at least through the silence and denial of racism that critical race theorists contend propagates racial oppression.

Similar patterns influenced Francophones in Alberta, since linguicism against them lessened during that time, and they were increasingly considered full citizens. Events such as Morinville's support of the petition against Black immigration into Alberta demonstrated overt anti-Black racism on the part of Francophones. In addition, they continued to distance themselves socially—and economically—from Blacks. As Francophones continued to fight for their language rights, their mobilization in no way opposed racism, which once again indicated their silence and denial of racism. Racism tainted Blacks and went unnoticed by many, but not by Blacks themselves. Much like rural Black pioneers, urban Blacks did not tolerate racism, as they, too, worked hard to improve their plight.

Urban Blacks established physical structures and organizations that culminated in the creation of geographic areas of concentration. Among other things, they founded the Colored Protective Association in Calgary in 1910, the first Black organization in urban Alberta. The association fought for Black civil rights and opposed the aforementioned Victoria Park petition that sought to segregate Blacks within Calgary. Furthermore, urban pioneers also established three unified associations under the auspices of the Universal Negro Improvement Association (UNIA), which Marcus Garvey had founded in New York in 1916. The first was the Negro Welfare Association of Alberta (NWAA), which was formed in 1921. Like the UNIA, the NWAA was dedicated to Black self-improvement and reducing unemployment rates in Black communities (Hooks 1997). The second was the Negro Political Association, which fought to improve civil rights among Black Albertans, and lobbied government officials to obtain equal rights legislation. The third was the Alberta Association for the Advancement of Colored People, which was established in 1947 and fought for equal employment rights for Blacks throughout the 1940s and 1950s. These organizations also aimed to enhance education and leadership skills among Black youth, which they did by providing scholarships and establishing social clubs, such as the Black Girl Guide Company and the Colored Boys' Athletic Club. Furthermore, the pioneers built infrastructure, including churches, and all these enterprises fostered tight-knit Black concentrations in Edmonton and Calgary. Edmonton's Black concentration was in what is now the Oliver neighbourhood downtown, and it was centred on the Shiloh Baptist Church. Calgary's Black neighbourhood was in Inglewood and was quite large. It was centred on the Calgary branch of the Standard Church of America, which the pioneers built in 1947. Utopia Hall was also built in Inglewood and became the secular hub of Blacks in Calgary. Like the community rural Black pioneers built, its counterpart in urban

Alberta fostered an enriching social life. It hosted a multitude of cultural activities and forums that debated the welfare of Black people in Alberta. The ensuing solidarity allowed Blacks to fight together to eliminate discriminatory practices in the workforce and put the concerns of Black Albertans before the provincial government. Their resilience resulted in milestones; for example, they pushed the Government of Alberta to pass the *Fair Employment Practices Act* in 1955 and the *Equal Pay Act* in 1957. These acts afforded Blacks more opportunities. Additionally, their mobilization led to progress in education and the economic realm, since some Blacks were able to become entrepreneurs and business owners (Foggo 1990).

The aforementioned discussion illustrates Fanon's (1967) theorization of Black identity, since anti-Black racism had plagued Blacks since their early settlement in Alberta. In Fanon's (1967) terms, that identity was tainted with "objectification," since it was associated with pejorative stereotypes. The denial of Black history was more subtle, since it was entrenched in Eurocentric ideologies that treated Blacks as an inferior race, a race with no culture, civilization or history. That identity was in turn negotiated through the exclusion of Black pioneers from social spaces and resources. Again, in Fanon's (1967) view, the pioneers countered identity annihilation, since the structures they created empowered them and provided them with a strong sense of solidarity. In CRT's terms, they enacted "political solidarity," a collective community action through which they became subjects and actors. They also redefined Black identity in a positive manner that combined sociocultural and political expression with community development. The negotiation of that identity echoed the ability to organize and establish structures and areas of concentration. They reinstated Black history by replicating Black organizations created previously to salvage it, in this case UNIA. They made history, Black history, which became an important identity source (Kelly 2001). For example, Amber Valley continues to be an iconic source of Black identity; it is highly esteemed as symbol of pride, spirituality, and dignity that honours Blacks' achievements in the pursuit of social justice. Though the number of Black pioneers in Alberta dwindled by the end of the 1950s, their legacy remains empowering. Their overall struggle cultivated Black heritage, projecting Black history as an integral part of Alberta's history. Thus, the pioneers' legacy inspired future generations of Blacks in Alberta, including Black Francophones. This is because the following decade, the 1960s, marked a turning point in Black lives. Larger waves of Blacks immigrated to Alberta, altering both the demographics and the identity of Blacks and the larger Alberta society.

From the 1960s to the present

The liberatory movements of the 1960s that prompted Canada to improve its treatment of Francophones also resulted in its willingness to combat racism. To this end, Canada made major changes to its legislation and enacted new policies, which impacted Canada's approach to immigration and multiculturalism issues, the Charter, employment equity, and antiracism initiatives. Thus, Canada modified its immigration policy in 1962, when the Canadian government admitted that immigrant selection was based on racist assumptions, but that these criteria would be removed. In 1967, Canada introduced the points system in the *Immigration Act*, which replaced the aforementioned racist selection criteria—i.e., race and nationality—with largely objective criteria. These included educational background, fluency in English and French, and job skills. However, we must be critical of this rhetoric, because social justice was not the only factor that spurred these changes. Political calculations pressured Canada to open up to racial diversity, since it sought to play a major peacemaking role in the world and become a model for tolerance and inclusion. It was evident that Canada's blatant racist immigration policies would jeopardize that goal. Canada also faced labour market shortages inasmuch as, as Mensah (2010) states, by the early 1960s, European skilled immigration to Canada decreased as a result of economic prosperity in Europe. In addition, there was a massive emigration of Canadian professionals to the US, and Canada sought to compete with the US for scarce skilled labour. Canada could no longer rely on traditional sources of immigration—white Europeans and Americans; thus, it had no choice but to open its doors to the developing world. In this regard, critical race theory's tenet of the centrality of race informs us that race has shaped Canada's immigration policy since its inception, including in the context of positive social change and the support of human rights. However, regardless of the intention behind these measures, they allowed visible minority immigrants to enter Canada. These waves of immigration strengthened Canada's diversity and made it more multicultural, and, in that climate, Canada took action regarding multiculturalism as well. I showed earlier that multiculturalism has four interconnected meanings—fact, ideology, policy, practice (Fleras & Elliott 2002), and that all these meanings are demonstrated in Canada. At this juncture, I elaborate on these issues by indicating that multiculturalism is a fact in Canada because of the country's racial, ethnic, and cultural diversity. Multiculturalism is also a policy because, as stated previously, Canada has adopted its Multiculturalism Policy (the Policy) in 1971. It bears noting that the Policy aimed to:

recognize and promote the understanding that multiculturalism reflects the cultural and racial diversity of Canadian society and acknowledges the freedom of all members of Canadian society to preserve, enhance and share their cultural heritage ... recognize and promote the understanding that multiculturalism is a fundamental characteristic of the Canadian heritage and identity and that it provides an invaluable resource in the shaping of Canada's future ... promote the full and equitable participation of individuals and communities of all origins in the continuing evolution and shaping of all aspects of Canadian society and assist them in the elimination of any barrier to that participation ... encourage and assist the social, cultural, economic and political institutions of Canada to be both respectful and inclusive of Canada's multicultural character ... encourage and assist the business community, labour organizations, voluntary and other private organizations, as well as public institutions, in ensuring full participation in Canadian society, including the social and economic aspects, of individuals of all origins and their communities, and in promoting respect and appreciation for the multicultural reality of Canada ... assist ethno-cultural minority communities to conduct activities with a view to overcoming any discriminatory barrier and, in particular, discrimination based on race or national or ethnic origin (Government of Canada 1985b).

The Policy posits that Canada's recognition of diversity is so integral to Canadian society that it equates multiculturalism with Canadian identity. Not only does the Policy associate Canadian identity with pluralism, it embraces multiple identities. This allows immigrants—and other Canadians—to maintain and develop specific—cultural, ethnic, racial—affiliations. Furthermore, multiculturalism in Canada is a matter of ideology because the Policy is largely influenced by liberal multiculturalism and somewhat shaped by critical multiculturalism. "The freedom of all members of Canadian society" and "ensuring full participation in Canadian society" echo the previously stated principles of liberal multiculturalism, such as freedom and equality. The terms such as "race," "racial diversity," and "discriminatory barrier ... based on race" in the above quote mirror the precepts of critical multiculturalism because they name and contest structural inequities, in this case racism. Moreover, multiculturalism in Canada is a practice because the Policy culminated in programs aimed at achieving its goal. I indicated earlier that the Policy evolved in three phases, and in this context it is useful to provide greater details about these phases to better understand their implications. Each phase targeted a specific social problem and offered a specific solution. The solution encompassed a specific model of education and drew on a specific multicultural ideology.

The first phase, "ethnic multiculturalism," took place in the 1970s, and the social problem it identified was immigrants' concern that their contributions to Canadian society were not appreciated. We recall that these immigrants were white Western and Eastern European Christians—i.e., Germans, Ukrainians, and Poles. The solution was to accommodate them by celebrating their heritage. For that reason, cultural diversity was at the heart of Canadian identity (Caidi et al. 2010). The Government of Canada contributed funding to ethnocultural organizations and activities that promoted heritage cultures, languages, and folklore. This phase was also marked by multicultural education. Ethnic multiculturalism facilitated the inclusion of these immigrants in Canadian society, but their identities overlapped with those of mainstream white Canadians. A focus on culture, even within the depoliticized liberal approach to culture, was sufficient to guarantee them inclusion. Again, white privilege served to leverage their status in society.

Nevertheless, the aforementioned changes in immigration policy increased the number of visible minority immigrants, including Blacks. An influx of Black immigrants began in the late 1960s, and their numbers in Canada experienced an unprecedented increase, from 34,400 in 1971 to 239,500 in 1981 (Mensah 2010). First, English-speaking Caribbean Blacks from Jamaica, Trinidad and Tobago, and the Bahamas arrived in eastern and central Canada, while French-speaking Haitians settled mostly in Quebec. Subsequently, Blacks from African countries, such as Nigeria, Ghana, Sudan, Ethiopia, and Congo, began to arrive. Scholars note that racism continued to rise as the proportion of Blacks increased (Govia 1988). It bears noting that, although none of the research participants were in Canada during the ethnic multiculturalism phase, Black Francophones who were in eastern Canada at that time disclosed facts that align with the scholarship. They endured multiple layers of anti-Black racism and felt that they were not considered full citizens (Madibbo & Maury 2002). It is argued that racism persisted because ethnic multiculturalism did not challenge structural barriers, especially racism, and these claims led Canada to enter the second phase of multiculturalism, equity multiculturalism, in the 1980s. This phase focused on racism as a social problem, and the solution was improving the well-being of racialized immigrants by eliminating structural discrimination in the labour market and other institutions. Government funding supported programs that aimed to improve minority representation and employment equity, such as antiracist workshops and support for entrepreneurship among racialized minorities. Equity multiculturalism was largely guided by the principles of critical multiculturalism

(CM) inasmuch as the programs, initiatives, and discourses during that phase echoed the aforementioned precepts of CM, including the urgency to challenge inequitable power relations and structural dynamics such as racism. Antiracism increasingly became a public issue and was entrenched in the education system. The type of education in Canada during that phase was termed "anti-racism education," which is very similar, if not identical to critical multicultural education. Anti-racism education in Canada might have been labelled critical multicultural education elsewhere. The difference between the two types of education is that antiracism education focuses on racism and anti-racism, while critical multicultural education explores issues of gender and identity in addition to racism. Thus, education in Canada was at least partially critical multicultural education. At this juncture, it is important to emphasize that a few of the research participants were in Canada during the equity phase. They were younger and were therefore students, which means that equity multiculturalism mainly influenced their educational experiences. These participants reported positive outcomes in the school system at that time. For example, one participant said: "For once, we had a Black teacher in . . . school, and learned about Black history." Their narratives also point to positive outcomes for other Black Francophones, which we can see in the words of a participant who stated: "We heard the echo, some [Black Francophones] found good [commensurate] jobs." As such, equity multiculturalism created a space for antiracism to emerge and fostered some inclusion for the racialized. Unfortunately, that progress did not continue, because equity multiculturalism was not afforded sufficient time to achieve the intended social transformation. Canada cut the phase short and moved on to the third phase of multiculturalism in the 1990s, civic multiculturalism, which is still in effect today.

The social problem that civic multiculturalism tackles is a series of debates that are labelled the "national unity argument" (Bissoondath 1994). Concerns were raised that equity multiculturalism weakened the sense of belonging to Canada because it encouraged ethnic separatism and created divisiveness between immigrants and the rest of Canadian society. The solution provided to rectify that problem is to strengthen social inclusion by building a shared Canadian identity that people of all backgrounds would adhere to. This allegiance connotes a civic identity based on shared citizenship and is intended to combat racism and other forms of discrimination by fostering equality, tolerance, and social cohesion among citizens. In particular, civic multiculturalism invites citizens to engage with each other, with communities, and with "the real social, political, and economic structures within . . . society or culture" (Knefelkamp 2008, 2). Civic multiculturalism program funding prioritizes intra-community initiatives that boost civic participation and civic engagement, such as volunteerism, charity work, community clean-up programs, and voting. The type of education prioritized during the civic multiculturalism phase is citizenship education, which aims to educate future citizens—children and youth—to enhance their understanding of the principles and institutions that govern their country, and raise awareness about the human and political issues that are at stake in their society (Banks 2006). To this end, citizenship education inculcates the principles of democracy, such as freedom, liberty, and non-violence (Wright 2012). It trains children to understand, respect, and apply the rights and obligations of citizenship. It asks schools to instill a democratic culture and advocate respect for all participants—students and teachers, administrators, and other employees. It requests that schools allow students to express their views freely and contribute to the decision-making process. Citizenship education postulates that racism, and conflict in general, is rooted in cultural ignorance that leads people to value some cultures over others. According to citizenship education, the solution to racism lies in the promotion of respect of cultural differences in daily life at school. Pedagogically speaking, students are encouraged to mingle with their classmates, learn about various cultures, create a dialogue, and take an interest in their peers' family lifestyles, social habits, and cultural practices. Thus, we see an overlap between civic multiculturalism and the liberal multiculturalism ideology.

Therefore, I argue that CM's above-mentioned critique of liberal multiculturalism applies to civic multiculturalism as well. Similarly, CM's reluctance concerning liberal multicultural education speaks to citizenship education as well (May & Sleeter 2010). Thus, civic multiculturalism does not effectively address and redress inequitable power structures, including racism. This is because civic multiculturalism stresses the ethos of freedom and equality devoid of structural barriers. As the critical multiculturalists would put it, civic multiculturalism dissociates culture from the power inequities that shape it because it considers conflict a cultural misunderstanding that can be salvaged by interactions between individuals. This approach overlooks the institutional factors that marginalize minorities. It is important to note that most of the research participants immigrated to Canada during the civic multiculturalism phase, and their lives are unfolding during the current civic multiculturalism phase. Therefore, their trajectories will reveal the impacts of this phase on Black-African Francophones.

In addition to the above changes, in 1985, Canada added a new section to the Charter that specifically denounces racism. Under the heading "Equality Rights," section 15 stipulates that:

> 15. (1) Every individual is equal before and under the law and has the right to the equal protection and equal benefit of the law without discrimination and, in particular, without discrimination based on race, national or ethnic origin, colour...

> (2) Subsection (1) does not preclude any law, program or activity that has as its object the amelioration of conditions of disadvantaged individuals or groups including those that are disadvantaged because of race, national or ethnic origin, colour, religion... (Government of Canada 2016).

While the Charter refutes racism in all layers of society, the *Employment Equity Act* (EEA) that Canada passed in 1986 targets racism in the labour market. The Act requires employers to take proactive action with regard to the four designated groups. The rationale is that these groups suffered historical disenfranchisement that requires specific additional measures to make up for. Thus, the Act was endorsed to guarantee the designated groups equitable access to the labour market. Moreover, in 2005, Canada implemented an antiracist action plan titled "A Canada for All: Canada's Action Plan Against Racism" (the Plan) (Canadian Heritage 2005). The Plan was essentially a response to the recommendations of the third World Conference Against Racism, Racial Discrimination, Xenophobia and Related Intolerance convened in South Africa in 2001, in which Canada took part. The conference called on the participating governments to take action to fight racism by implementing the conference's recommendations and the International Convention on the Elimination of All Forms of Racial Discrimination, which were both interrelated. The governments were also asked to report to the United Nations Committee on the Elimination of All Forms of Racial Discrimination (UN Committee) on the implementation of the recommendations. Canada appeared before the UN Committee in 2002 and, while the Committee commended Canada for the many antiracist initiatives it had endorsed, it identified key areas of concern about the persistence of racism in Canadian society. Shortly afterwards, in 2003, the UN Special Rapporteur on Contemporary Forms of Racism, Racial Discrimination, Xenophobia and Related Forms of Discrimination visited Canada. The Rapporteur praised Canada for having embraced antiracist measures—i.e., the Multiculturalism Policy, the Charter, and the *Employment Equity Act*—but noted wide socioeconomic gaps in Canadian society that particularly plagued Aboriginal people and racialized minorities. To improve this situation, the Rapporteur iterated the need for a strategy to complement the policy framework. In particular, he advised Canada to take action to fight racism. As a result, Canada implemented the Plan, a five-year initiative which lasted from 2005 to 2010. The Plan explicitly acknowledged that racism against racialized minorities, especially Blacks, is prevalent in Canada. It stated that:

> nearly 50 percent of Blacks reported discrimination or unfair treatment. By contrast, 33 percent of South Asians and 33 percent of Chinese respondents reported experiencing discrimination or unfair treatment (Canadian Heritage 2005, 8).

> [A] clearer picture comes into view about the economic, social and political nature of race and its impact on different groups (9).

As critical race theorists would argue, the Government of Canada named race explicitly in the Plan, considering it a social construct that influences citizens in terms of access to resources, or lack thereof. The Plan specified the severity of anti-Black sentiment, suggesting that Blacks face more racism than other racialized minorities. However, as we will see, the Plan's engagement with antiracism was more discursive than practical. Since the Plan is the only anti-racist federal action to date, a close look at the programs and initiatives it envisioned to counter racism reveals how Canada deals with racism concretely. Table 1 illustrates these initiatives.

TABLE 1
Description of the initiatives funded under Canada's Action Plan Against Racism

Initiative	Department	5-year planned budget	Purpose/description	Status
Inclusive Institutions Initiative (III)	PCH (Department of Canadian Heritage) (Multiculturalism Program)	$12,124,700 over 5 years; $2,847,200 ongoing	Aims to support and encourage federal institutions to take the priorities and needs of ethno-cultural and ethno-racial communities into consideration when developing new policies, programs and services and implementing existing ones	Cancelled in 2006
Anti-Racism Test Case Initiative (ARTCI)	PCH (Human Rights Program)	$268,784 for year 1 (excluding funds for implementation)	Was envisioned to provide funding to challenge provincial/territorial legislation, practice or policies that allegedly violated the racial equality provisions of the *Canadian Charter of Rights and Freedoms* where such cases were expected to be of potential national significance	Not implemented
Nationally Standardized Data Collection Strategy on Hate-Motivated Crime (Data Collection Strategy)	PCH (Multiculturalism Program), CIC (Multiculturalism Program)	$2,289,200 over 5 years; $332,200 ongoing	The Canadian Centre for Justice Statistics (CCJS) implements the Data Collection Strategy. Through the Strategy, police report hate-motivated crime to CCJS. The goal of the strategy is to provide both the public and policy makers with key indicators on racial discrimination.	Ongoing
Law Enforcement Aboriginal and Diversity Network (LEAD)	PCH (Multiculturalism Program)	$575,800 over 4 years	LEAD was founded in 2003 as a non-profit network of law enforcement agencies and individuals from all jurisdictions in Canada to raise the professional standard in serving Aboriginal and ethno-cultural and ethno-racial communities.*	Cancelled in 2008
Welcoming Communities Initiative (WCI)	CIC (Immigration Settlement and Adaptation Program)	$17.6 million over 5 years; $4.4 million ongoing	WCI aims to create a true sense of belonging and shared citizenship for immigrants. The Initiative focuses on working with non-governmental organizations and provincial partners to foster a welcoming environment for newcomers in communities.	Ongoing

Initiative	Department	5-year planned budget	Purpose/description	Status
Racism-Free Workplace Strategy (RFWS)	HRSDC (Labour Program)	$13 million over 5 years; $3 million ongoing	The goal of RFWS is to facilitate the integration of skilled individuals in Canadian workplaces by developing tools, guidelines, and educational materials for employers, practitioners, managers, employees, and the general public. Activities are intended to reduce discriminatory barriers faced by visible minorities and Aboriginal people in Canadian workplaces.	Ongoing
Race-Based Issues in the Justice System (RBIJS)	DoJ (Justice Partnership and Innovation Fund)	$6.7 million over 5 years (distributed among the three Justice Initiatives); $500,000 ongoing	Aims to improve the fair treatment of Aboriginal people and visible minorities in the justice system	Ongoing
Interventions for Victims and Perpetrators of Hate Crimes (IVPHC)	DoJ (Justice Partnership and Innovation Fund)		This initiative aimed to identify and respond to the special needs and requirements of victims of hate crimes	Ongoing
Countering Internet-Based Hate Crimes (CIBHC)	CoJ (Justice Partnership and Innovation Fund)		Was intended to detect and address the issue of hate speech on the Internet. The initiative also aimed to provide public legal education and information on the definition of hate propaganda to enhance the capacity of the public and Internet service providers to recognize hate speech.	Not implemented

Source: Citizenship and Immigration Canada 2010, 5-6

* Under CAPAR, PCH signed an agreement with the Canadian Association of Chiefs of Police to support a number of LEAD-based activities on a 50-50 cost sharing basis. Funding included support for a coordinator and activities such as administrative functions/supplies and meetings, communication plans and tools, research, consultations, and website development.

I will refer to this table repeatedly in the remainder of this book because the Plan was implemented during two years of the research fieldwork (2008-2010) and is of the utmost relevance to this analysis. In this context, I stress that, although the Plan stipulated that Blacks face more racism than other racialized groups, it did not address anti-Black racism properly for a number of reasons. First, as Table 1 reveals, the Plan did not include action against anti-Black racism specifically. Second, the Plan did not even counter general racism properly because the Government of Canada devoted only $53.6 million to execute the Plan over five years. That amount of money was not sufficient to identify structural barriers in the vast Canadian system, let alone remedy racism. Third, Canada did not renew the Plan after 2010, which prevented any follow-up of the Plan's goals and implementation. Overall, the Plan did not improve the material conditions of Black Canadians inasmuch as, while the demographics of Blacks in Canada continued to increase, anti-Black racism continued to unfold, if not increase. For example, the number of Blacks in Canada jumped from 504,300 in 1991 to 662,200 in 2001 (Statistics Canada 2004), then to 662,215 in 2001, to 945,665 in 2011, and to 1,198,540 in 2016. Similar patterns occurred in Alberta, where the proportion of Blacks more than doubled, jumping from 31,395 in 2001 to 74,435 in 2011, which represented a little less than 5% of the province's total population (Statistics Canada 2017). That makes Alberta the province with the third largest Black concentration, after Ontario and Quebec. In addition, the 2016 Census indicated that four census subdivisions in Alberta had Black populations higher than the national average (3.5%), namely, Brooks (14.3%), Edmonton (5.9%), Wood Buffalo (5.8%), and Calgary (4.2%) (Statistics Canada 2017). As such, Canada's immigration policies allowed Blacks to move to Canada, but the law did not improve their status after they settled in Canada. As we stated previously, the first large waves of Black immigration suffered racial oppression. Racism continues to afflict Blacks during the current civic multiculturalism phase. The literature (Foster 2007; Mensah & Williams 2015) and human rights reports (Ontario Human Rights Commission 2003) document anti-Black racism, for example, in obstacles to access to education and skilled employment, and in problems with structural and cultural incorporation. Anti-Black racism is severe because the socioeconomic status of Blacks continues to deteriorate compared with that of other racialized immigrants. For example, in 2008, Statistics Canada revealed that Black immigrants earned $51,317 a year, less than white immigrants ($65,000), Japanese immigrants ($58,294), and Chinese immigrants ($55,270). In addition, it was found that:

for [B]lacks ... there is little or no economic mobility across generations...

[B]lacks languished, with third-generation immigrants earning less than newcomers...

The census findings also suggest that [B]lacks experience more discrimination and difficulties in the labour market than others... [even though they] do fairly well in terms of education (Jiménez 2008).[8]

While in the past Blacks and Asians were both placed at the bottom of the racialized hierarchy of desirability (RHD) (Satzewich & Liodakis 2013), Asian groups such as the Japanese and Chinese experience significant generational mobility. This pattern supports CRT's tenet of differential racialization, in this case among visible minorities. Asian groups were leveraged, while Blacks continue to be relegated to the bottom of the socioeconomic ladder. This is another illustration of anti-Black racism that illustrates deep-rooted hostility and bias towards Blacks. Similarly, the increase of the Black population in Alberta did not translate into openness to this population, since it also had to deal with anti-Black racism. In spite of the absence of scholarship about Blacks in Alberta from the 1960s to the mid-1990s, there is reason to believe that they encountered similar, if not more severe, racism in comparison to their counterparts in other Canadian provinces. The literature showcases racial discrimination against Blacks in Alberta as of the second half of the 1990s. A study conducted in Calgary in 1996-1997 (Danso & Grant 2000) ascertained that Black Africans in Calgary encountered racism in the housing industry. Whether renting or buying, Blacks were shown fewer properties than whites and other visible minority groups, and landlords offered excuses to avoid renting to Blacks. Other studies assert that anti-Black racism was also prominent in the labour market and education system in the late 1990s and early 2000s (Madibbo 2012a; Zaami 2017). Blacks are also the target of law enforcement, especially racial profiling by the police. Furthermore, it is difficult for Blacks to obtain bank credit, which hinders the creation of entrepreneurship and businesses (Akrofi-Obeng 2015). In particular, Black youth are subjected to racism in the "justice" system and the education system, which leads many to drop out of school. Moreover, Blacks are underrepresented in Alberta's institutions inasmuch as the political representation of Blacks is so minimal that there was only one Black member

---

8.   There is no evidence to suggest that this situation has improved significantly or at all since 2008.

of the Legislative Assembly of Alberta in 2016. There are no Black city councillors in Alberta, and no Blacks representing Alberta in the Parliament of Canada. Aside from elected office, Blacks are also underrepresented in other leadership positions, whether in the civil service, academia, or the private sector, as well as in Alberta's mainstream media, with less fewer five television, radio, and newspaper journalists. There are only a handful of Black-owned businesses, which are mostly small-scale enterprises (Akrofi-Obeng 2015). If Blacks are almost totally absent on the political scene and in the public and private sector, where are they? There are a few middle-class Blacks in Alberta who are employed in education and other institutions, but the vast majority are blue-collar workers. Thus, Blacks did not benefit from the economic boom in Alberta, and their drastic under-representation in the highest institutions minimizes their voice, because it means that there are no established Blacks to advocate on their behalf. These trends contribute to the overall poverty of the Black community in Alberta and generate problematic outcomes for Black youth. These young people suffer alienation that jeopardizes their sense of belonging to Canada. It is worth noting this occurs in Brooks (Merin 2012), Calgary (Lewis 2017; Madibbo 2016), Edmonton, and other places in Alberta (Tettey & Puplampu 2005). As we will see, these types of racism are exacerbated by the racial hatred that revealed itself in the resurgence of white supremacist organizations in the mid-2000s. It is important to acknowledge that Alberta made an effort to fight racism; for example, it passed the *Human Rights, Citizenship and Multiculturalism Act* in 1996. Nevertheless, the continued racism in Alberta indicates that this act did not have a significant impact on the struggle against racism.

We see that, in modern times, the forces of domination have not stopped objectifying Blackness to diminish Black identity. Blacks have challenged contemporary anti-Black racism in a number of ways. In particular, they created organizations and associations in many places, including Alberta. Some of the organizations bring together expatriates from a single country living in the same city, such as the Grenada-Canada Social and Cultural Association of Calgary and the Sudanese-Canadian Community Association of Edmonton. Others bring together groups of Blacks, such as the Caribbean Community Council of Calgary. There are province-wide Black organizations, including the Jamaican-Canadian Association Alberta and the Council of Canadians of African & Caribbean Heritage. There are also a few Black institutions, such as the Africa Centre and the African History Library in Edmonton, Black youth-established student associations, sports teams, and cultural groups, but there are no

Black religious institutions in Alberta. The existing organizations share the goal of fighting anti-Black racism through sociopolitical activism. They promote Black history and youth empowerment, along with immigrant integration. These are two of the goals of the Africa Centre (n.d.), which states that it "supports African immigrant and refugee families." Other organizations implement educational and cultural productivity programs. Once again, these initiatives tell us that contemporary Blacks are refuting the imposition of identity by redefining Black identity and restoring Black history. However, it is appalling that contemporary Blacks are less organized than the pioneers. Not only are there no a Black geographic concentrations per se in Alberta, there are no provincial or local Black organizations that unite Blacks and fight for them collectively the way the pioneers' organiz- ations did. This issue merits attention that extends beyond the scope of this book, but it is sufficient to suggest that anti-Black racism seems to plague Blacks more in the contemporary era than in the past. Black resist- ance is jeopardized by racism, making contemporary anti-Black racism an intricate issue, a vicious cycle that strangles Blacks so much that it prevents them from organizing effectively to move forward effectively.

Thus, Black Francophones arrive in Alberta in a context where Blacks continue to suffer the anti-Black racism that has historically subjugated them, and they attempt to fight it. White Francophones are still subject to linguicism, but they have achieved a stage of institutional completeness (Breton 2005) that places them in a strong position to claim and acquire additional rights and resources. Up until the 1990s, white Francophones did not build bridges with Blacks inasmuch as they either oppressed them or distanced themselves from them. However, the immigration of Black- African Francophones to Alberta requires interaction with Francophones already there. Because the trajectories of both white Francophones and Blacks influence Black-African Francophones, the legislation that concerns Blacks and Francophones impacts Black-African Francophone identities. We saw that Canadian policies produced differential racialization—to use CRT wording, because they guaranteed many white Francophones, but not Blacks, prosperity. For example, the OLA afforded Francophones $2.2 billion for one action plan over five years, while Canada's Action Plan against Racism was awarded $56 million for the same period of time. The Charter gave Francophones publicly funded French-language schools and autonomous boards of education, but, while it condemns racism, it does not specify actions or resources to fight it. The same critique extends to the Multiculturalism Policy and *Employment Equity Act*, since neither has improved the alienation of Blacks in Canada. Francophones have built a space that strengthens their struggle, while Blacks are struggling to survive. Consequently, there are not sufficient resources to combat racism within La Francophonie and the broader Canadian society. CRT's precept concerning "contradiction-closing cases" is relevant here, because the policies generate asymmetric power relations and status that advantage white Francophones—and some racialized minorities—but afflict Blacks. These intricate dynamics confront Black-African Francophones as they construct and negotiate their identities. We will uncover these dynamics as we analyze the identities that the research participants construct and negotiate, starting with Canadian identity.

CHAPTER 3
THE CONSTRUCTION AND NEGOTIATION OF CANADIAN IDENTITY

"Either I am Canadian, or the word means nothing"

George Elliott Clarke (2002).

ll of the participants expressed a sense of belonging to Canada that they generally constructed as follows:

> Participant:[1] To me, being Canadian is a privilege.... It means acquiring a lot of things, citizenship and also safety. It means having the opportunity to be a [Canadian] citizen...the freedom to travel...obtain employment. It means living in a political and social system that has values I respect. I am happy to be in a democratic system that provides me with the freedom to think, express myself, and move around...where I am able to flourish and achieve my goals [of immigration to Canada].

> Participant: Canadian identity means accepting differences, other cultures and ways of being... It is multiculturalism. I am keen on the issues of my new country, Canada. It means do[ing] our best to be a good Canadian, and help[ing] our [Canadian] society achieve its goals.

The participants perceive their relationships to Canada positively in terms of the legal rights and social benefits this country offers. They cherish the values of freedom and fairness, along with the ethos of multiculturalism, such as accepting people of various backgrounds and the opportunity to

---

1.   I do not indicate the participants' gender, sending country, education, etc., to respect their confidentiality. Any identifier could disclose their identity in La Francophonie.

retain and develop their racial, ethnic, and cultural identities. They also admire the relative safety and the employment opportunities that Canada offers. They consider Canada their country, one where there is potential for them to meet their migration goal, which is to build a rich social and economic life. However, their relationship to Canada is not confined to these advantages, because they also describe Canadian identity in terms of their respect for the main duties that come with citizenship, such as voting, respect for Canadian political institutions and civic involvement through volunteerism. However, the problem of racism in Canadian society at large gives rise to the perception that participants are not considered genuine Canadians:

> Participant: I am Canadian, but I don't feel accepted as such.... When you are Black, people have all these ideas [stereotypes] about you.... We don't see Black Francophones in Alberta political [scene] ... or in high [key] jobs [positions]. I myself faced problems [racism] ... with the police, many times. And in the work place.

> Participant: Naturally, like all immigrants, I started with a survival job in a sector [which] was not in my field of expertise. The job was not rewarding given my level of education and [work] experience. But I had to do it in order to survive ... also, there is a language barrier.

The participants teased out the numerous types of racism that they encounter, ranging from negative stereotyping to racial profiling by the police and discrimination institutionalized in the basic structures of society. They find the complete lack of political representation of Black-African Francophones striking. This is because none of these people has occupied political office in Alberta to date, or on the public scene, such as in the Anglophone media. This marginalization inhibits their ability to voice their concerns and needs. In particular, participants raised two forms of racism: 1) exclusion from Alberta's labour market, and 2) the presence of neo-Nazi white supremacist organizations. As the quotes above illustrate, racism in the labour market manifests in the devaluation of credentials, linguicism, underemployment, and discrimination in the workplace. With regard to the non-recognition of credentials, it is important to note that 19 of the 42 participants moved to Canada directly from their sending countries or neighbouring African states. As Appendix A shows, they all obtained undergraduate or graduate degrees there: 17 studied and worked in French-speaking countries, while 2 were trained in English-speaking states. They all had employment in African countries where the vast majority of them (17) obtained commensurate employment. They specialized in various fields, ranging from medicine to education, engineering to pharmacy studies, development to human resources, information technologies to economics, and accounting to business and media. Twelve participants studied in France before they relocated to Canada, where a few of them were unemployed and a majority were underemployed. One first settled in Europe and one Asia, where they conducted studies, but neither obtained employment. Two individuals came to Canada as international students, where one obtained a BA and the other a BA and graduate degree. One acquired a commensurate job while the other worked for a Black Francophone organization. Seven grew up and were schooled in Canada; three of them obtained a bachelor degree, one dropped out of school, one had a college diploma, one obtained two bachelor degrees, and one received an undergraduate and graduate degree. Thus, we note that the participants who were trained abroad had more schooling than those who grew up in Canada.

Overall, none of the qualifications of the 33 participants who were trained abroad in Africa, Asia, France, other European countries or Canada were recognized. This factor forced many participants to accept low-paying employment for which they were overqualified in their first years in Canada, and endured unfavourable working conditions. To improve their socio-economic status, 31 of the 33 participants who were trained abroad pursued additional studies in Canada. They upgraded, regraded, repeated degrees or earned new degrees. They devoted money and years of their lives to gain additional qualifications that were unnecessary and volunteered to gain Canadian experience because their work abroad was not acknowledged. While the credentials acquired abroad were devalued, those obtained in Canada were no more highly regarded. Both participants who studied in Canada as international students and those who grew up and were educated in Canada suffered similar outcomes. Upon graduation, they all ended up doing similar, menial jobs. Three of these nine participants earned more than one degree in Canada. However, for the most part, their efforts did not translate into rewarding employment, since the vast majority of the 42 participants were underemployed. This state of affairs draws our attention to anti-Black racism in relation to the devaluation of Blacks' credentials. Although there were differences in the participants' profiles in terms of the country of education, work experience, language of education, and field of expertise—both regulated and unregulated professions—there is one striking similarity. The credentials of all the participants were rejected both in predominantly Anglophone Canada and in Quebec.

Arguably, the credentials obtained in Africa were discredited because of the general tendency to undervalue and devalue training acquired in the developing world (Reitz 2013). According to the literature on immigration, while racialized immigrants are more educated than their Canadian-born counterparts, a majority ended up in jobs requiring only a high school diploma (Galarneau & Morissette 2008; Girard et al. 2008). This extended to credentials obtained in Africa, which demonstrates institutional racism fuelled by negative Eurocentric stereotypes about these regions of the world. They reflect generalizations both about the Western world—considered superior—and the developing world—perceived as inferior in the realm of knowledge and innovation. However, the credentials that the participants acquired in France were not accepted either. In general, whites with French credentials (from France or Canada) receive accreditation, which is not the case for Blacks (Gallant 2011). The credentials of the research participants who hold equivalent French degrees were rejected in both Quebec and other Canadian provinces, and the participants were underemployed or unemployed in both Quebec and the Francophone labour market in Alberta. Moreover, it is striking that the young people who grew up in Canada did not achieve commensurate employment even if they had one or more Canadian degrees. These cases reveal how ubiquitous anti-Black racism is; the geography changes—Africa versus Europe versus Asia versus Canada—but racist ideologies prevail. Blacks are permanently associated with negative stereotypes regardless of their field and where they study and work. Thus, in the case of Blacks, credentials are not the issue, race is. CRT's precept concerning the saliency of race underscores that race determines these outcomes. The participant who said "naturally . . . like all immigrants, I started with a survival job" illustrated an irony inasmuch as, in some cases, entire communities are marginalized: Blacks are underemployed. It is noteworthy that, at the time of the fieldwork (2008-2011), only one of the 42 participants had commensurate employment in an English-language institution (see Appendix 1). Two obtained good-paying but contractual bilingual positions, which reveals that, although in Canada bilingualism, knowledge of both of Canada's official languages, is considered social capital (Bourdieu 1986), it does not result in positive outcomes for the participants. Furthermore, two participants were employed in mainstream French-language organizations, and two had small businesses. A few were employed in Black-African Francophone-led organizations which did not offer high income and whose future was uncertain because they relied on government funding that was both scant and insecure. The vast majority of participants in Brooks worked at the meat plant, Lakeside Packers, which was known for its precarious work conditions at the time. The others—a majority—were under-employed. Similarly, a majority of participants experienced downward mobility, physicians working as nurses, and engineers as taxi drivers. Thus, anti-Black racism prevented Black-African Francophones from benefiting from Alberta's economic boom; they were rewarded only with underemployment!

As stated, in addition to the non-recognition of credentials, a linguistic barrier inhibited participants' inclusion in the labour market. The discrimination in question is what I described earlier as racialized lingui-cism, in which the use of language is associated with race and triggers racism. Participants faced discrimination in the form of generalized stereo-types about them as lacking proficiency in the English language, and this is because they were French-speaking immigrants. It is important to emphasize that, while a few participants were not fluent in English upon their arrival in Alberta, they all were at the time of the fieldwork. This is because some grew up in Canada, and the others learned English as an Additional Language (EAL) or lived in other English-speaking Canadian provinces before moving to Alberta, which means that they had had suffi-cient time to acquire the language and practise it. Linguicism creeps into racism because language is perceived through the lens of biological deter-minism in a primordial manner, as being genetic and fixed. It is assumed that the participants would never speak English properly because they were not born into it. One participant contended that: "they [employers and other Canadians] don't like our accent." This statement describes the aforementioned discrimination that targets racialized people who do not speak with the standard white-Canadian accent. The participants were discriminated against because their English accent diverged from the normative white-Canadian accent. However, participants who had the standard Canadian accent, those who grew up in Canada, were not guar-anteed inclusion either. Once again, this proves that linguicism collides with racism to include some speakers and preclude others. One participant revealed another type of language discrimination: "I was once told I speak English with a French accent." But white Canadians who speak English with a French accent are not discriminated against in the same way as Blacks are. Racialized linguicism extends to French to the extent that the participants who settled in Quebec first were not included in the labour market although they were fluent in French, which again reminds us that language is racialized. These outcomes reveal a consistent racist ideology; the patterns change but the ideology does not. Notwithstanding their fluency and accent, all participants experienced racialized linguicism that contributed to their exclusion in the unilingual English, unilingual French, and bilingual labour market. Unfortunately, racism did not end with the lack of recognition of credentials and racialized linguicism, since the few participants who overcame these challenges also suffered another type of racism: workplace discrimination. In this regard, one participant had this to say:

> Though I am a Canadian citizen, there are many forms of discrimination ... though I have the same rights as any [white] Canadian, there are barriers. My job is good, but I am over-qualified for the position I am doing now. I can't obtain certain positions. Some doors open, but we can't go far. Nevertheless, we are Canadians, and we have the same qualifications and training [as white Canadians].

This participant studied at university in an African country in addition to receiving an undergraduate and graduate degree in Canada. Although the job they got upon hiring was commensurate, they did not advance in the institutional hierarchy as they deserved. The participant was not promoted, while their white co-workers, who had the same qualifications as the participant, reached higher positions. In the end, the participant had a supervisor who was less qualified than them; thus the participant remained in a position for which they were over-qualified. The participant became underemployed in the institution, facing racism in the form of a glass ceiling that confined them to a lower rung. In this regard, it bears noting that numerous types of racism that occur in the workplace inhibit institutional advancement for Blacks, and one participant illustrated the most prominent ones as follows:

> I had a job that did not even correspond to my knowledge [qualifications], people under-estimated me. They thought that, because of my skin color [Black], I couldn't do a good job ... they kept me away from [positions that involve handling] money ... they created problems for me [harassed them] and when I protested they kept harassing me ... this prejudice keeps you [Blacks] down.

The aforementioned pejorative stereotypes about Blacks being criminals, thugs, and so on, led employers to limit participants to rudimentary tasks including those that did not involve dealing with money. They were excluded from positions with bigger responsibilities, which also means that they did not get promoted to these positions. When one participant protested against differential treatment, their courage was met with another problem that prevented their progress in the institutional hierarchy. They were harassed and intimidated, and rumours circulated that they were not a good employee or colleague. The incident resulted in an unfavourable evaluation of the participant's performance. Knowing that these actions were meant to "keep Blacks down," the participant further challenged the racism. They took the complaint to a higher level in the institution, which only culminated in additional support for the participant's supervisors and further condemnation of the participant. The participant said: "I wasn't going to give up. I wanted to turn it into a legal issue [action]. But I have to say I realized I couldn't afford the legal expenses and that sort of things [sic]." This incident speaks to the severity of anti-Black racism that Blacks are subjected to in the workplace. We are harassed, bullied and belittled, surveilled and intimidated. Negative stereotypes are used to prove that we lack ethical and professional rigour. When we contest such unfair treatment, we are punished further. Taking anti-racist action generates a stigma because it can bring more exclusion; our job will be threatened, and we are subjected to retaliation (Das Gupta 2009). When the institutional provisions did not accord the participant justice, they considered protesting through legal means, i.e., hiring a human rights lawyer and/or filing a complaint with a human rights commission. The participant did not pursue that avenue because, although these legal means are meant to defend the marginalized, they are often more of a dilemma than a solution. They are costly, time consuming, mentally distressing and, above all, difficult to prove in the way Canadian laws perceive "evidence." Evidence should be concrete and tangible, but racial harassment is often subtle, disguised in coded language, such as ignoring someone, and is implied covertly through the distribution of tasks and responsibilities. If a complainant wins a case of racism, that victory does not occur without losses, including financial and mental health strains.

Thus, the participants encountered racism in the labour market in both Quebec and predominantly Anglophone Canada. Unfortunately, anti-Black racism is not confined to the research participants, other Black Francophones being subjected to it in Alberta (Madibbo 2016; Moke Ngala 2005) and other provinces, including Ontario (Huot 2017) and British Columbia (Jacquet et al. 2008). Marginalization is so severe in Quebec (McDonald 2009) that, in 2011, the unemployment rate of Haitians there was twice as high as that of the total population (15.9% compared with 8.2%) (Gouvernement du Québec 2005). It is not limited to Black Francophones either since, as we stated earlier, other Blacks encounter racism in the labour market and other institutions. These constraints galvanized the participants, resulting in "financial problems [poverty]."

This is a chronic problem that the literature refers to as "racialized poverty" (Galabuzi 2006). Racialized communities in Canada experience disproportionate levels of poverty that stem from institutional racism (Allahdini 2014; Stapleton et al. 2012). In particular, this poverty hits Black Canadians hard (Canadian Press 2017). The challenges also caused the participants mental distress, which was revealed in contentions such as: "I even have trouble sleeping," "We always worry about the future of my children," "I was depressed... then I had high blood pressure, which I didn't have before." Once again, these outcomes are echoed in the literature, which considers racism a social determinant of health (Shishehgar et al. 2014). For these reasons, racism in the labour market hindered the participants' identification with Canada. I previously indicated that participants repeatedly emphasized their exclusion from the labour market, indicating that employment a determinant of identity. For them, getting a good job meant that they "were respected as Canadians," while not getting one meant that they "were not considered genuine Canadians." This aspect is in line with the literature, which corroborates the close relationship between socioeconomic status and identity (Goodman et al. 2007). Employment is an identity (re)source (Hall 2000; Kelly 2001) that gives people dignity and makes them feel welcome. This aspect is illustrated in contentions such as "I am working, you know, I feel like I am someone." Conversely, one participant stated: "After all these efforts I can't find a good job. It is as if I don't exist," which indicates that lack of employment or underemployment generates identity exclusion.

My follow-up on the employment status of the participants in 2016 revealed another troubling aspect of anti-Black racism in the labour market. There had been more regression than progression. I reached 38 out of the 42 participants, since 3 of them returned to their sending country in the hope of finding commensurate employment, and the other I could not manage to reach. None of the participants made strides inasmuch as no one enjoyed upward mobility or advancement in the institutional hierarchy. Even the few participants who had commensurate jobs during the fieldwork had lost them by 2016. Most experienced downward mobility, since many lost their jobs or were underemployed, occupying lesser jobs than the ones they had had during the fieldwork. One participant moved back to another Canadian province in search of better opportunities. This situation was largely the result of the economic downturn that began in Alberta in 2014 in the midst of the global oil market collapse, which hit Alberta's economy hard; for example, "Alberta lost 63,500 jobs in the first eight months of this year [2015]" (Younglai 2015), the most jobs the province had lost since the 1980s recession. Companies and businesses closed, and thousands were laid off. Although many Albertans lost their jobs, the ratio of participants who did was too high (36 out of 38), which suggests that that outcome was differential. The crisis was more severe for Blacks. This number includes the two participants who had businesses during the fieldwork but had closed them by 2016. We should emphasize that the businesses were established during the economic boom and were then met with the challenges that face Black businesses in general. For example, in a study about Black-African English-language businesses in Alberta, Akrofi-Obeng (2015) explains that there are only a handful of Black businesses, and they are small in scope and tend to collapse within a short period of time. The author maintains that this is triggered by racism, because banks refuse to offer Blacks credit, and lack of a sustainable clientele. Ironically, the general public considers these businesses ethnic, or Black, even when they involve general services, such as car washing.

While the participants' businesses met hurdles during the economic boom, the recession brought them to a halt. Not only did Blacks not benefit from the province's economic prosperity, they also suffered more drastically during the financial downturn. "[B]lacks are the last hired during periods of economic growth and the first fired in recessions" (Couch & Fairlie 2010). These trends are not new, for they were present in Alberta in the past. In a previous section, I indicated that white Francophones survived the Great Depression, Black pioneers were afflicted to the extent that the economic crisis contributed to the decline of Black rural settlements. Unfortunately, once again, this discrimination is not confined to Alberta or to the rest of Canada. It surfaced in the US during the same period, as the unemployment rate of Blacks exceeded that of whites (Sundstrom 1992). The discrimination also extended to Europe, including France, Germany, and the UK. This accentuates the global nature of anti-Black racism (Mazrui 2002), which afflicts Blacks worldwide. Thus, the participants did not intentionally distance themselves from the Canadian identity, they were excluded from it. This phenomenon substantiates and is substantiated by the trajectories of other Blacks in Canada. For example, in a study titled "'I am Canadian,' Challenging Stereotypes about Young Somali Canadians" (Berns-McGown 2013), the research participants:

> self-identify as Canadian and want very much to be a part of this country, which they see as their home (1).

At the same time, respondents did not always believe that other Canadians saw them as Canadian or accepted them as such, and they described encountering... colour racism (11).

The participants, Black Somali youth in their late teens and early to mid-twenties, felt a strong sense of belongingness to Canada, but racism alienated them. This exclusion extends to other striking occurrences, such as the one confronted by the notable George Elliott Clarke (Clarke 2002). An employer in Ontario once asked Clarke for his passport, which indicated that the agent took for granted that Clarke was not Canadian. Yet Clarke's grandfather had arrived in Nova Scotia in 1898, which makes Clarke a third-generation Canadian. That Clarke is famous and a talented artist who has enriches the cultural life of Canada did not matter, for he was considered an outsider. Both Clarke and the Somali youth were excluded from belongingness to Canada. Once again, this plight reveals the ubiquitous character of anti-Black racism. These people differ in age, nationality, generation, and official language status, but they were all denied Canadianness. The few Blacks, such as Clarke, who surmount endless hurdles and make it in Canada are not exempt from this racism either. Since the research participants suffered this identity exclusion, how did they challenge it? They refuted the dominant perception of Canadian identity as being white European Christian, and reconstructed it in an inclusive manner. They poignantly stated:

> Participant: Being Canadian means that some of them [their friends] are white, some are like me [Black-African], some are Indian [from India]. There are also First Nations... and I also have a friend from Yugoslavia. They speak different languages.... Some are born in Canada, others are like me [first-generation immigrants]. And we hang together, we eat pizza and Thai. We attend [multicultural] festivals. And we go to the movies together.

The participants associated Canadian-ness with diversity in all its senses, in particular with multilingualism, whereby an English or French speaker is considered Canadian, as is someone who speaks Punjabi, Swahili, or Cree. They also reconstructed it through ethnic and geographic diversity, and numerous trajectories of people, both those who have lived in Canada for a long time and those who are newcomers. This view of Canadian identity is entrenched in multiculturalism, the participants associating this identity with multiculturalism more than any other term. Their stance supports both CRT's and critical multiculturalism's standpoint on identity as being fluid and dynamic. It reminds us that the current social fabric of

Alberta society is increasingly racially and ethnically diverse. Diversity is not just a fact of society; it is negotiated in practice as participants incorporate it into the ties they form with people of different backgrounds in various social settings, including in restaurants and at multicultural celebrations. In so doing, the participants joined other Black Canadians who took similar action, such as Clarke. When Clarke's Canadian-ness was questioned, he uttered the phrase at the beginning of this chapter: "Either I am Canadian, or the word means nothing" (2002). Clarke's words speak volumes, because he redefined Canadian identity to centre on Blackness as an integral aspect of this belongingness, and the participants followed suit. Thus, the preceding analysis reveals Fleras' (2014) description of "How racism works in a contemporary Canada":

> Systematically, they [the various types of racism] are deeply embedded within normative values and institutional relations, practices, and policies... infrastructurally, in terms of the founding assumptions and foundational principles of a society's constitutional order (265).

> [R]acism in Canada tends to be relatively muted, politely conveyed, and often reflecting the use of coded words to reflect attention away from put-downs that potentially deny, exclude (216).

> [R]acism is publicly rejected yet privately popular; racism is socially unacceptable yet pervasively persistent; people are in denial over racism, yet there is more racism than ever before.... Open racism is widely condemned in advancing an inclusive multiculturalism, yet acts of racism still frequently occur and undermine a commitment to a multicultural inclusiveness (267).

Like classical racism, contemporary racism is omnipresent; it is systemic, structural, institutional, individual, and so on. Unlike classical racism, which was largely overt, modern racism is largely covert. It is disguised in discourses and policies that project Canada as one of the most tolerant societies in the world, if not the most tolerant. Canadians' seeming politeness conceals vicious racist ideologies and practices, and Canada's legislation further obscures racism. Fleras (2014) echoes critical multiculturalism by stressing that contemporary racism discerns "the founding assumptions and foundational principles" about Canada. These master narratives continue to construe a dominant construction of Canadian identity that is also negotiated through exclusionary praxis, including in the labour market. As CRT would put it, the master narratives normalize both white supremacy and white privilege in the labour market, favouring whites and excluding Black-African Francophones. The latter worked hard to fight their plight but did not overcome it because that endeavour requires official government support that was not provided. As we observed, one participant planned to take legal action against the institution that discriminated against them but did not pursue that avenue because of a lack of resources. We noted earlier that Canada's *Employment Equity Act* (EEA) aims to eradicate racism in the labour market. Admittedly, since its enactment in 1986, the EEA has improved the inclusion of some groups. But it falls short when it comes to Blacks (Essed & Goldberg 2001).

In essence, the EEA applies to all federally regulated employers—the public sector, Crown corporations, and federal contractors—with at least a hundred employees, that bid for government contracts worth $200,000 or more. How the government ensures the application of the EEA is that it requires all these employers to file an annual progress report about the composition of their workforce, the number of members of designated groups employed, and the types of job they have. Any employer who fails to produce this progress report is liable to a fine of up to $50,000. However, it is not clear how the government follows up after the submission of the annual reports, i.e., what it does if institutions do not hire sufficient numbers of members designated minorities, if these are not represented in the institutional hierarchy or if they face racism in the workplace. The preceding discussion shows that both underemployment and unemployment and language-based discrimination persist, in this case with regard to Black-African Francophones. This allows us to argue that the word "equity" in the act's title is superfluous. As Mensah (2010) holds, "For the most part, the Act [EEA] is enforced based on complaints made to the Canadian Human Rights Commission" (242). But who is likely to do something about human rights complaints against the EEA's treatment of Black-African Francophones (and Blacks in general)? We certainly do not expect the very institutions that exclude Blacks to take such actions on behalf of them, nor do we anticipate similar actions on the part of the Canadian public (at least this has not occurred to date). It is up to Blacks themselves to bear that burden, yet, as we observed, it is very difficult for them to do that. If the EEA did not improve the employment status of Black-African Francophones and that is difficult to protest against, what about the Multiculturalism Policy (the Policy)?

In this regard, Mensah (2010) holds that "despite its pitfalls, multiculturalism has been beneficial for Blacks" (235) "to the extent that it has been used as a tool to battle racism" (236). In a previous section, I highlighted the four interpretations of multiculturalism that Fleras and Elliott (2002) put forth, which describe multiculturalism as a fact, ideology, policy, and practice. I specified that the four meanings of multiculturalism are inter-connected and complement each other to help achieve inclusion. At this juncture, I specify that Mensah's (2010) account reflects two meanings of multiculturalism: practice and policy. Mensah suggests that Blacks used (practiced) the policy of multiculturalism to achieve their desired goals. To corroborate, Blacks drew on the policy's wording about overcoming racial barriers to full participation in society to contest their marginalization and demand justice. This means that multiculturalism strengthened Blacks' identity politics, since it created a space for them to make claims. Therefore, I concur with Mensah that multiculturalism has been beneficial to Blacks. However, I argue that they benefited too little since, at this point in time, multiculturalism should, and could, have offered Black Canadians more than a tool for making claims. It should have guaranteed them rights and a better status in Canadian society the way the OLA does for white Francophones. Even the benefit of multiculturalism for Blacks as a practice is not complete. Although Blacks capitalized on the Policy to demand justice, the goals of the Policy are far from being a reality for Blacks. As we observed, Blacks continue to face numerous types of racism and are largely underrepresented in Canada's institutional hierarchy, a situation that the Policy should have improved. Furthermore, there is negligence in terms of the meaning of multiculturalism as a fact with respect to the fact of Blackness in Canada. Because, as is the case with other Canadian legislation, the Policy considers all racialized groups as one single designated group: "visible minorities." It does not treat Blacks as a specific designated group and therefore does nothing about the anti-Black racism that targets Blacks specifically. Thus, it simultaneously ignores and enhances "differ-ential racialization" which, as critical race theorists would put it, benefits some racialized groups while marginalizing others—in this case Blacks.

Moreover, it is in the current civic multiculturalism phase that the participants and other Blacks suffer the aforementioned racism, which indicates that multiculturalism does not improve the participants' or other Blacks' inclusion in Alberta and Canadian society. Critical multiculturalists would argue that this is because civic multiculturalism does not address the racism underlying societal structures and therefore does not redress it. The same criticism applies to the Charter and Canada's Action Plan Against Racism (the Plan). I mentioned earlier that these provisions do not prove to be adequate for Blacks in general, and in this context I add that this situation also extends to Black-African Francophones, who remain largely excluded in Alberta (I will discuss the impacts of the OLA on Black-African Francophones in a later chapter). Blacks are left to remedy these problems on their own, but the racism they suffer does not facilitate the task. Citizens should make an effort to bring about justice, and the research participants did just that. But it is primarily the responsibility of the government to ensure the proper application of its own laws. As we pointed out, the Canadian government assumes this responsibility towards white Francophones, implementing poignant measures that allow Francophones to thrive. This reveals that the Canadian government is capable of endorsing similar provisions to improve the lives of Blacks, but it does not. In fact, it abolishes measures that could have helped to achieve this goal, i.e., the equity phase of multiculturalism and the Plan. This analysis confirms what Mensah (2010) posited as the Canadian government's complicity in racism, contending that "the Government and White society . . . are not in any rush to change the status quo to alleviate racism" (183). Not only did the Canadian government fail to guarantee Black-African Francophones justice, it makes it worse for them. These forms of racism are largely subtle, but contemporary racism is also overt, and interpreting this type of racism offers us a more thorough understanding of the problematics before us. This is because a blatant case of overt racism surfaced during the fieldwork, reflecting the identity alienation that the research participants suffered: the rise of neo-Nazi white supremacist organizations.

THE POLITICS OF RACIAL HATRED: PERSISTING WHITE SUPREMACY IN CONTEMPORARY CANADA

The research participants spoke at length about white supremacist organizations that were visible during the fieldwork and brought up the topic even when we did not allude to it. They were shocked that white supremacy was alive in Canada in the 21st century. It threatened their very existence, and made them feel that they were not considered Canadian. Although supremacist organizations surfaced in Alberta in the past, I will examine them in chronological perspective in relation to the organizations that emerged during the fieldwork. The various waves of white supremacy constitute a continuum in which each wave of white supremacy feeds into a previous one, which means that the wave that emerged during the field-work was not an isolated phenomenon. Investigating the interplay between the various waves allows us to better understand how they reproduce racist ideologies and tactics so that we can identify efficient ways to eradicate them. In *Web of Hate: Inside Canada's Far Right Network*, one of the most thorough sources on white supremacist groups in Canada to date, Warren

Kinsella (2001) states that, whether we call these groups and organizations "white supremacists," "white nationalists," "white power," or "far right,"[2] they are all similar because they all share two fundamental criteria: 1) they are neo-Nazis, and 2) they are white supremacists. They are neo-Nazis because "they embrace traditional National Socialist ideology, in particular, anti-Semitism," and they are white supremacists because their "immediate concern is race" (Kinsella 2001, 6). Although white supremacists first organized in Canada officially in the middle of the 1920s, their presence in the country extends back to an earlier time (Sher 1983). I divide white supremacy in Canada into four waves, the first of which organized in the mid-1920s. The second surfaced in the 1970s, the third in the early 2000s and coincided with my research fieldwork, and the fourth is the current one, which emerged around 2015. The first wave was established by white supremacists who crossed the US border into Canada where they found a home in most—if not all—of its regions (Sher 1983). This wave was a show of neo-Nazism, glorifying Adolf Hitler, depicting him as "a man who wanted the best for one of the world's greatest empires. A man who dared to envision a new white race which strove for success and new heights" (Kinsella 2001, 315). It also embraced white supremacy, since it was inspired by the related philosophy of Friedrich Nietzsche, taking pride in his contention that: "It was white men of courage, white men of strength, white men of fury and blazing anger that conquered the world, and it is exactly the same type of WHITE MEN that will win it back" (Kinsella 2001, 267).

Thus, this wave of white supremacy affirmed the aforementioned classical racism; it embraced biological determinism inasmuch as it categorized people in Canada into separate races. It stressed the racial superiority of the Aryan race and constructed this racial group *à la canadienne*. According to this wave, the Aryan race consisted of the white people of Canada, Great Britain, Australia, New Zealand, and the US, and white northern Europeans, who are comprised of the Anglo-Saxon, Celtic, Germanic, Scandinavian and "related people" (Hage 2012). It projected white supremacy by associating the Aryan race of Canada with the highest standards of civilization, contending that this racial group was physically, intellectually, and morally superior to the members of other races—racialized people. They considered the Asian and Indigenous races apart, labelling them "pre-human." While the supremacists considered the Eastern Europeans lesser than the Aryan race, they perceived them as

---

2.   In this book I refer to them as white supremacists.

superior to racialized groups. Thus, they revitalized what critical race theory refers to as differential racialization. In particular, white supremacists inherited the dehumanization of Blacks, derogating Blacks and ranking them far from humans, closer to animals. They proclaimed that:

> The African people [are] completely primitive (Kinsella 2001, 254).

> Blacks are inferior to whites because they evolved much later (379).

> We [white supremacists] hold it is obligatory for the negro race... in Canada to recognize that they are living in the land of the white race by courtesy of the white race (44).

> The plain truth is, our race is losing. We are losing our schools to [B]lack savagery, losing our hard-earned pay to [B]lack welfare, losing our lives to no-win red treason and [B]lack crime... [B]lack degeneracy (238).

White supremacists were galvanized by anti-Semitism, since they perceived the Jews as a race apart, an inferior one. They used this classification to spread prejudiced propaganda about Jews as communists whose aim was to destroy the Aryan race of Canada. To strengthen the superiority of the Aryan races and the inferiority of the racialized people, they espoused the doctrine of "racial purity." Their desire to preserve the myth of the "racial purity" of the Aryan race in Canada can be no clearer than in their slogan "We stand for the supremacy of the white race [in Canada]" (Kinsella 2001, 1). To that end, supremacists stood against inter-racial marriages and intermingling between whites and other racial groups. They considered these social relations a conspiracy to contaminate the "racial purity" of the Aryan race and dilute its right to dominate, control, subjugate, elim-inate, and even exterminate other racial groups. Furthermore, this wave of supremacy was openly anti-Catholic in order to safeguard Protestantism, the religion of the Anglo-Saxons whom the supremacists perceived as the promoters of the Aryan race. It is noteworthy that this first wave of organ-ized white supremacy actively practised its neo-Nazi, racist, and anti-Catholic sentiments, establishing white supremacist organizations across Canada, including the Aryan Nations, the Heritage Front, the Alliance for the Preservation of English Canada, and Montreal's "The famous Ku Klux Klan." It organized in the Atlantic provinces, Ontario, Quebec, Alberta and Saskatchewan, and in cities such as Moncton and Vancouver, as well as in rural areas. White supremacists displayed their ideologies explicitly through anti-Semitic and racist discourses and praxis. In the process, "[t]hey pass out leaflets at street corners, they paint swastikas on synagogue walls, they burn crosses at night rallies, they set up hate lines, they deny the Holocaust. Some of them beat people up; some of them kill people" (Kinsella 2001, 1).

The white supremacists took heinous action, murdering Sikhs and Aboriginal people, organizing neo-Nazi rallies, provoking riots, and engaging in bombing plots. Their tactics also included cross burning and threats of lynching and murder aimed at eliminating racialized minorities, including Blacks. They also targeted French Canadians whom, as stated earlier, they considered the largest Catholic group in Canada and thus a threat to Protestantism. The white supremacists' racial and religious bigotry found ripe environments across Canada, as their number and popularity continued to increase. For example, in 1925, there were 1,100 Ku Klux Klan (KKK) members in Ontario, and more still in Western Canada. In Saskatchewan, the KKK created 125 local clubs, and they were so popular in Manitoba that the national treasurer of the KKK in that province, Walter Davey Cowan, was elected as a Conservative to the House of Commons and became a Member of Parliament for Regina in 1930. Alberta was one of the most welcoming provinces to white supremacy, if not the most welcoming, and white supremacist organizations lasted longer in Alberta than in any other Canadian province. This can be explained by a number of reasons, including, as stated previously, the fact that Alberta had been conservative since its formative years. As Palmer (1982) points out, many KKK members in Alberta were expatriate Americans who moved to Alberta from the Midwestern United States, where the KKK had achieved considerable influence by the 1920s. But this does not mean that their exclusionary ideologies were imported from the US to Alberta. The conservatism that permeated Alberta at that time meant nothing less than a welcoming home for white supremacy. By the time white suprem-acists reached Alberta in the early 1920s, white Albertans were extremely hostile to racialized people, including Blacks. In addition, by that time, the Orange Order of Alberta had already spread its anti-Catholic tradition, which it demonstrated in anti-French sentiment. Understandably, the KKK "sprang up in areas where the Orange Order . . . had been established" (Palmer 1982, 106).

The Orange Order, other white segments of Alberta's population, and the KKK encouraged each other. They combined their forces to strengthen racism and halt Catholicism, especially through anti-French sentiment. Aside from the wide public support the KKK had received in Alberta, it enjoyed significant official backing. The Government of Alberta granted it a charter, the only charter of its kind in the entire British Empire (Baergen 2000). Granting the KKK a charter meant that it would not be subjected to police surveillance, which afforded the KKK additional power and legitimized its activities. The only opposition to the KKK came from some Alberta newspapers, which criticized the KKK openly but did not denounce the Orange Order. That meant that the KKK continued to enjoy overwhelming support because the Orange Order was a major ally. Like the national organizations, Alberta's KKK echoed anti-Semitism and did not hide its anti-Catholic sentiment, which, like the Orange Order, it demonstrated through hostility towards Francophones. The KKK also opposed the immigration of Eastern Europeans to Alberta, and exhibited racist doctrines as it stirred up racial prejudice and fostered the myth of "racial purity." In this regard:

> [The Alberta KKK's] first recorded set of principles . . . forever maintain the supremacy of the Anglo-Saxon race . . . keeping eternally a blaze the sacred fires of a true patriotism to Canada . . . and the white Race . . . the devout impulse of an unconquered race (Baergen 2000, 109-110).

> [T]he ten questions that formed the admissions test stressed racial purity . . . with questions like . . . "Do you believe in and will faithfully strive for the eternal maintenance of Racial Purity?" (Baergen 2000, 216).

Alberta's KKK also resented the immigration of racialized groups, at that time mainly the Chinese and Japanese (Black immigration had by then already been banned in Alberta). The KKK continued to grow in Alberta and, by 1927, it became a highly structured organization and political movement. It had thousands of members and formed chapters across Alberta, including in Edmonton, Calgary, and Red Deer. It carried out public activities similar to the ones organized by white supremacists in the rest of Canada. Not only did Alberta's KKK engage in frequent speaking tours across the province, it perpetrated overt violence in the form of cross burning, kidnapping, beating, and threats by posters and written messages (Appleblatt 1976). Thus, in this first wave of organized white supremacy, Canadian identity was racially and ethnically bound. Canadian-ness was constructed of interlocking notions of whiteness, Aryan race, and Protestantism. Although white supremacists were not the only ones to embrace this identity construction at that time, they were unique in negotiating it in explicit acts of racial hatred and racial violence.

The first wave of white supremacy waned in Alberta in the mid-1930s, and in the rest of Canada a few years before that. Some social changes contributed to its demise, including the virtual cessation of immigration in the early 1930s, the deepening of the economic depression, and the coming of war later in the decade. These events also contributed to the decline of anti-Catholicism, since the so-called "Catholic threat" was no longer the main concern of Albertans and other Canadians. It was difficult to convince Canadians that the Pope was succeeding in taking control of Canada. In Alberta, additional factors peculiar to the KKK contributed to its demise, such as the weakness of the KKK's leaders, fraud charges against them, and the imprisonment of some of them, which shook the organization. Nevertheless, while the KKK and like-minded organizations—i.e., the Orange Order—dwindled, their ideologies did not. A second wave of neo-Nazism and white supremacists surfaced in Alberta and the rest of Canada in later decades, during the 1970s and 1980s. When it comes to Alberta, Baergen (2000) states that the prominent organization at that time (1970s and 1980s) was an identity Christian Movement (the Movement) that brought the Aryan Nations Movement to Alberta. The Movement was primarily white supremacist, since it sought to fill "the void in identity," associating Canadian identity with the "true chosen White Europeans" (Baergen 2000, 263). Although the Movement was modern, it reproduced the classical racism that the previous white supremacists had embraced. It adapted biological determinism to its construction of Canadian identity, perceiving race and culture as genetic and static. It, too, called for "racial purity," and this bigotry was clearly stressed in the Movement's discourse. A section in the Movement's Certificate of Incorporation titled the "Objects of the Society," declared that the Movement aimed:

(a) To provide . . . a kinship of race . . .

(b) To attempt to preserve . . . the traditions and ideals of the Celtic and Anglo-Saxon races, or more generally, the traditions and ideals of the White Races . . . . To advocate racial purity among its members (Baergen 2000, 229-230).

The Alberta government approved the Movement's Certificate of Incorporation in spite of its explicit racial hatred. The government granted the Movement a charter in 1972, which marked the second time that a hate group was granted a charter in the entire British Empire (the first being when the Alberta government granted the KKK a charter). However, it is important to mention that the second charter was met with some resistance. Some people in Alberta advised then Premier of Alberta J.E. Brownlee to not grant the Movement a chapter because of its openly racist and xenophobic declarations. But the Premier refused to ban the Movement under the pretext of freedom of expression (Baergen 2000). That recognition made the hate group a legal entity and further legitimized it. This meant that a basic human right was given to a hate group, that white supremacists received both public and official governmental support time and again. This blatant racism which, as the above quotes illustrate, prioritized white culture as the basis of identity, was embraced and normalized. It bears noting that the Movement targeted racialized minorities, especially Blacks, explicitly pointing to them as one of the groups who "were not eligible to join [the Movement]" (Baergen 2000, 270). The Movement did not display animosity towards Francophones because, anti-Catholicism had waned. It did not marginalize Eastern European immigrants because they had already been accepted in Canada as desirable citizens. However, the Movement remained anti-Semitic, which it demonstrated in statements indicating that Jews should be killed en masse. In general, the Movement displayed its white supremacist ideologies publicly through acts of racial hatred that included cross burning, and that were expressed at rallies and meetings. It also projected signs and symbols of white supremacy, since it was once again given permission to organize public events, such as the Aryan Fest held in Provost. It showcased signs stating "KKK WHITE POWER!" and "ARYAN NATIONS." In particular, the organization demonstrated white supremacy in its vehement opposition to the previously mentioned immigration and multiculturalism provisions that Canada endorsed in the 1960s and 1970s. White supremacists perceived the immigration and multiculturalism policies as being interconnected, the former allowing racialized people to immigrate to Canada and the latter seeking to improve their integration into society. They believed that immigration and multiculturalism issues combined to materialize "the Death of the white race." Alberta's Movement joined other white supremacist organizations in Canada to denounce these policies. Together, they declared:

> Never has our Race had such a challenge as today . . . . They [the federal government] have opened the floodgates of immigration diluting our blood (Kinsella 2001, 371-372).

> [T]he federal government's policy of multiculturalism is a political means of controlling whites . . . . [Multiculturalism] was the road to ruin Canada (75).

With regard to immigration, while most, if not all, white supremacists were themselves immigrants to Canada, they racialized immigration. They resorted to the terms "immigrants," "non-whites," "the colored immigration," and "Third World immigrants" interchangeably to project racialized immigrants as aliens who invaded "their" country. They resented multiculturalism from the outset, and I argue that this is because, even soft, liberal multiculturalism is incompatible with everything white supremacists stand for, let alone critical multiculturalism. Multiculturalism ideology cherishes diversity (Fleras & Elliott 2002), which is the opposite of the monoculturalism white supremacists long for. The multiculturalism policy seeks the inclusion of racialized groups, which does not sit well with the supremacists because they are solely concerned with white race. The fact of multiculturalism acknowledges the co/existence of people of various backgrounds, which counters the supremacists' imagined utopian society that does not hold any place for the racialized. The practice of multiculturalism encourages interactions among the various groups, which clashes with the supremacists' intention to keep the races apart so as to safeguard the "racial purity" of Canada's Aryan race. The supremacists sought to ignite a backlash against racialized immigrants and multiculturalism, which they did by spreading racist prejudice and stereotypes about these immigrants. They maintained that:

> The current wave of Third World immigrants can never be assimilated with any value to Canadian culture, they only serve to weaken our national direction and value system (Kinsella 2001, 274).

> [I]f an immigrant [from the developing world] comes into Canada and gets a job for $150,000, he is taking jobs away from us... the Gentile people, the white people (22).

> [Racialized] Immigrants exploit Canadian social programs and shoplift a lot (45).

> [They] are more prone to violence, they bring drugs wherever they go. When you talk about modern-day problems, when you talk about the drug problem, when you talk about the rise in crime, when you talk about problems in the economy, so much of that is connected to the tremendous percentage of non-whites (266).

White supremacists propagated the mythical racist connection between the immigration of racialized people and economic problems. They first manifested racism of elimination towards racialized immigrants when they called for their segregation, then embraced racism of extermination when they demanded that they be deported to "their places of origin." It is worth noting that this second wave of white supremacy dwindled in most places in Canada in the early 1990s, once again lasting longer in Alberta. The demise of this wave was mainly due to weakness in their leadership. Thus, we see that Canada's second wave of white supremacy propagated the same anti-Semitism and racism of the first wave. It differed from the first wave in that it was not anti-Catholic and therefore did not exhibit hostility towards Francophones. Both waves were anti-immigrant, but the first wave targeted Eastern European and racialized immigrants, while the second one focused on racialized immigrants and the multiculturalism programs that sought to improve their status in society. These patterns confirm CRT's assertion about white privilege, since they reproduced the advantages that white minorities, in this case Francophones and Eastern European immigrants, enjoyed since they were increasingly accepted in Canadian society. This is not the case with racialized minorities, in this case Blacks, who continued to be marginalized. Like the first wave of white supremacy, the second resorted to racial hatred tactics to achieve its goals, i.e., cross burning, and utilized racist language to intimidate the racialized and spread propaganda about them. Both waves of white supremacy enjoyed public and political support. It is because of these patterns that they resurfaced in our contemporary era in the form of the third wave[3] of white supremacy that was particularly active from the mid-2000s through 2013. This contemporary wave was particularly visible in Alberta and coincided with the three years of the fieldwork (2008-2011). Understandably, the emergence of a third wave of white supremacy threatened citizens' and the research participants' safety and sense of belongingness.

For the participants, the visible presence of white supremacist organizations in Alberta seemed more like fiction than reality, a perspective they shared in statements such as: "We can't believe this is happening" and "We never thought such a thing would occur in Canada at this time, there is not just one [white supremacist organization] but many." This is because the participants had a different image of Canada prior to immigration, one that projects Canada to the world as a tolerant society. The participants expected that, at the turn of the 21st century, Canada would have achieved much more in terms of social justice. That white supremacy persisted in contemporary Canada contradicted everything Canada represented for them. The participants confirmed the presence of "many" white supremacist organizations because there were three organizations in Alberta at that time. These included: 1) the Aryan Guard, 2) the Western European Bloodlines, and 3) Volksfront. The Aryan Guard was created in Calgary in 2005 when its founder moved from Ontario to Alberta and chose

---

3.   I also refer to the third wave of white supremacy as the contemporary wave.

Calgary as the organization's headquarters because, in his words, "Calgary, with its skinhead scene and ample job opportunities, was ripe for the movement... was a fertile ground" (Wingrove 2011). The organization chose Alberta over other Canadian provinces as their base because of the support that they expected to receive there. They believed that Alberta's image as the Bible belt of Canada and as a bastion of conservatism that welcomed white supremacy in the past prevailed and that it would consider a white supremacist organization a desirable ally. Furthermore, they were interested in the economic opportunities that were available in Alberta during its economic boom. Once again, Calgary in particular attracted white supremacists because the concentration of the oil and gas companies in the city made for a larger labour market, and because Calgary is believed to be conservative. The founder of the Aryan Guard led the organization out of his Calgary townhouse, which he also used as a waystation for new recruits when they arrived in the city. The organization also offered to help pay for other white nationalists to move to Calgary from other Canadian provinces and cities, which allowed it to grow and attract additional members. A few years later, in 2010-2011, the Aryan Guard reorganized and rebranded itself as Blood and Honour/Combat 18.[4] The number 18 is a code for Adolf Hitler, representing his initials—"1" for "A" and "8" for "H." The second organization, Western European Bloodlines (WEB), was formed in 2011, and its members were identified by spiderweb tattoos. It was believed to be volatile and violent (Martin 2015). The third organization, Volksfront, was also formed in 2011. It was an underground group that originated in the US and moved to Calgary where it set up a branch (Huffpost 2013). Although all three organizations organized activities to spread their propaganda, the Aryan Guard remained the most prominent, active and visible, which is why I focus on it in this section.

Like the two previous waves of white supremacy, the Aryan Guard professed neo-Nazism and white supremacy. One of the group's leaders declared: "We're... the intellectual types if you will. Blood and Honour is more of a philosophical group" (Babiak 2011). The Aryan Guard's philosophy is that of Adolph Hitler, in whom it found a hero for which it exhibited public admiration. As a member of the Aryan Guard stated: "It was a pretty good platform he [Hitler] ran on and got elected" (Martin 2015). Members appreciated Hitler's exclusionary beliefs and tactics. Their anti-Semitism was visible in contentions that alluded to the "conspiracy

---

4. Notwithstanding the change of the organization's name, I will refer to it in this book as the Aryan Guard.

of the Jews" and that ascertained that "there is no greater threat than the Jews" (Wingrove 2011). The Aryan Guard exhibited white supremacy in its "White Pride" slogan that was displayed publicly. In this respect, Van McVey (2008) reminds us that "White pride is a motto, slogan, term used by white separatist, white nationalist, neo-Nazi and white supremacist organizations in order to signal racist or racialist viewpoints." Thus, "White Pride" is a badge that symbolizes a racist project. It is imbued with power and coined with white privilege to incite white racist movements, such as the Aryan Guard. By displaying the "White Pride" slogan, the Aryan Guard reproduced the classical thinking about race. In the current era where race is increasingly considered a social construct, Alberta's contemporary white supremacists continue to perceive it through the lens of biological determinism. Other scholars assert that contemporary white supremacists interpret race in a primordial manner; for example, Ezekiel (2002) states that "The organized White racist movement rests on the following ... axioms: that race is real, that white is best" (67). Ezekiel (2002) goes on to say that white supremacists consider race "a biological category with absolute boundaries, each race having a different essence—just as a rock is a rock and a tree is a tree, a white is a white and a [B]lack is a [B]lack" (53). Again, as in the case of the two previous waves of white supremacy, the Aryan Guards put their neo-Nazi and white supremacist ideologies into practice. They gave their organization names, i.e., the Aryan Guard and Blood & Honour, that put forward white racial superiority and the desire for "racial purity." They embraced these ideologies as a way of life:

> [Name of one of the Aryan Guard's leaders] has assembled the requisite image of a skinhead leader. He has a pit bull named Thor and a three-year-old daughter named Aryanna. He shaves his head, wears all black and is covered in tattoos: "white power" on his chest, "skin" and a swastika on his left hand, "kill" on one leg and "Jews" on the other (Wingrove 2011).

The Aryan Guard displayed the most atrocious symbols of neo-Nazism and white supremacy. They bore the Swastika, Nazism's most symbolic icon of racism, hatred, and mass murder (Martin 2015). They also wore "skinhead" tattoos referring to a music subculture largely tied to white nationalism. Thus, they felt safe exhibiting their xenophobia in the public space. While they relied on the Internet to recruit new members and distribute hate propaganda, they organized beyond the Internet in 2008. They reached a broader arena inasmuch as "they leaflet neighbourhoods throughout Calgary in an attempt to recruit like-minded people" (Martin 2015). Recruitment materials reiterated racist ideologies such as their determination to preserve the "racial purity" of white Canada. That public exposure was galvanized when the Aryan Guard started holding annual marches that they termed White Power rallies in Calgary on March 21 of every year, from 2008 to 2011. One of the Aryan Guard's leaders made the following statements about the annual White Power rallies:

> It's one thing where everyone says you can't do it [hold a march] but I'm showing you that you can. Everyone has always said for years—'The gays have their march, the Blacks have their march, why don't we have ours?' Simple. Because you haven't organized it (Wingrove 2011).

In these rallies, white supremacists intended to prove that they had reached a sophisticated level of organizing, and to affirm that their organization had members and supporters who were capable of setting up such activities. They used the rallies to spread their principles and encourage people to join them. Their choice of March 21 to display their support for "White Pride" was not random, because it is the International Day for the Elimination of Racial Discrimination (IDERD). White supremacists resent the fact that people around the world gather on March 21 to commemorate the struggle against racism. A coalition called Calgary Anti-racist Action (CAA) holds an antiracism rally on March 21 every year in support of anti-racism and social justice. The CAA is committed to exposing and eradicating white supremacists in Alberta, in particular through their March 21 rallies. Arguably, the Aryan Guard held its annual marches on the same day, March 21, in a cynical attempt to contest the anti-racism that the IDERD rallies represent. Every March 21, white supremacists marched down the streets of downtown Calgary and gathered on the steps of City Hall. More disturbingly, "[t]hey ... wave flags, carry signs and chant slogans, all broadcasting an unmistakable, unsettling message: White pride" (Wingrove 2011). Not only did they display neo-Nazi and white supremacist emblems, they resorted to violence.

They instigated violent confrontations and clashes with anti-racist activists by scaring them away and giving their own organization more legitimacy. However, their violence was not limited to clashes at the rallies; it was an integral aspect of their beliefs and activities. A statement by one of the Aryan Guard's leaders reveals that they did not hide their support for violence: "I'm fine with violence . . . . If someone's in our way, we'll move them out of our way" (Wingrove 2011). The Aryan Guard's acts of coercion included making explosives and "possession of a weapon dangerous to the public," to which one of its leaders pled guilty in 2011 (Wingrove 2011). In this case, devices were found in the leader's home during a police search. Arguably, this aggression represented racial hatred, since the white supremacists used it to exhibit racism and xenophobia. In this climate, the Aryan Guard's enmity was directed at both racialized minorities and white anti-racist activists. Among other things, in 2011, a member of the Aryan Guard was charged with a racially motivated assault after he attacked a Japanese woman. In particular, the Aryan Guard targeted opponents of racism in Calgary, notably the CAA spokespersons Jason and Bonnie Devine.

The Devines first received threats online and in person, but the intimidation soon escalated into severe attacks. On one occasion, in 2008, the couple's home was vandalized and firebombed with a Molotov cocktail, while on another it was spray-painted, and projectiles were thrown into their children's rooms. These incidents were aggravated in 2010 when masked people armed with hammers and pipes invaded the couple's residence. Not only did they damage property, they attacked another member of the CAA who was at the Devines' residence at that time, and severely beat Jason Devine about the head in an attempt to kill him. The Devines' home was also vandalized more recently in 2013, when a large rock was thrown at the residence and smashed a window pane. This incident was considered a warning to the Devines—and other like-minded people—who stood up to the white supremacists. The CAA used the rallies to update participants on the status of white supremacists in Calgary and, at the 2013 rally, Jason Divine stated that "neo-Nazis are not active in our city [Calgary] right now. They're not organizing and this is a thing to be happy about" (Massinon 2013). Devine also suggested that the number of white supremacists was dwindling and that they were not as strong as they were in previous years. What led Devine to make these statements is that white supremacists have not held an annual "White Pride" rally in Calgary since 2011, and their public exposure has decreased. This led the Devines and others to the conclusion that the white supremacist organization had weakened and was disappearing. However, the Devines' home was attacked shortly after Jason Devine made the comments, which was a reminder that white supremacists were alive and well. Although they no longer held annual "White Pride" rallies, they were still organizing other activities, including opposing their opponents by violent means. It bears noting that white supremacist violence was not confined to Calgary, and that it extended to other locations in Alberta. For example, in 2008, they once again demonstrated their racial hatred by tarageting Aboriginal people on the Siksika First Nation reserve. A mall on the reserve was vandalized, and it was confirmed that white supremacists were connected to the attack. The "RCMP say four white supremacists punched holes in the walls of the building, likely using pipes or baseball bats," that the suspects were arrested and that they were "members of the Aryan Guard in Calgary" (CTV News Calgary 2008).

Furthermore, the Aryan Guard extended its violence to Edmonton inasmuch as, in March 2011, "the Edmonton police hate crimes unit charged four men with assault and other offences. The men were distributing flyers for a white nationalist organization called Blood and Honour" (Babiak 2011). Wingrove (2011) added that there were also "other offenses" and that they were all "hate-motivated attacks." As such, overt racial violence was a key facet of white supremacists' work up to 2013 when they attacked the Devines' home. This attack and other violent incidents led to the arrest of most of the organization's leaders, and some were put in jail. These events weakened the organization, but they did not wipe it out. The remaining white supremacists confined their actions to online activity. There was no public discussion about white supremacists until 2015, when two incidents drew attention to them again. The first incident unfolded during the March 21, 2015, anti-racist march in Calgary, when a man crashed the event outside City Hall, "yelling 'white power' at rally-goers" (CBC News 2015). The man pulled out a pipe, threatened to attack rally participants, and refused to comply with the police, causing the police to shoot him. It was thought that the man might have been linked to the white supremacists in Calgary because of the white power slogan that he shouted and his violent behaviour. Following the shooting, white supremacists in Calgary offered to help the man, whom they considered a "police shooting victim." In Wood's (2015) words:

> [Shortly after the shooting,] a poster on an online white pride community said "We would like to start a collection once we know who he is if he is in jail and needs bail and for some pocket money once he is out because he will not be able to work for a while after being gunned down . . . . But first we need to find out who this guy is and what is going on with his situation."

Whether this was the Aryan Guard or another group, the poster's language echoed the organization's rhetoric and confirmed that white supremacists continued to exist, that they followed up on events and defended members and sympathizers. Similarly, the incident reminds us that, whether the man was a member of an organized group or not, there continue to be people who adhere to white supremacist ideologies and do not shy away from open violence. The other incident for which the Aryan Guard made the news in 2015 concerned an Indigenous man's accusation of one of the Aryan Guard leaders. The man stated that the Aryan Guard member attacked and pepper sprayed him because the "man... insulted Adolf Hitler" (Martin 2015). In response, "Calgary white supremacist [name] denie[d] [the] assault" (Martin 2015) and was acquitted. Regardless of the outcome of this charge in particular, time and time again the Aryan Guard, and possibly other white supremacist groups, continued to operate in Calgary at least until 2015. In this regard, it is important to emphasize that the Aryan Guard's activities were not limited to Alberta either, sine their ideologies and activities expanded nationwide. The Aryan Guard reproduced the strategy of the two previous waves of white supremacy by solidifying its organizing at both the provincial and national levels. The organization's leaders went as far as to affirm that they were going to revive white supremacy and neo-Nazism in contemporary Canada. Shortly after the Aryan Guard established its headquarters in Calgary in 2005, it collaborated with other white nationalists and co-founded the National Socialist Party of Canada (the Party) in 2005. The Aryan Guard officially affiliated itself with the Party and declared it a national political organization. Understandably, the Party was openly neo-Nazi and white supremacist, as evidenced by the following statement:

> [The Party aims to] [c]hallenge by any and all legal means the Jewish influence [in Canada] ... [and] revive the European-Canadian foundations. It praises Adolf Hitler [who is a] gift of an inscrutable Providence to a world.... only the blazing spirit of this heroic man can give us the strength and inspiration to bring the world a new birth of radiant idealism, realistic peace, international order and social justice for all men (Metapedia 2015).

The similarity between the Aryan Guard's and the Party's ideologies in terms of anti-Semitism and racism, and the time of the establishment of the two organizations (2005), were not non-coincidental. The white supremacists sought to posit that they were well organized, collaborated nationally, and that the Aryan Guard played a key role in that process. It is this xenophobia that made the participants fear white supremacists. Participants in the three cities—Calgary, Edmonton, and Brooks—alluded to white supremacists in the interviews, contending:

Participant: I didn't believe it [the presence of white supremacists] is actually happening... until I saw them on the news. So we have to be careful when we go around.

Participant: We fear for our safety because they don't hesitate to do anything. Whether you are in Calgary or Edmonton or somewhere else, you know they can be anywhere. They don't like immigrants and what immigrants bring, like diversity [multiculturalism]. They don't like people who don't look like them [white]. So we have to be careful. I worry about my kids [safety].

White supremacists created an atmosphere of fear and insecurity because their tactics and hostility took racism to the extremes of racial violence and hatred. The danger of explosives, assault, beatings, and murder became life threatening. The participants felt intimidated and insecure in a situation where they could be attacked because of their skin colour or affiliation with an anti-racist collective. The Aryan Guard's violence made white supremacists' lynching of Blacks in the past a possibility in the present. The above quotes show that this violence left a scar on their soul. They felt that they were targeted because they were visibly Black and immigrants, which also implied that they supported multiculturalism. This is because, as in the case of the previous waves of white supremacy, Alberta's contemporary white supremacist organizations opposed both racialized immigration and multiculturalism. However, while the previous organizations refuted racialized immigration and multiculturalism overtly, contemporary organizations disputed them in a different manner. They entrenched them in their basic emblems and doctrines, in particular in their "White Pride" slogans. Scholars emphasized that:

[The] [u]se of white pride as an identity marker (Van McVey 2008).

[A]ffirmations of white pride... serve to mask and perpetuate white privilege (Ingram 2004, 55).

"White pride" would, of course, be a politically distasteful goal, given that whiteness is not a personal... identity, but has been a strategy to maintain inequities of privilege and power (Mayo 2004, 311).

[T]he idea of "white pride" in contemporary US has developed in contrast to an "immigrant" against the backdrop of recent immigrant influx of people from the developing world into the US (Swain & Nieli 2003, 5).

"White Pride" also serves "as an identity marker" to reinforce an exclusionary image of belongingness, in this case, of Canadian identity. As in
the case of the previous white supremacists, their contemporary counterparts confine Canadian-ness to the Aryan race; it is void of the diversity
that characterizes our contemporary society. It grants whiteness identity
normativity (Jensen 2005), opposing it to immigration and, I would add,
multiculturalism. To corroborate Swain and Nieli's (2003) assertion, the
"White Pride" movement in the US disputed immigration by refuting
policies that encourage it, such as affirmative action policies. For white
supremacists, these provisions took employment away from "Americans"—
meaning white Americans—which labels racialized immigrants non-Amer-
ican. I argue that the logic of American white supremacists applies to
Alberta's—and Canada's—contemporary white supremacist organizations
as well. They use "White Pride" rhetoric to denounce the immigration of
visible minorities and multiculturalism. Another incident that occurred in
Calgary during the fieldwork also indicates that contemporary organizations oppose racialized immigration and multiculturalism. In March 2009,
the Annual National Metropolis Conference was held in Calgary for the
first time. The conference is devoted to immigration issues in Canada; it
brings together academics, government officials, policy makers, and community partners to discuss a wide range of topics about immigration. It
deliberates on issues ranging from refugee protection to transnationalism
and immigrant family reunification. It also discusses immigrant integration
policies, especially multiculturalism. As Canada's largest immigration
forum, the conference represents a willingness to facilitate immigration
and integration in Canadian society. The ideals and goals of the conference
did not sit well with white supremacists, who expressed resentment about
both the conference and that fact that it was being held in Calgary. A few
days prior to the conference, flyers containing racist anti-immigration
propaganda were left on parked cars in downtown Calgary. Figures 1 and
2 show both sides of the flyers.

FIGURE 1

It Is Time to Put Canada & Canadians First

- Canada's immigration policy caters to the noisy immigrant lobby...
- Canada is in harsh recession. The stock market tumbled nearly 50% last year. People's savings have dwindled.
- Unemployed is soaring. "Canada's unemployment rate is now 6.2% of the labour force." ... The OECD estimates that Canada's unemployment rate will rise to 7 per cent next year and then grow to 7.5 per cent in 2010... [a]n increase [which] means that about 183,000 more people will be out of work....
- Yet while Canadians are losing their jobs, the heartless government continues to flood the country with more immigrants... foreigners flooding into Canada just as unemployment soars.
- Where are they going to work? They will either take Canadians' jobs or go on welfare.

Immigration costs
Stop Immigration & Put Canadians Back to Work

... **They will either take Canadians jobs or go on welfare.**
Subscribe to the **Canadian Immigration Hotline** (monthly; $30 per year.)
Write: **Canadian Immigration Hotline**, P.O. Box 332, Rexdale, ON., M9W 5L3
Http://www.canadafirst.net [emphasis in the original]

FIGURE 2

Canadafirst.net is an online national white supremacist organization that proclaims to "fight for the ignored Canadian Majority in immigration matters" (Canadafirst.net 2018a). It alleges that Canada's immigration system is not working because it "is changing Canada to what more resembles a third world country" (Canadafirst.net 2018b). Therefore, the organization aims to reform the immigration system in order to "preserve" Canada and Canadians, alluding to white Canadians. The unwelcome immigration is that of racialized people and people from the developing world. The Canadian Immigration Hotline belongs to Canadafirst.net, and it uses it as a platform to propagate anti-immigration rhetoric. More than once, it is wrongly stated on the flyers that immigration is costing Canada because it is a burden on the health system, that immigration increases the crime rate because the immigration system allows illegals to enter Canada. The flyers perpetuate the classic stereotype of immigrants as job-stealers who take employment away from nationals (Lapshina 2015). The image of immigrants that the flyers convey can only reinforce racist prejudice. Note the stark similarity between the language of the flyers and the racist stereotypes about racialized immigrants that the previous white supremacists embraced. Why do I believe that Calgary's and Alberta's white supremacists were connected to the flyers?

Although the flyers do not disclose the name of any Albertan white supremacist organization, the xenophobia in the flyers is a hallmark of the Aryan Guard and other white supremacist organizations in Alberta. In addition, given the aforementioned cooperation between Albertan and national organizations, such as between the Aryan Guard and the National Socialist Party of Canada, it is possible that one of Alberta's organizations is associated with Canadafirst.net. The method of distributing the flyers was similar to the way Alberta-based white supremacists have disseminated their propaganda. It also resembles the Aryan Guard's tactics of choosing specific occasions, such as International Day for the Elimination of Racial Discrimination (IDERD), to publicize their agenda. In this case, the conference is equivalent to IDERD because of its relevance to immigration and multiculturalism. At any rate, the flyers were intended to achieve what Alberta's white supremacists would have sought, which is to denounce the immigration conference and the support of multiculturalism it represents. Thus, the Aryan Guard revived white supremacy, but by no means did its demise in 2013 signify that its neo-Nazi and white supremacist ideologies disappeared. This is because they were spread shortly afterwards in an even more pronounced manner. As the Aryan Guard waned, similar organizations surfaced across Alberta and the rest of Canada at the end of 2015. They represent what I term the fourth wave of white supremacy in Canada, which is larger in scope, membership, and support than the Aryan Guard and the previous waves of white supremacy. For example, an organization called the Soldiers of Odin (SOO) continues to grow, and other alt-right groups are following suit (Metapedia 2015). They are all provincial (Alberta) chapters of national organizations. Like the previous white supremacists, the fourth wave propagates white supremacy and neo-Nazism across Canada, which they displayed in acts including a poster campaign called "Hey, White Person" that an alt-right group launched in Toronto in 2016 (Siekierska 2016).

The campaign aimed to ignite racial hatred by conveying messages such as "tired of being told you're 'racist' for celebrating your [white] heritage?" We note that that campaign added anti-immigration and anti-multiculturalism wording such as "Wondering when immigration will stop?" and "Wondering why only white countries have to become 'multi-cultural'?" This is because the current and fourth wave of white supremacy resurrected the initial waves' plausible attacks on racialized immigration and multiculturalism. However, the fourth wave also spreads anti-refugee and anti-Islamic rhetoric. These developments are in line with contemporary events that brought large influxes of refugees and Muslims to Canada and the Northern hemisphere in general. This time, white supremacists have reached even larger arenas, since they also cooperate internationally. There are chapters of SOO and similar white supremacist organizations in Europe, the US, and Australia. This is evidence of the expansion of white supremacist doctrines globally, with the overarching goal of eroding diversity and emphasizing whiteness as the normative identity. Once again, these xenophobic ideologies are negotiated through racial and ethnic hatred. In Canada in particular, hate crimes increased as the number of white supremacist organizations continued to grow. Islamophobia escalated to the extent that "[i]n 2015, police across the country recorded 159 hate crimes targeted at Muslims, up from 45 in 2012, representing an increase of 253 per cent" (Minsky 2017). The hate crimes against Blacks also increased drastically, as "members of the [B]lack community in Canada remained, by far, the most targeted group in terms of police-reported hate crimes, representing 17 per cent of all hate crimes" (Minsky 2017), which suggests that racial hatred in the form of anti-Black racism continues to grow as well.

A thorough investigation of the current and fourth wave of white supremacy goes beyond the scope of this book, but this brief analysis is of relevance because it reveals that white supremacy in Alberta and Canada is deep-rooted and continues to reproduce racial hatred. If it is not curtailed, it will continue to spread xenophobia, possibly on a larger scale and in more violent ways. Although the fieldwork only explored the third wave, the preceding content analysis of the other waves proves Kinsella's (2001) contention that these organizations are characterized by two constant criteria: white supremacy and neo-Nazism. They all resort to violence and are all zealous to maintain the "racial purity" of the Aryan race. Thus, they all construct Canadian identity in an exclusionary manner that centres on whiteness. Furthermore, they all cooperate with national organizations to strengthen their agenda. I added new nuances in the differences between the four waves of white supremacy in that anti-Catholicism towards Francophones and Eastern European immigrants decreased, if it continues at all. Nonetheless, white Francophones joined white supremacist organizations and created new ones. In the past there was the "Famous KKK of Montreal," and at present there are numerous alt-right groups in Quebec (Milton et al. 2018). This factor allows us to conclude that white Francophones contribute to white supremacy and, by implication, disenfranchise racialized minorities. Although we cannot prove that Eastern Europeans participate in such organizations, we cannot confirm that they are fighting white supremacy either. Thus, the seemingly positive change that lessened hostility towards these two groups remains racially differential because white supremacy continues to plague racialized groups. Furthermore, we noted changes in the tactics concerning immigration and multiculturalism, since the first wave overtly denounced immigration and the second openly opposed both immigration and multiculturalism (multiculturalism was a new development at the time). The third wave denounced these two aspects indirectly, entrenching them in their "White Pride" slogan. The fourth and current wave returned to the strategy of explicitly denouncing immigration and multiculturalism, while adding anti-refugee and anti-Muslim sentiment. These convergences suggest a change of tactics but not of ideologies. The ideals remain xenophobic, but the methods may differ, largely a protest against emerging social and demographic shifts.

Similarly, white supremacists' standpoint on anti-Black racism changed in form but not in content. The first and second waves displayed anti-Black racism openly, while the two latest waves implied it in their xenophobia towards racialized immigrants. There is a specific difference in the third and fourth waves of white supremacy: their use of the Internet. Again, this is in line with social developments, in this case the technological innovations that mark the postmodern era. It reminds us that the digital revolution is a double-edged sword, since white supremacists have found a welcoming home on the Internet. They rely on the Internet to achieve their goals, such as organizing, recruiting, and distributing propaganda. They have even created Internet service providers to bolster their organizing, which means that the new technologies facilitate their work. What sets the fourth wave apart is that it replicates global white supremacy directly. This suggests that the groups may be communicating via the Internet, but definitely indicates that white supremacy is currently widespread. As such, white supremacy in Canada projects critical race theory (CRT)'s assertions about the saliency of race and racism, and the interpretation of white supremacy as cruel violence. CRT would warn us that we are in an era of racial hatred and violence that is not disappearing but proliferating. This is because it is rooted in a long-established tradition of bigotry. We noted earlier that its longevity is also made possible because white supremacy receives public and official support. Now the Internet is a contributing factor to the persistence of white supremacy.

If we link this discussion to the literature on immigration, we find that white supremacy becomes increasingly threatening as the numbers of racialized immigrants continue to rise. It is for this reason that the research participants voiced concern both for themselves and their children, suggesting that white supremacy will not disappear unless we take serious actions to stop it. I agree, and add that it is useful to analyze how the previous waves of white supremacy were countered. This allows us to identify which strategies may work and which may not. I described how the first and second waves were countered, and now I lay out how the third wave, which unfolded during the research fieldwork, was fought. This endeavor allows us to decipher ways to help eradicate the current and fourth wave of white supremacy and hopefully prevent it from being reproduced.

COUNTERING CONTEMPORARY WHITE SUPREMACY

Commenting on who should fight white supremacy, Perry and Scrivens (2019) corroborates that "must counter-extremism initiatives be multi-dimensional, drawing upon the strength and experiences of diverse sectors: law enforcement . . . education" (2019, 121). The authors rightfully remind us that fighting white supremacy is a collective responsibility that involves numerous actors. In line with this contention, I stress that Alberta's white supremacist organizations did not go unchallenged, for specific actors took action to fight them. We will see that the research participants, the anti-racist organization Calgary Anti-Racist Action (CAA), and the media opposed white supremacists, and that the legal system should deploy more efforts to help eradicate white supremacy. The research participants denounced white supremacy vehemently:

> Participant: If I am talking to you about them [white supremacist organizations] it is because one should talk against them. It is racism, but it is violent racism. They should know ... they can't just take all this space.

> Participant: I took part in last year's [March 21, 2010, anti-racist] rally. I felt I needed to be there because we have to do something [about their racism] .... I marched with many others, and we showed them [white supremacists] that extremist racism does not intimidate us. Fortunately, others fought it too.

In line with CRT, the participants practised the "critique of liberalism," explicitly calling the acts of the white supremacist organizations "racism," "violent racism," and "extremist racism." Their discourse refutes white supremacy and demand justice to rectify it. In addition, the participants took part in the aforementioned annual CAA anti-racist rallies on March 21 to counter white supremacy. Thus, they resisted white supremacy in their discourse and through their actions. This was made easier by the fact that, as the participants put it, "others" contributed to the struggle against white supremacy. These included civil society actors—the CAA, the media, and law enforcement. The CAA created a space to voice concerns about white supremacy and deployed considerable efforts to ensure the effectiveness of the anti-racist rallies. For example, it launched a campaign to encourage people to participate in the rallies. Given the paucity of antiracist literature about white supremacist organizations in Alberta, long excerpts from the campaign's emails that the CAA sent out prior to March 21, 2011, anti-racist rally are worth our attention:

> It cannot be denied or ignored: the neo-Nazi movement in Calgary is alive and growing, with three groups now actively organising. But we cannot give into fear!

> ... The March 21, 2010 rally was successful and was held to commemorate March 21, to denounce the continued presence of racist gangs in our community, to bring attention to systemic racism, and finally to
> . celebrate our diversity. Since that day many events have occurred here in Calgary, events which have shown that the struggle against the neo-Nazi movement in Calgary is far from over ....

> In continuing its tradition, CAA Calgary is organising again for March. However this year, with a revitalised movement, [name of a Aryan Guard

leader], on behalf of B&H, has stated they will be holding a "White Pride March" in downtown Calgary on March . . .

Thus we are organising to rally . . . and, if the neo-Nazis do indeed march, we plan to meet them and prevent them from freely marching down our streets.

Thus, in order to truly form a tradition of open and militant anti-racism in Calgary, we need to move to include as many people as possible on a critical basis and respect for a diversity of tactics . . . among those who want an end to racism."[5]

The "struggle" that the email alluded to is the CAA's mobilization of people to confront white supremacy. This struggle epitomizes CRT's strategy of "political struggle," whose aim is to eradicate racism. The CAA's preparatory campaign for the anti-racist rallies included communication and discussions with its members and supporters. In so doing, the CAA created a platform to drive racial justice, establishing a dialogical approach to opposing racism. The CAA's "political struggle" made a strong coalition, a race-conscious mobilization which proved that racism will not be tolerated. Significantly, the CAA demonstrated CRT's viewpoint about the power of coalitions when they assemble actors banded together in the name of social justice. CAA members and supporters demonstrated this power because they were united by specific "contextual factors" (Chong & Rogers 2005), namely racial consciousness, awareness of racism, and a commitment to anti-racist action. The rallies formed a multiracial movement in which both racialized people and whites took part, which leads us to comment specifically on the participation of whites in the anti-racist rallies. In *Race and the Politics of Solidarity*, Juliet Hooker (2009) states that, in order for anti-racism to be successful, any related social solidarity movement must make whiteness visible. This visibility showcases whites' direct involvement in anti-racism because they have the power to effect change. In addition, such commitment enables white people to challenge and correct the unearned white privilege they enjoy. As Fleras (2014) asserted:

Those persons called "white" have a particular obligation to fight racism because it is ours, created in its modern form by us, for the purpose of commanding power over resources and opportunities at the expense of people of colour. Furthermore, all whites . . . have to address the internalized beliefs about white supremacy from which we all suffer (223).

---

5.   I received the email because my name was on the CAA's mailing list.

Whites should take anti-racist action because they are contributors and the primary beneficiaries of long-standing injustices—i.e., slavery, colonialism, and the ensuing racism. These inequities granted them material and psychological benefits that they have enjoyed for centuries now. Not only does racism afford whites economic benefits, it boosts their collective sense of superiority and satisfaction with their dominant status in society. The whites who participated in the anti-racist rallies assumed that responsibility, they helped make whiteness visible and unveiled white supremacy and the associated white privilege that allowed their organizations to occupy such a central public space. Although the whites who took part in the rallies were only a small proportion of Calgary's white population, they displayed commitment to anti-racism. As such, the CAA cultivated a multiracial decolonizing space to dismantle racial hatred and xenophobia. It challenged subordination and the unjust immigration controls entrenched in white supremacist organizing. Furthermore, the CAA's "political solidarity" has been successful because of its continuity. The CAA's email made reference to both the 2010 and 2011 anti-racist marches, and invited citizens to plan for upcoming rallies and consider additional tactics. This pattern suggests a high level of organizing, since the CAA builds on previous anti-racist rallies to strengthen upcoming ones. It also demonstrates constancy, since not only were the rallies held in 2010 and 2011, they continue to be held today. The contention in the above email that "the struggle against the neo-Nazi movement in Calgary is far from over" brings to light both the prolonged existence of white supremacy and the need to broaden the struggle to fight it. This is because the CAA is aware that fighting racism requires an all-encompassing strategy—to use CRT's wording. Luckily, this goal was partially achieved, since the media also helped oppose Alberta's white supremacist organizations.

With regard to the media's coverage of the news about white supremacist organizations in Alberta, the numerous media sources that I quote in this book reveal that the media provided a platform that informed the public that white supremacy persists in Alberta and in Canada. In particular, English-language print and online newspapers and a few TV news channels provided information about racist groups. Not only did the media put forth documentation that facilitated anti-racist studies, such as this book, they also educated the public about the xenophobic ideologies that guide white supremacist organizations. In addition, they warned about the danger that white supremacists pose to individuals and society. Statements the research participants made in the interviews, such as "it is good that the media talked about them [white supremacists]" and "Once

I heard about it [the White Power March] in the news, I decided to do something about it," indicate that the media helped to mobilize public opinion against white supremacy. Before we praise the media further, let us not forget that they are a double-edged sword. On one hand, the media perpetuate racism towards racialized minorities because they are totally absent in media institutions or underrepresented in important areas of decision making and staffing and overrepresented in less important roles (Henry & Tator 2002). This pattern of exclusion pertains to Alberta's mainstream English media vis-à-vis Blacks. None of the research participants were employed in these institutions and, more generally, no Black Francophones in Alberta are employed in any of these media. This exclusion is not confined to Black Francophones, for, as I explained earlier, only a handful of Black Anglophones are employed in these media and fewer, if any, occupy decision-making positions (I will subsequently show that the Francophone media are equally exclusionary).

Furthermore, the media perpetuate negative reporting about racialized minorities that exacerbate racism. When it comes to Blacks in particular, the media associate them with entertainment and sports, as being void of intellectualism and professionalism. They also portray Blacks as criminals and a hazard to society, and in so doing promulgate anti-Black racism. On the other hand, the media can inculcate social justice but, as Fleras and Elliott (2007b) suggest, this endeavour requires society to "multiculturalize the media." From the perspective of critical multiculturalism, the media can be "multiculturalized" by correcting the aforementioned shortcomings. The media should assume an educational and representational responsibility, offering constructive coverage and raising awareness about the benefits of diversity for society. With regard to our analysis, the media "multiculturalized" itself to some extent, since they informed the public about the racial hatred and xenophobia of white supremacists and pushed people to protest against them. Although Alberta's (and Canada's) media remain too far from the stage of inclusion that would make them fully "multiculturalized," they did provide much-needed anti-racist knowledge and education about white supremacists. This factor also illustrates Perry and Scrivens' (2019) aforementioned statements about the relevance of education to the struggle against extremism. While the participants alluded to the contribution of the media, they also called out other actors in the legal system.

Kinsella (2001, 434) rightfully stated that "[t]he law remains our best instrument in restricting, and eventually stopping, the dramatic growth in racist ideologies in Canada." The legal system is crucial for eradicating white supremacy because it is the ultimate authority to stop racial hatred. To be sure, Canadian laws do limit racial hatred and organized racism. Both the Charter and the *Canadian Human Rights Act* forbid any kind of discrimination based on race, colour, national origin, ethnicity or religion. In addition, Canada's *Criminal Code* prohibits hate crimes and hate propaganda. When it comes to white supremacy in Alberta, the legal system penalized members of the Aryan Guard in some ways. A few were charged with offences, namely, assault and the possession of weapons dangerous to the public, and were sentenced to jail as a result. Nevertheless, these outcomes were not achieved in a timely manner, nor were the measures sufficient. For example, it took the police a long time to charge the white supremacists for the aforementioned attacks on the Devines. Jason Devine confirmed that "it [the series of violent incidents on their residence] has been happening for the last six years [2008-2013]—and the trail always leads back to members of Calgary's white supremacist movement" (Huffpost 2013). The police themselves maintained that Mr. Devine was "100-per-cent targeted" (Wingrove 2011). Nevertheless, no one was charged for the attacks until 2013, when one of the leaders of the Aryan Guard pled guilty to making "racist motivated threats" to Jason Devine (Huffpost 2013). These "threats" proved white supremacist involvement in the offences against the Devines. The 2013 charges finally put an end to the violence targeting the anti-racist activists. However, the charges of attempted murder and racially motivated assault were dropped. In particular, the white supremacists were not charged for hate crimes and hate propaganda, nor were their Internet activities considered cybercrime. Thus, they were not penalized for the main threat that is embedded in their ideologies and practices: racial hatred. Why was this the case? Because white supremacists are protected under the auspices of freedom of speech. It is for this reason that, in the past, as we indicated earlier, the Government of Alberta granted racial hatred groups—the KKK and the identity Christian Movement—charters that made them legal entities, justifying their decision on the pretext of freedom of speech. Unfortunately, the legal response to white supremacist organizations in the contemporary era is still the same. According to Babiak (2011), a police constable opined that the Aryan Guard's distribution of hate flyers in Edmonton was not a criminal act because: "We [the police] do strongly advocate for freedom of speech," said [name of Constable] of the … police hate crimes unit. "We have no trouble with people having white nationalist views"" (Babiak 2011).

How can Canadian legislation both prohibit and permit racial hatred? The answer is in the subjective interpretation of "freedom of speech," which confuses hate propaganda with liberty. This is because Canada's legal system itself mixes "white nationalist views" with "freedom of speech." The laws define neither "freedom of speech" or "hate crime" in a manner that makes it possible to clearly distinguish one from the other. As it stands, the law blurs the line between freedom of speech and racial hatred. It allows the police to consider white supremacists acts "views," but we can see that these "views" are explicit examples of racial hatred. They used oppressive language—to use Tony Morrison's (1992) words—and symbols, such as the swastika, the Nazi insignia, and other white power and neo-Nazi symbols. Thus, they endorsed both coercive and symbolic violence (Bourdieu 1986). The materials that they distributed incite hatred against specific racialized groups, which makes them "hate crimes and hate propaganda." Similarly, the above-stated charges laid on some white supremacists were much more than "minor assaults"; they were "hate crimes." Since Canadian law does not condemn these acts as hate crimes and hate propaganda, we have reason to believe that the law functions in intricate ways to tolerate such behaviour. Hate becomes freedom of speech, while freedom of speech represents the most racist ideologies and praxis. Fleras (2014) describes these contradictions as follows:

> As societies [Canada] become more diverse and inclusive, they must grapple with the dual prospect of restricting racist speech and associations to protect diversities, yet preserve core constitutional values related to speech and association.... How... to balance these values when confronted by those who use liberal democratic freedoms to justify their racist acts? (226-227).

As it happens, white supremacists rely on Canadian laws to validate their actions. In fact, Alberta's white supremacists did just that when they contended that their activities were their "Charter rights." Unfortunately, law enforcement and white supremacy are mutually enforcing. As Wingrove (2011) notes, "the Charter protects much of what neo-Nazi groups say and do." White supremacists interpret their racial hatred and hate propaganda as freedom of speech, and the law supports them. While we agree with Fleras (2014) that Canada "grapples" with these inconsistencies, we do not see any reason why Canada has not yet come to terms with these contradictions. Why is it taking Canadian legislators so long to explicitly define the limits of freedom of speech when this "freedom" is imbued with racism and has adverse consequences for citizens? Why has Canada not clearly defined "hate crimes" and "hate propaganda," leaving the terms open to interpretation and allowing the propagation of white privilege? We believe that Canada has had sufficient time and the necessary resources to sort out these contradictions, but it chose not to. Canadian legislation has a double standard when it comes to condemning some and tolerating others, and this dynamic is racialized. While Canada overlooked the hate crimes of white supremacy even though the perpetrators should have been held accountable, it has not hesitated to sentence innocent racialized minorities for similar offences.

A perfect example of these patterns are the anti-terrorism measures Canada enacted in the aftermath of September 11. Ironically, these provisions came into effect during the fieldwork. They were initially implemented in November 2001, when Canada passed the *Immigration and Refugee Protection Act* (IRPA), then the *Anti-Terrorism Act* (ATA) in December 2001. Canada was caught up in the wave of the Islamophobia that resurfaced in the Western world at the time. The IRPA was not exactly intended to "protect" immigrants and refugees as its name suggests; it aimed to protect Canada from racialized refugees and immigrants. In the climate of the time, Canada considered terrorism an imported—not Canadian—phenomenon brought into Canada by immigrants and refugees. The sudden association between terrorism and immigration and refugees was justified by the need to protect the security and safety of Canada and "Canadians." Canada considered "terrorism" a threat to both its national security and human security, in this case "the importance of making individuals and their communities secure" (Crocker et al. 2007, 1). The immigrants and refugees who were considered a threat were from the Muslim world. The measures did not only regulate the immigration of people and refugees who had not yet entered Canada, they curtailed the rights of Canadian citizens who were already in Canada. As it happened, Canadians who "looked Muslim" or had Muslim-sounding names experienced atrocious discrimination. That description fit many visible minorities, including the participants, and those who were suspected were profiled, surveilled, fired from work, and deported to their sending countries (Zine 2008), despite the fact that they were Canadian citizens. They were terrorized by the very state that should have protected and ensure their "human security" in the first place. They were not included in the category of "Canadians" that Canada seek to protect; thus, they were not identified as Canadians. Their exclusion from the terrain of Canadian identity meant that their human security does not matter, and that the terrorism they faced from Canada was justified.

Canada did not accuse white supremacists of terrorism, despite the fact that they threatened the human security of the racialized people they targeted. In essence, it rewarded them, since they walked away with their racial hatred and hate propaganda. While the racialized were penalized in multiple ways, they were not protected from white supremacy and were the target of the anti-terrorism legislation because of how they looked. It is for this reason that one participant said: "we are cornered. The [white supremacists] tell us we are not Canadians... but the law [anti-terrorism legislation] is not better." Therefore, I argue that Canada's "grappling" with white supremacy is not justified. A welfare state should not allow actors to abuse "democratic freedoms." Since it punishes some, it should condemn others. It could have solved this problem a long time ago in the same way it rushed to fight "terrorism." Canada passed anti-terrorist legislation and made sure it was properly applied when it penalized the racialized. It did not ensure that the existing legislation—the Charter and the *Criminal Code*—was clear enough and be applied properly to protect the racialized. This perspective extends to other diversity-related legislation, such as the *Multiculturalism Act*, which did not serve to fight white supremacy either. Canada's Action Plan Against Racism (the Plan) could have potentially reduced white supremacy, especially because it included two initiatives that could have helped achieve that goal: 1) the Nationally Standardized Data Collection Strategy on Hate-Motivated Crime (Data Collection Strategy), and 2) Interventions for Victims and Perpetrators of Hate Crimes (IVPHC). However, in practice, these initiatives did not lessen white supremacist activities. Alberta's white supremacists were active during three years of Plan (2007-2010), meaning that they had the freedom to carry out their activities. We are reminded of CRT's tenet of the "critique of liberalism," stating that liberalism can propagate racism. In this case, the liberal premise of freedom of speech is twisted to tolerate racial hatred. I therefore argue that Canada does not "face contradictions"; it creates its own contradictions and, in so doing, it reproduces racism. Thus, the forces of dominance construct and negotiate Canadian identity to cater to whites, while they annihilate the racialized, in this case Blacks. Unfortunately, these exclusionary patterns are not confined to Canadian identity, since they extend to other affiliations, including Francophone identity.

CHAPTER 4

THE CONSTRUCTION AND NEGOTIATION OF FRANCOPHONE IDENTITY

"La Francophonie is this integral humanism . . . this symbiosis
of . . . all the continents, of all the races".

Léopold Sédar Senghor 1962

I t is important for Black-African Francophones to identify with La
Francophonie, which has been an integral part of their sociocultural
heritage and contemporary life for a very long time.

Participant: Being Francophone is very important to me, because it has
always been a part of who I am . . . Africa has a long history with French
[La Francophonie]. French was obviously my language. I lived in French,
I went to school in French, then I worked in French.

Participant: After I immigrated [to Canada], I also see myself as a
Francophone of Alberta. Here, we continue to be Francophone . . . there
are some changes . . . Being Francophone means living in French, in our
[Francophone] community . . . We become members of the Francophone
associations, we attend [Francophone] events and festivals . . . we are an
integral part of the Francophone [space].

Participant: In Alberta, we [the Francophones] are a linguistic minority.
One has to deploy a lot of efforts to maintain French language and
culture. The Francophone struggle in Alberta and Canada is a long one,
and we have joined it . . . . If we have to take a political action, we will.
If we have to take any [other] action, we will. For example, the Caron

Case is a priority.... It is detrimental to the Francophone destiny. It is our fight, and we will fight it.

Participants' relationships with French and La Francophonie began in their sending countries, where French is either one of the official languages or the only official language. There, they studied in French and used it in work and public life and as a medium of communication. In addition, they incorporated French into pop culture, including music and poetry. Their Francophone identity is deep-rooted because Africa itself has a centuries-long engagement with La Francophonie. It is evident that this rapport involves inequitable power relations between France and Africa, including slavery, colonialism, and the ensuing racism. Nevertheless, Africans used language—French—as a means of decolonization to oppose their marginalization. Their standpoint mirrors the aforementioned facet of critical multiculturalism, language as a means of resistance, in this case the subversion of a colonial language into a decolonial instrument (Habashi 2008). Using French, Africans created a strong place for Africa within the Francophonie Internationale,[1] the global entity that brings together Francophone countries around the world. As a result of such decolonizing efforts, the French language is no longer the property of France or other former European colonial nations. Rather, French is the language of the Francophonie Internationale. This entity is governed by the Organisation internationale de la Francophonie (OIF),[2] the global political agency that consists of 58 member states and governments, and 26 observers. The OIF aims to maintain and expand the French language globally, enhance solidarity among French-speaking countries and peoples, and strengthen their political and economic power (OIF n.d.). The OIF is to the Francophone world what the Commonwealth is to the Anglophone world. It plays a crucial role in all Francophone affairs and cannot achieve its purpose without Africa's input. The continent accounts for 29 member states and a few observing states, more than half of the organization. African countries and peoples have strengthened La Francophonie; they promoted French by giving it official language status, using it and participating in various Francophone organizations. As such, while in Africa, the participants constructed their Francophone identity along historical, cultural, educational and sociocultural lines, which they negotiated in public and daily life praxis.

---

1.   The International Francophonie.
2.   The International Organization of the Francophonie.

In Alberta and in Canada the participants' construction of Francophone identity reflects both continuity and change. In terms of identity continuity, when they were in Africa, the participants attached a persistent symbolic and actual value to La Francophonie. The change adapts this identity to the new immigration context. As the above quotes reveal, the participants felt an attachment to La Francophonie in Alberta and in Canada, embracing its collective histories, cultures, struggles, and aspirations. While French is a prestigious language in Africa, it is a minority language in Alberta and the rest of Canada, and the participants are conscious of the ambivalent social and political position in which Francophones in Canada find themselves. Their awareness of the minority status of French and Francophones encouraged them to adopt the Francophone struggle as their own. For these reasons, they aimed to continue to live in French, and to be able to use this language as a means of communication at work and in daily, institutional, and community practices. They are keen on passing on the French language and Francophone culture to their children. They negotiate these aspects of identity in practices such as sending their children to French-language schools and using French-language services. They also organize and attend Francophone events. It bears noting that the Alberta Francophonie vibrates with a polyphony of activities that constitute the cornerstone of the social life in La Francophonie. These include the Festival des Sucres,[3] which is celebrated every year in Calgary and Edmonton (and other cities across Canada). There is also the Calgary-based biennial Gala de la franco-phonie[4] and Brooks' annual Franco Festival.

These events are particularly significant in the Francophone minority context because they serve to expand the Francophone space and enhance the visibility of La Francophonie and bilingualism in society. Therefore, the participants' contribution to these initiatives boosts the growth of La Francophonie. Furthermore, the participants practise political activism as they partake in the promotion of La Francophonie and bilingualism in Alberta. The reference the participants made to the Caron case in the above quotes is not coincidental, since the case unfolded during the field-work. The analysis of this case extends beyond this book, but suffice it to say that it resembles the aforementioned Paquette Affair. It was launched by an individual, Caron, who believed that his language rights had been breached and who took legal action that was eventually supported by the

---

3.   The Maple Festival.
4.   The Francophonie Gala.

ACFA. This organization mobilized Francophones in a collective struggle to support the case. As the above quotes show, the case held special significance for the participants, who considered it fundamental to the well-being of La Francophonie. They followed the case developments closely and publicly voiced their support, including during mainstream and community events. Many other Black Francophones took similar initiatives with the overarching goal of supporting the political claims of Francophones. Thus, we note that the demands for French-language rights are made in the name of all Francophones, and Blacks remain true to this responsibility. Participants' commitment and contributions to La Francophonie mean that they deserve to be included in the Francophone space and have their fair share in the gains of the Francophone struggle. It is for this reason that the participants also constructed Francophone identity in terms of being "an integral part of La Francophonie," which they wish to be negotiated through their inclusion in the institutions and resources that constitute the Francophone space. Nevertheless, racism within La Francophonie lead the participants to believe that they are not considered genuine Francophones, a perspective that they explained as follows:

> Participant: We [Black-Africans] are part of La Francophonie, our kids attend French schools... but when people [white Francophones] here talk about Francophones, they mean Franco-Albertans, they mean people who are French Canadian. They don't mean [visible] minorities or people who came from other [developing] countries.

> Participant: Then you realize that we don't get the same opportunities [and resources] as white Francophones. We don't get good jobs in organizations, radio or TV... schools... Our status in La Francophonie is impacted by our race.... However, you don't see [white] Francophones paying attention to it.... [We] want to talk about it [race]. Do you hear them talk about racism? No... La Francophonie is not what it should be: the image of this colourful multicultural Francophonie... in business, etc., etc.

These statements allude to the identity exclusion the participants experienced as a result of the dominant construction and negotiation of Francophone identity. Hegemonic ideologies construct a racially, religiously, and culturally fixed homogeneous understanding of Francophone identity. The participants' reference to "Franco-Albertans" and "French-Canadian" affiliations echoes the dominant imaginary about the Francophone identity. In this case, this identity is synonymous with being white, Catholic, Quebecer or French Canadian, being in Quebec or elsewhere in Canada for generations, and having roots in France and French as a mother tongue (Dalley 2003; Knight 2001). This construct "confirms what many Quebecers have always believed," that "they, the descendants of original French settlers, are the only true Quebecois" (Tandt, in Angry French Guy 2009). These expressions are politically and culturally charged inasmuch as they suggest "racial purity" in a manner commensurate with white supremacists' perception of the biological determinism of race. They are intended to recognize whites as the only legitimate Francophones. In minority contexts outside Quebec, the dominant identity construct is replicated through similar identifiers that consist of the term "Franco" followed by a form of the name of a Canadian province, i.e., Franco-Saskatchewanian, Franco-Ontarian. The participants' use of the qualifier "Franco-Albertans" in the above discourse indicates awareness that this notion accepts white Catholic Albertans of French Canadian origin as the genuine Francophones. It diminishes the participants' capacity for identification, depicting them as "immigrants" and "foreigners" (Shahsiah 2006), pushed outside the Francophone space of belongingness. Thus, the exclusion associated with Francophone identity echoes CRT's tenet of the centrality of racism, in this case in relation to identity. We can see that racist ideologies serve to disenfranchise Black-African Francophones.

The dominant construction of Francophone identity is negotiated in three forms of racism mentioned by the participants: 1) the under-representation of Black-Africans in the mainstream Francophonie, 2) the silence about racism, and 3) Francophones' opposition to multiculturalism. The underrepresentation of Black-Africans implies the marginalization of the racial and ethnic diversity of La Francophonie in both the public and private sector. In the public sector, Black-Africans are excluded from mainstream Francophone institutions and key positions of power and decision making. As stated earlier, there are many autonomous mainstream Francophone institutions; however, only two of the forty-two participants were employed in these institutions during the fieldwork. Of these, only one had commensurate employment; the other had a contract-based position. The participants actively searched for employment in Francophone institutions, but that did not guarantee them commensurate work. Some participants were interviewed for jobs that they did not obtain and indicated that the same jobs were filled by white candidates who were less qualified than them. Others were informed that they were overqualified for the positions for which they applied. Thus, qualifications were used as an excuse to justify racism, since the participants were punished for being highly qualified. We see that the mainstream Francophone institutions did not recognize the French-language credentials obtained in African countries, France, and Canada. Overall, underrepresentation in employment was not confined to the research participants, since it also extended to other Black Francophones in Alberta (Madibbo 2016; Moke-Ngala 2005). Only two Black Francophones occupied key positions in mainstream institutions, though both lost their job a few years later. As the above quotes reveal, the participants stressed underrepresentation in Francophone institutions but pointed to two institutions in particular, the media and the school system. This illustrates the key role these institutions play in society in general and in the Francophone minority context in particular. With regard to the media, we asserted that critical multiculturalism stresses that the media must have representational and educational significance. There are a few mainstream Francophone media outlets in Alberta: a radio station (CBC French), a television station (ICI Radio-Canada Télé), and the weekly newspaper, *Le Franco*. For the most part, these media did not assume this responsibility, since they replicated the aforementioned exclusion of Black-African Francophones. None of the participants were employed by these media outlets, although a handful had training and skills in journalism. Again, this lack of representation was not limited to the research participants. During the fieldwork, only one Black Francophone was employed as a journalist with *Le Franco*, and they eventually lost their job.

When it comes to the exclusion of Black-African Francophones in the French-language school system, we indicated earlier that these schools are key in the struggle for language rights, since Francophones consider them the guardians of the French language and the Francophone identity and culture against the backdrop of linguistic and cultural assimilation. The participants' discourse revealed the contradictions inherent in the mainstream Francophonie. White Francophones control the system, while Black-African Francophones are largely excluded. The participants supported this school system in a number of ways, including by sending their children to French-language schools. Other Black-African Francophones followed suit, providing the schools with a much-needed student population that justifies the Francophone demands for these schools in the first place. However, two participants who were qualified to teach did not obtain regular employment in these schools, ending up working there as supply teachers. One of these participants said that, after they were employed, the school hired full-time teachers and did not offer them a full-time position. That led the participant to believe that the school did not wish to offer Black-African Francophones long-term employment. The underrepresentation of the participants in the French-language school system extended to Black Francophones in general, since very few were employed there during the fieldwork. Thus, Black Francophones ended up being clients of these schools, while they were underrepresented as teachers and administrators. The participants in Edmonton, Calgary, and Brooks noted the contrast between the student population on one hand, and the teachers and administrators on the other. There were a large number of Black students in the French-language schools, but very few or no Black teachers or principals. It is important to emphasize that there are no specific statistics about the ethnicity of teachers and staff in these schools because the French-language school boards do not collect or release race-based data. However, CRT's precept of "experiential knowledge" confirms the participants' contentions, because the participants had profound knowledge of these schools. The participants examined the schools closely because they approached them seeking employment and because their children attended these institutions. In addition, the younger participants who were schooled in Canada attended these schools and corroborated that underrepresentation. They also brought to light additional barriers caused by their underrepresentation. They recalled stigma associated with the placement of Black students in lower educational levels and devaluation by the predominantly white teaching staff and administration in phrases such as: "The teachers treated us differently." They recounted a lack of material pertaining to Black history and other social aspects in contentions such as: "I didn't learn Black history, we didn't really talk about Black [Canadians]." Racism left lasting scars on the participants that led them to make comments such as: "I don't have good memories about my school in [city in Alberta]."

Most participants feared the influence of these barriers for their children, and they iterated their fear in statements such as: "I don't want my kids to think that jobs such as a school teacher are not for Blacks." They worried that the lack of role models in schools would lead their children to develop low self-esteem and limit their future aspirations. Another participant added: "Our kids drop out of schools, and this is a big problem," drawing attention to the high rate of school non-completion that plagues Black youth in particular. The participants' concerns align with the literature, which stresses that school racism has an adverse effect on Black students' achievements and aspirations (Dei & McDermott 2014) and pushes Black youth to drop out of school (Zaami 2017). These patterns were also documented in the French-language school system in Alberta (Moke-Ngala 2005), and has been observed in other Canadian provinces such as Saskatchewan (Carlson Berg 2011). Thus, we see contradictions in French-language schools in that they confine their historical mission to facilitate the formation of a Francophone identity to the dominant construction that perceives whiteness as the norm. As the critical multi-culturalists would put it, French-language schools replicate the master narrative about white Francophones as a "founding people of Canada," which serves to bolster the identity of white Francophone students while it pushes their Black counterparts to the margins. One participant validated this outcome by saying: "When in school I felt I wasn't included as a Francophone." The French-language school system reproduces a host of racist obstacles that adversely affect Black-African Francophones' self-perception and their inclusion in society.

The exclusion of Black-African Francophones in mainstream public Francophone institutions extends to the private sector. The two participants who owned small businesses during the fieldwork had closed them down by 2016. The exclusion of the participants in the private sector replicated that of other Black Francophones, since this sector remained predominantly white. Content analysis of the research data confirms this contention in materials such as the Annuaire Francophone de l'Alberta,[5] which maps the socioeconomic and cultural landscape of Alberta's Francophonie. Not only do these directories list the names and contact information of schools, school boards, and other mainstream institutions and organizations, they identify businesses ranging from accounting and translation to real estate, bakeries, restaurants, insurance, and daycare. They also provide information about psychologists and dentists, lawyers and translators, among other entrepreneurs and professionals. Although these directories do not include all Francophone businesses, they provide information about key agencies that citizens resort to in daily life. For example, the 2009 Directory of Calgary and region (ACFA Régionale de Calgary 2009) contained 25 businesses, none of which were Black-owned. Content analysis of the newspaper *Le Franco* revealed an identical pattern. The "Annonces et services"[6] sections of *Le Franco* do not include all Francophone businesses, but list large numbers of important services. These sections, too, depict a white Francophone business world that is monopolized by whites and gives the impression of a community void of racial diversity.

If this marginalization occurred during the fieldwork, my follow-up with the participants in 2016 unveiled more unfortunate facts. Racism in the Francophone marketplace was as bad if not worse. I indicated

---

5.   Alberta's Annual Francophone Directory.
6.   Advertisement and Services.

previously that the participants experienced drastic downward mobility in the Anglophone labour market by 2016, and this exclusion was replicated in La Francophonie as well. The two participants who worked in mainstream public Francophone institutions during the fieldwork lost their job by 2016. None of the other forty participants were employed in a mainstream Francophone institution in 2016. In fact, very few—fewer than five—Black Francophones worked in these institutions at that time. Similarly, the education system also continued to marginalize Black Francophones. Although a few Black-African teachers were hired in French-language schools, this is a minor achievement because both the number of schools and Black-African Francophone students grew in Alberta. There should have been more Black-Africans in these institutions. The same trend extended to the media, since in 2016 there was only one Black-African radio journalist in the Francophone media. Thus, the underrepresentation in La Francophonie that the participants pinpointed as a cause of their identity alienation did not decrease; it hit them harder than during the fieldwork. The 2016 follow-up with the participants demonstrated that identity exclusion did not diminish but might even have increased. It bears noting that the downward mobility that the participants endured in the Francophone public sector in 2016 extended to the Francophone private sector. No participants had businesses in 2016, nor were any of them employed in Francophone businesses. Admittedly, the economic recession had an adverse effect on La Francophonie, as some businesses collapsed. However, the majority survived the economic downturn. Once again, the recession impacted Black-Africans more severely. In 2016, there were only two Black Francophone-owned businesses in Alberta, and both were small in scale. Overall, the Francophone private sector had not changed much since the fieldwork, and was still overwhelmingly white in 2016. Our content analysis corroborated this fact, since the 2016 Alberta Directory (Annuaire 2016) included 148 businesses and, again, none were Black-owned.

With respect to the participants' contention about the silence about racism as another signifier of Francophone racism, it is noteworthy that this type of discrimination can occur anywhere, but that it is more prominent and systemic in La Francophonie. Micheline Labelle (2011) termed this phenomenon "the Franco-centric approach to anti-racism" (103), alluding to the silence about racism that permeates France and extends to Francophone Canada. Significantly, the participants endured silence about racism in both France and Francophone Canada, a fact that appeared in declarations such as: "I lived in France, but the word 'race' is taboo. Quebec and other provinces are no different." "The Franco-centric approach to anti-racism" resembles CRT's conceptualization of the silence about racism, and this contention cannot be truer than in France. France's Republican ideal (Citrin & Sears 2009) affirms that all citizens are equal without regard to race. France adopts colourblind legislation that makes it illegal to use the term "race" in any official manner in France and therefore prohibits collecting any race- or ethnic origin-based data, whether it is about education, housing, or employment. France extends its colourblind rationale to identity, arguing that citizens' allegiance should be directed only to the Republic. For this reason, France's constitutional principles stress that there is only one, unique national French identity that guarantees equality to all French citizens. It holds that all people in France are French, and this is a monolithic designation that supersedes any racial, ethnic, or religious affiliation. It is important to emphasize that it is the weight of national history that led France to erase the discourse of race. The French Revolution entrenched rights as universal and natural benefits of being human. France sought to distance itself from the African slave trade in which it actively participated by ushering in a new era of respect for universal human rights. In addition, Nazi Germany's occupation of France during WWII pushed France to denounce discrimination based on race throughout the post-war period. However, these ideals remain slogans more than reality, since France has breached them repeatedly. France waged war against Algeria[7] and continued to embrace its race-neutral rhetoric, which produces the adverse outcome that CRT cautions against: propagating racism.

France's official banning of the term "race" for the sake of equal citizenship means that it endorses the assimilationist approach to immigrant integration under the pretext of allowing immigrants to become equal French citizens. However, it is evident that France's mythology of national unity disguises deep-rooted structural and systemic racism, for it did not guarantee its multicultural population equitable treatment. On the contrary, these people endure severe racial oppression that, among other things, is illustrated in the trajectories of the population of North African descent. Although this populace has been in France for generations, it suffers drastic socioeconomic and political marginalization. Racialized stratification and geographic segmentation plagues this people (Montague 2013), and their

---

7.   Emmanuel Macron, President of France, aims to acknowledge the atrocities that France committed towards Algerians, but his efforts are being contested, especially by right-wing conservatives in France.

plight extends to other racialized minorities, especially Blacks. The participants' quotes illustrate this exclusion, indicating that they faced racism in France. As such, France's republican ideal turns into nativism, while the official silence about race delegitimizes any formal debate about racism. Because of a lack of race-based data,[8] the French government does not monitor racism, which means that it does not define how it occurs, nor does it implement measures to fight it (Hunter 2007). It is noteworthy that France's stance on race does not apply to gender, since the country collects gender-based data and publicly debates gender-related affairs. This means that banning the use of the term "race" in France is more about escaping accountability for racism than a confirmation of a unified national identity. France's "Franco-centric approach" to race and racism (Labelle 2011) is replicated in academic discourse as well, which tends to ignore race. Again, this is not the case with gender, and it hinders the analysis of racial problems and relevant solutions.

France's constitution initially stipulated that "France … shall ensure the equality of all citizens before the law, without distinction of origin, race or religion." In 2018, France removed the term "race" from its constitution when the National Assembly of France ratified an amended article which states that France shall "ensure the equality of all citizens before the law, without distinction of sex, origin or religion" (Le Monde 2018). This move was intended to fight racism, it being argued that using the term "race" can incite racism because it legitimizes the dated concept of biological determinism and racist ideologies about race and racial differences. However, we can also argue that refraining from using the term "race" can trigger racism. In line with the previous contentions about the need to continue to use race as a social construct and an analytical category, we emphasize that, despite the fact that the term "race" was removed from the constitution, racism persists in society and there are no explicit official

---

8. The Institut national d'études démographiques in France has collected data about immigrant origins and other social factors, including income, to examine correlations between origin and socioeconomic status. The data were gathered from 26,500 participants from 2019 to 2020. Though this is a positive step towards social inclusion, it is not comprehensive. The number of participants included in the survey is very small compared with France's total population (65,365,824 people). In addition, the survey doesn't include questions about race, which seems to have been replaced by nationality/origin and immigration status. A more efficient solution requires gathering official statistics from the entire population of France and adding explicit questions about race.

ways to identify racism and redress it.[9] France's stance on racism did not significantly improve and was exported to La Francophonie in Canada.

We noted that Canada's federal government occasionally embraces race and anti-racist discourse and actions, which is demonstrated in provisions such as Canada's Action Plan against Racism (the Plan). This openness to anti-racism, albeit it minor, is more prevalent in Anglophone Canada than in Francophone Canada, since the denial of racism permeates the latter space. Quebec denies race in a number of ways, for example, the Ministère de l'Immigration et des Communautés culturelles,[10] which is responsible for anti-racism matters, rarely employs the term "race" (Labelle 2011). More generally, Quebec's political and public discourse avoids using the terms "racism" and "race," instead employing the notion of "cultural communities" to denote racial minorities, and discrimination as a substitute for racism. Like France, Quebec's colourblind approach extends to academic analyses. Apart from the work of very few authors (Labelle 2011; Maillé 2015; Potvin 2006), the literature in Quebec ignores race. Like France, Quebec is not silent about gender the way it is about race. In particular, Quebec is not silent about language; on the contrary, the French language is at the heart of all policy and discourse. In the end, Quebec's silence about race did not reduce the incidence of racism. Rather, it complicated it by letting it persist without addressing and redressing it. Again, to corroborate the tenets of CRT, "the experiential knowledge" of people of colour proved the veracity of racism in Quebec. There, the research participants faced racism in the labour market and the education system, as well as in other institutions. Haitians and other Black Francophones also encounter anti-Black racism in Quebec (Femmes Africaines Horizon 2015 2006). As such, Quebec's silence about racism mirrors the construction and negotiation of a homogeneous white identity that does not accommodate the diversity of society.

La Francophonie outside Quebec, in this case in Alberta, showcases the "Franco-centric approach" (Labelle 2011) to race in a number of ways. Mainstream Francophone public and political discourse does not use the term "race" or related concepts. It substitute the term "ethnicity" for "race," "cultural diversity" for "racial diversity," and "immigrants" by

---

9.   Similarly, France implemented a National Plan Against Racism and Against Anti-Semitism (2018-2020), which also aimed to "fight hate on the Internet." This is another positive initiative that could generate inclusion, especially if it culminates in initiatives that address the three types of discrimination—racism, Anti-Semitism and cyberhate—separately, and appropriate follow-up policies and mechanisms.

10.   The Ministry of Immigration and Cultural Communities.

"racial minorities." By implication, this discourse does not allude to the racism and inequitable power relations suffered by Blacks. For example, the mainstream Francophone media did not cover the aforementioned white supremacist organizations in Alberta. For the most part, Francophone academic discourse denies racism, although very few scholars counter this tendency by stressing race, racism, and antiracism (Carlson Berg 2012; Madibbo 2006; Sall 2021). The silence about racism prevails, which means that Black-African Francophones are caught up in a vicious cycle of racial oppression. The reality of racism—to use CRT's wording—plagues them, while the silence about racism renders it invisible. In the end, this silence benefits white Francophones because it allows them to escape the ethical and political responsibility that the recognition of racism generates. Such recognition exposes white Francophones as oppressors who reproduce discrimination towards Black-African Francophones. The recognition of racism would change the image that white Francophones have historically projected as a minority, and they will no longer be the primary beneficiaries of the associated rights and resources. Anti-racism means that white Francophones would have to give up the white privilege they enjoy because they will no longer control the power in the Francophone space because they will have to share it equitably with racialized minorities. However, there is a hope that current and future generations of white Francophones, including those who are cited in this book, will refute anti-Black racism and share the Francophone space with Black and other racialized Francophones in more equitable ways.

The cycle of racism that faces Black-African Francophones is galvanized by the third type of racism the participants brought to light: Francophone opposition to multiculturalism.

In this regard, it is noteworthy that La Francophonie in Canada has historically resented multiculturalism. We stated earlier that the *Official Languages Act* (OLA) came into force in 1969 and that Canada issued its Multiculturalism Policy (the Policy) shortly afterwards—in 1971. In essence, the two should be complementary, because one sought the inclusion of a linguistic minority while the other targeted the inclusion of racialized minorities. However, the inception of the Policy signaled the beginning of an antagonism by La Francophonie towards multiculturalism. The literature reminds us that Francophone opposition to multiculturalism surfaced in both Quebec and the Francophone linguistic minority contexts in the rest of Canada:

[M]ulticulturalism causes a particular kind of insecurity for Canada's national minorities ... notably French Canadians ... [It] threatens their recognition (Taylor, in Couture 2002, 147).[11]

[French Canadians perceived the Policy as] a federal strategy to weaken Quebec's position [in Canada] .... [T]he special contribution of the French group in the creation of Canada is recognized but only to a certain extent ... keeping them equal with the other population groups (Government of Canada n.d.).

Since 1974, nearly all Canadian provinces have adopted some form of official multiculturalism, while Quebec is the only province that has formally rejected official multiculturalism. Before the inception of the Policy, Canada was considered a bicultural nation in which the British and French cultures formed the basis of society. This image of Canada advantages Francophones because it enhanced Canada's national identity as a dual—British-Canadian and French-Canadian—affiliation in which Francophones occupy a central place. It legitimizes the master narratives—to use critical multiculturalism (CM)'s terminology—about white Francophones as one of the two "founding peoples" of Canada. For Francophones in particular, any departure from the bicultural image of Canada threatens the privileges they enjoy. They perceived multiculturalism as a huge retreat from biculturalism, a threat to their status in Canada. Quebec in general, and the Parti Québécois in particular, refuted the Policy from the outset. They believed that it threatened the special status of French Canadians and Quebec as a "distinct society," because it promotes the "equivalence of cultures," a perspective that they argue makes all cultures equal to one another in status. Moreover, it equates Quebec/French-Canadian culture with "immigrant" cultures, which relegates French Canadians to "just another ethnic phenomenon" in a predominantly Anglophone Canada. Based on this rationale, Quebec rejected federal multiculturalism and replaced it with its own model of immigrant integration, interculturalism. Like multiculturalism, interculturalism promotes social cohesion and participation and prohibits discrimination. Unlike multiculturalism, interculturalism seeks to reconcile a "common culture" and "cultural diversity," which raises questions about the place of diversity in the "common culture" (Charest 2019). In addition, interculturalism prescribes the socioeconomic integration of immigrants in one language only: French. Furthermore, interculturalism refers to two categories of actors: 1) a Francophone majority

---

11.   My translation, since I translated all the French citations into English.

and 2) minorities, which some critics perceive as a binary between genuine Quebecers and "Others—minorities" who are precluded from this identity (Joppke 2018). In this regard, Talbani (1993) states:

> stress was increasingly laid on the linguistic and cultural assimilation of minorities [in Quebec]. By law, minorities were directed to French-only schools. The assimilationist interpretation of intercultural education has created racial antagonism in schools and minority students feel their rights have been endangered (407).

Thus, interculturalism's provisions led some critics to suggest that interculturalism favours Quebec's mainstream culture and the French language at the expense of the cultures and languages of racialized groups and therefore encourages their assimilation into the mainstream society and language.

Outside Quebec, white Francophones in minority situations also concur that multiculturalism reduces their status to that of "just another ethnic group." They believe that multiculturalism hinders the achievement of the bilingual project and the building of the Francophone space (Carslon Berg 2011; Huot 2017; Madibbo 2012b). Francophones believe that any focus on multiculturalism takes attention and resources away from French language rights. They believe it inhibits the primacy of La Francophonie because Francophones will no longer be a "special" minority that deserves "special" language rights, since racial rights will also be an issue. As in other Canadian provinces, the mainstream Francophonie in Alberta uses such discourse to convey its rejection of multiculturalism. White Francophones are silent about multiculturalism, rarely using this term or its derivatives—e.g., multicultural diversity. They do not acknowledge the multicultural aspect of La Francophonie, nor do they clarify how to accommodate it. The Francophone discourse substitutes interculturalism or immigration for multiculturalism, which falls short in bringing about true social justice. This is because the discourse embraces equality without addressing the power inequities that both CM and CRT invite us to challenge in order to effect real institutional and societal transformation. In this case, we can infer that La Francophonie's rejection of multiculturalism resembles its silence about racism in that both perspectives resort to the same technique: avoiding using the term in question and substituting seemingly neutral notions. The outcomes are also similar in that both perpetuate racism.

Does multiculturalism actually subvert English-French biculturalism to the extent of jeopardizing the status of French Canadians? The answer is no, because of policy and Francophone strategic nationalism. With respect to policy, it is useful to recall Pierre Elliott Trudeau's declaration that "Although there are two official languages, there is no official culture [in Canada]" (Laing & Cooper, 2019). Canada meant to separate language from culture; the OLA was intended to promote the two official languages, while the Multilingualism Policy (the Policy) sought to acknowledge immigrant cultures and languages without giving them official status. Nevertheless, one law—the OLA—associates language with culture in a manner that privileges white Francophones, while the Policy dissociates them in a fashion that marginalizes racialized groups—including Black-African Francophones. This is because of the way the OLA treats language—French—and embodies culture. The OLA does not regard French from the purely linguistic perspective of syntax and grammar but encompasses the speakers—Francophones—and their rights and associated resources. It is evident that these matters are related to identity, which means that the OLA respects the relationship between language, culture, and identity. At the same time, the OLA does not include provisions about racism and anti-racism within La Francophonie, which means that it challenges linguicism but not racism. Thus, the OLA serves the interests of white Francophones, while failing to redress the specific barriers, in this case racism, that inhibit their Black-African counterparts. At the same time, no racialized minority language is given official status, which is why racialized minorities do not enjoy equivalent recognition. On the other hand, the Policy does not assign official status to any culture, which harms the cultural/identity issues of racialized minorities because they cannot use the Policy to claim specific cultural and linguistic rights that impact their identities. The Policy does not stress the multicultural aspect of La Francophonie, let alone redress the racism that permeates this space. Thus, I argue that the separation between language and culture is true for racialized but not white Francophones. At this juncture, I contend that multiculturalism *should* subvert biculturalism, because the latter is a master narrative that ignores the racial and ethnic diversity of Canadian society.

As critical multiculturalists maintain, this narrative is "manifestly a racial story" (Razack 2007, 74), replicated in white Francophones' dichotomy of "distinct society" and "founding nation" on the one hand, and "immigrants" and "just another ethnic group," on the other. This distinction illustrates CM's perception of the self/other identity binary that Ella Shohat (Shohat & Stam 2013) considers a "characteristic of

Eurocentric discourses . . . of Western colonialism" (209). This perspective views identity as the alterity of the other, which white Francophones propagate by drawing a line between themselves as a "founding people" and the racialized as "just other ethnic groups," "immigrants," and ethnic others. White Francophones reproduced colonialism by portraying themselves as the bearers of civilization who built and modernized Canada, while the racialized are considered late arrivals who need to be civilized by enlightened white Francophones. In so doing, white Francophones project a Eurocentric and racist approach to identity, assuming that the "founding people" cannot be ethnicized and that the "ethnic others" cannot become a "founding people." White Francophones forget that they themselves immigrated to Canada and are an ethnic group by virtue of their shared language and culture. They are as ethnic as any group in Canada. They are ethnics who became a founding people, but they deny "ethnic others" this same transition. By perceiving Black-African Francophones as "immigrants" and "ethnic others" who do not belong to the "founding people" of Canada, white Francophones imbue the founding of Canada with whiteness and white privilege.

Indeed, the identity binary that white Francophones have established reveals racism inherent in Francophone strategic nationalism. We stated previously that white Francophones utilize strategic nationalism to claim recognition as a "founding people" of Canada. They use the same strategic nationalism to contend that multiculturalism is detrimental to La Francophonie without providing evidence to back this claim. At the beginning of this book I asked whether strategic nationalism was successful because it was efficient and whether it would be accepted should any minority group employ it to claim a "founding people" status. The answer is clearly that, though white Francophones employed it effectively, it was fruitful because it was made by whites and advantages whites. White privilege enhanced the success of strategic nationalism, and white Francophones did not even acknowledge Black Francophones as part of the Francophone "founding people." Instead, they used strategic nationalism to refute multiculturalism and relegate Black-Africans to a lower status. Thus, I call Francophone strategic nationalism "exclusionary nationalism," since it remains Eurocentric. It is used to claim language rights but does not demand racial justice for racialized Francophones; it embodies anti-Black racism.

Thus, there is reason to believe that multiculturalism does not jeopardize La Francophonie. Indeed, the recognition of white Francophones as a "founding people" of Canada preceded the inception of the Policy and has prevailed since it was implemented. Multiculturalism did not harm Quebec's status in the Canadian federation, since it continues to enjoy autonomy. Not only did Quebec choose its own immigrant integration model, interculturalism, it has power over the selection of immigrants and other immigration aspects inasmuch as "[t]he 1991 Canada-Quebec Accord gives the French-speaking province the right to set its own immigration policies, with minimal input at the federal level" (Immigration.ca 2020). Similarly, multiculturalism does not inhibit La Francophonie in minority contexts, such as in Alberta. The opposite is true, because multiculturalism helps to boost the numbers of Black-African Francophones, which in turn increases the overall proportion of Francophones in Alberta. In addition, while white Francophones are in denial of the racism that Black-Africans endure, the latter support the Francophone struggle against linguicism wholeheartedly, in favour of the bilingual project and the Francophone space. Thus, white Francophones continue to prosper with or without multiculturalism, while racialized minorities continue to languish even with the Policy in place. In essence, the Policy did not result in better outcomes for Black-African Francophones because it did not change their status. In addition, the relatively quick shift from equity multiculturalism hindered any efforts that could have improved the plight of these minorities.

The three illustrations of Francophone racism, underrepresentation of Black-Africans in the mainstream Francophonie, silence about racism, and opposition to multiculturalism, tell us that the OLA and the Policy are not the only things that could better protect Black-African Francophones, since other provisions, especially in the Charter, project similar patterns. The Charter guarantees education in French and denounces racism, but it does not stress the intersection between these issues. It does not recognize racism within La Francophonie, including in the French-language education system. Canada's Action Plan against Racism is no different in this regard since, although it points to anti-Black racism, it does not allude to racism in La Francophonie. The *Employment Equity Act* replicates these inequities, failing to specifically mention the Francophone labour market or to provide measures to ensure employment equity in this sphere. Canadian legislation seems to consider whites the only genuine Francophones, since it addresses linguicism but overlooks its intersection with racism. This factor draws our attention to the white privilege that leads whites to work together to foster their interests. It is not a coincidence that white Francophones continue to prosper in Canada while their Black-African counterparts continue to suffer in spite of the policies in place.

This is because, although white Francophones and Anglophones were engaged in domination and subordination relations, they are becoming allies in a manner that once again stresses white privilege. In this regard, Fleras and Elliott (1992) stressed that "Quebec and Ottawa are first among equals in the corridors of power, with guaranteed rights to self-determination over specific areas of jurisdiction" (173). Again, these factors remind us that whites work together to protect their interests and dehumanize Blacks by strengthening white privilege.

This factor reminds us of CRT's tenet of " contradicting-closing cases." We get the impression that Canada has the most tolerant policies in the world that protect all minorities. But when we examine these policies closely we realize that, for the most part, they advantage whites while failing to come to the aid of racialized minorities, in this case Black-African Francophones. They subtly embody anti-Black racism, producing stringent, albeit differential, material outcomes in favour of white Francophones. The latter continue to maintain the structural relations of power—to use critical multiculturalism's wording—by controlling the apparatuses and institutional hierarchy of the Francophone space. Meanwhile, they continue to relegate their Black-Africans counterparts to the lowest rungs of this hierarchy. Thus, Francophone racism is structural, systemic, and institutional and a reproduction of the racism that permeates Canadian society. While encounters between white Francophones and Blacks in the past involved racism on the part of the former, the same is true of encounters in the Francophone space in Alberta. White Francophones constructed the dominant Francophone identity that alienates Black-Africans and negotiate it in the form of their exclusion from the resources allocated to Francophones. This exacerbates the identity exclusion that Black-Africans already endure regarding Canadian identity. Luckily, Black-Africans have challenged this racism, as we saw earlier. The participants redefined Francophone identity in more inclusive ways that stress multiculturalism and anti-racism as important components of this identity. Their perception of Francophone identity aligns with Senghor's (1962) quote at the beginning of this chapter, in that both interpretations acknowledge the diversity that characterizes La Francophonie. The participants negotiated this identity construct in practices that serve to sustain La Francophonie and strengthen its struggles. Their agency did not stop there, since they supported an anti-racism education program that unfolded during the fieldwork, the Caravane contre le racisme et la discrimination. Since Black-African Francophones, including participants, created this program to counter

Francophone racism, it makes for a suitable case study to decipher ways to enhance the desired inclusion regarding Francophone identity.

THE CARAVANE CONTRE LE RACISME ET LA DISCRIMINATION (THE CARAVAN)

It is for a good reason that participants spoke about the Caravan at length in the interviews, and this is because it was unique in many ways. The Caravan was an education program that was implemented in French-language schools[12] from 2005 to 2013. It was established by the Alliance Jeunesse-Famille de l'Alberta Society[13] (AJFAS), a Francophone community organization that was created in 1999 in Edmonton. It was officially inaugurated in 2004 and has since had its head office in Edmonton, in addition to two branches in Calgary and Grande Prairie from 2009 to 2013. The AJFAS focuses on education and crime prevention among Francophone youth and immigrant families. For this reason, it works closely with Black Francophones, a majority of whom are African. The founder of the AJFAS, Luketa M'Pindou, has for a long time raised concerns about the racism that Black Francophone youth face in school and the workplace and in the form of racial profiling by the police (M'Pindou 2002). M'Pindou contends that racism disenfranchises youth, making them an at-risk group, and that this plight contributes to their involvement with gangs and problems with the "justice" system. M'Pindou asserts that, since these problems are caused by structural barriers, the solutions must target structural change. For that reason, he worked with other Black-African Francophones to create the AJFAS, which was established and has been run by Black-African Francophones. To eradicate the anti-Black racism that is directed at youth, the AJFAS seeks to enhance the inclusion of Black Francophone youth in society. Therefore, the AJFAS':

> main mission is to [assist] Francophone immigrant youth and families ... help them find a sense of belonging in Albertan society and the work place (AJFAS n.d.a, 5).
>
> [It aims to] facilitate their integration and socio-professional integration into Alberta society ... [and] promoting and validating Canadian ... diversity ... [It] works in the fields of education and crime prevention

---

12. It was also implemented in some community activities, but in this book I focus on its activities in schools.
13. The Alberta Family-Youth Alliance.

> with Francophone immigrant youth and families living in Alberta . . . [and] through social development program . . . to sensitize . . . to multi-culturalism [and] to racism (AJFAS n.d.b).

> [It promotes] the values of . . . harmony, safety, integration, social cohesion and appreciation of the others (AJFAS, n.d.c, 3).

The AJFAS seeks to improve the socioeconomic conditions of youths and their families and strengthen their sense of belonging to Canadian society. For these reasons, it aims to enhance the understanding and application of multiculturalism, and to explicitly name and counter racism. To this end, the AJFAS implements a wide range of social programs in the fields of law enforcement, family rights, employment, and exchange programs bringing together youth and families from various backgrounds. Its anti-racist orientation makes it the most vocal Francophone organization in Alberta about racism and anti-racism. As such, the very creation of the AJFAS represents agency on the part of Black-African Francophones, demonstrating that they assumed their collective responsibility to promote anti-racism. The AJFAS' antiracist approach is in line with CRT's contention about the need to explicitly name racism in order to confront it. The AJFAS proved its commitment to anti-racism through numerous initiatives, in particular the Caravan.

Since the AJFAS documents its activities in social and print media, I obtained rich public data about the Caravan in a quarterly newspaper named *L'Écho de la Caravane*,[14] and the AJFAS' Facebook page (AJFAS n.d.c) and website http://www.ajfas.ca/caravane).[15] I also found information in the AJFAS' annual general meeting reports and in its bilingual print magazine called, *Alliance Jeunesse-famille de l'Alberta Society—our Programs and Services*. Furthermore, some of the participants were involved in the Caravan in many capacities, including as volunteers. The participants also provided me with internal documents about the Caravan that contained its annual evaluations. Put together, these sources provided in-depth perspectives that allowed me to capture the scope of the Caravan, its progress, utility, and impacts, and the important role it played in La Francophonie. Thus, I was able to analyze the relevance of the Caravan to Francophone identity. The AJFAS detailed the purpose of the Caravan as follows:

---

14.   Echo of the Caravan.
15.   Some of the information that was available on the AJFAS' website was deleted in mid-2018 when the website was restructured.

[to] promote ... the struggle against racism and discrimination ... the youth are crucial ... they are susceptible to having a critical look at the self and the world, solving conflicts and coming up with specific solutions ... [we aim to] educate the youth how to fight against racism ... prejudice, discrimination ... violence, hate and the dangers of intolerance ... [to understand] their origin, causes as well as their consequences ... and the serious dangers of intolerance ... to instill in young people a critical attitude ... to respect ... multiculturalism ... and the ... cultural diversity of Canadian society (AJFAS n.d.d).

[To prepare young people to build] a discrimination-free society founded on justice and empathy (AJFAS n.d.d).

... to respond to the ... [needs] of these institutions [French-language schools] and ... promote the diversity that characterizes a country as multicultural as Canada (Ndagije 2012a, 1).

[The Caravan seeks] to promote intercultural exchanges .... Alberta needs everybody to work for its development ... We all need others to grow and live in a society where we all have the same ideal: build our future and make our province, Alberta, rich and fully developed (AJFAS n.d.a, 14).

[The Caravan instills] the sense of belonging to this great nation, Canada (Ndagije 2012b, 2).

... to promote a just and equitable Canadian society free of discrimination (Pabu 2012, 3).

What is better than leading a peaceful life, side by side, in a diverse multicultural Canada, where human diversity would not be a threat to the interests of some, but ... a wealth (Tundula 2012, 1).

It is a program that is committed to promoting responsibility and citizen participation (Ndagije 2012a, 1).[16]

These statements remind us that the Caravan served as an anti-racist educational strategy to improve the plight of Black Francophone youth. It conveyed this message by stressing the need to fight racism, enhancing multiculturalism and the diversity of Canadian society in general and Alberta in particular, and strengthening identification with Canada. It strategically targeted education, associated school settings, and young people to reach this goal. The focus on education goes to the AJFAS'

---

16. Since I refer to these statements in the ensuing analysis I will hereafter call them: the quotes about the Caravan.

conviction about education as a means of emancipation, which resembles critical multiculturalism's perception of education as a tool of liberation and transformation (hooks 1994; Freire 2000; May & Sleeter 2010). The choice of schools shows the AJFAS' awareness of the key role that schools play in fostering identity and social justice. French-language schools exclude Black youth, and the AJFAS sought to show schools how to remedy this problem. The AJFAS' focus on young people reveals its understanding of this group as an extremely important proxy in society. Young people have the potential to develop new and inclusionary ideas, can play a decisive role in society, and can shape its future in positive ways. As such, the Caravan was intended to equip racialized youth with the necessary skills to overcome racial oppression and help white majority children to comprehend and fight racism. In particular, the Caravan included an elaborate anti-racist and anti-oppressive curriculum that was taught in a series of workshops in French-language schools.[17] The curriculum was related to various disciplines, including history, education, and sociology, and was produced by authors from various racial and ethnic backgrounds. Through this curriculum, the Caravan applied the goal of critical multicultural education: multidisciplinarity and the incorporation of diversity at all education levels in order to enhance inclusion. The educational materials were equally diverse, consisting of newspaper clips, films and documentaries, posters, flyers, paintings, and photos. This is in line with critical multicultural education's keenness to develop a social justice curriculum. This is because the Caravan's educational materials included "texts marked by cultural diversity [which] has attempted to transform a Eurocentric curriculum ... [and] offer modes of resisting domination" (Sharma 2010, 113). Thus, the Caravan intended to address CM's concerns about the dominance of Eurocentric perspectives and master narratives in education, in this case, in the curriculum taught in French-language schools. In addition, the Caravan's materials shared CRT's appreciation of the narratives and experiential knowledge of the marginalized group, since the documentaries, newspaper clips, and so on revealed the experiences of these groups in their own voices and from their own perspectives.

The AJFAS hired Black-African and other visible minority Francophones to teach students. As stated earlier, these were qualified teachers who were denied commensurate employment in French-language

---

17.   The Caravan was eventually introduced in a few French immersion schools. I focus on its work in the French-language schools because French-immersion schools are not managed by the French-language education boards.

schools. By doing so, the Caravan remedied another chronic problem in French schools: it filled the gaps in the representation of Black Francophone teachers. In addition, it provided schools with professionals who are cognizant of anti-racism and anti-oppression in general, while giving Blacks well-deserved recognition and allowing them to teach in French-language schools. When it comes to the Caravan's pedagogical approach to teaching and learning, the curriculum was divided into major themes such as prejudice, discrimination, and bullying in schools. Each theme was taught in a series of workshops delivered to groups of 20-30 pupils in sessions that did not exceed one hour. These arrangements were meant to take into consideration the correlation between age and learning capacity. Each series of workshops was devoted to a major theme, and for the purpose of this analysis I focus on the workshops that dealt with prejudice. My content analysis of the Caravan's educational materials revealed that the workshops about prejudice started with the interpretation of the word in a section titled "Prejudice: What is it?" The Caravan defined this concept as "a preconceived belief or opinion and is often based on generalizations... [and] stereotypes." Thus, prejudice is described in the same way as it is interpreted by CRT: as unfounded stereotypical judgments about entire groups of people that neglect individual characteristics. Then the session transitioned to the roots of prejudice in a section titled "Where does it [prejudice] come from?" Teachers helped the young people to understand that "[p]rejudice can come from information received from family, friends, the media, etc." Thus, the Caravan teased out social and institutional sources that exhibit prejudice. It also explained that prejudice is not a new phenomenon; rather, it is long-established and is historically situated in inequitable power relations that date back to colonialism and earlier times. After that, the instructors explained how prejudice manifests, informing the young people that prejudice is not just an abstract concept but is demonstrated in specific aspects of social life. The sessions defined numerous types of stereotypes that target people based on identity attributes, in particular race, language, religion, culture, gender, and ability. For the purpose of analysis, I focus on the Caravan's teachings about racial prejudice[18] and language-based prejudice.

To help young people to comprehend racial prejudice, the Caravan first delved into race as a socially invented category that accounts for differences in human character or ability, in order to deem some racial groups superior and others inferior. Thus, the Caravan followed CRT's

---

18.   The Caravan used the terms "racial prejudice" and "racism" alternately.

approach to race as a social construct. Young people are taught that racial prejudice generates racism because it forms opinions about people based on their skin colour, not on knowledge or experience about them, that racial prejudice is harmful because it has an adverse impact on people. Strategically, the Caravan accentuated examples of racial bigotry that are familiar in Canada, such as : "the Aboriginal peoples are alcoholic; Africans are lazy . . . . Immigrants steal our jobs." This approach is useful because it would have informed the young people that prejudice can surface in any place in the world, even in Canada. This is important because it would have assisted the students in forming a real and realistic idea about Canada that counters its overly romanticized image as being racism-free. In this way, future leaders would realize that racism exists in Canada and identify ways to eradicate it. Significantly, the Caravan explained that, though racial prejudice uses both "negative or unfavourable" and "positive or favourable" stereotypes, it still serves to marginalize some groups of people. To clarify this dilemma, the Caravan put forth the example : "Blacks are good at sports." It stated that, while this contention appears to be benign, it can be harmful to Blacks because, in this case, sport is racialized. Sport is considered non-intellectual, and that is why Blacks are capable of doing it. This image disparages Blacks in the public imaginary because it confines their abilities to physical activity and entertainment while precluding them from intellectual fields that require creativity and rationalization, such as science. Then the Caravan construed the negative impacts of the seemingly positive stereotypes, explaining that not only do these generalizations relegate Blacks to the bottom of the social ladder, they jeopardize the potential of Black children. They have an adverse effect on children's self-esteem and ambitions, which in turn hinders their future dreams. We see that the Caravan provided examples close to home, related to an age group with which the students could identify, in order to enhance their learning.

The workshops exposed serious racial prejudice in Canada, including historical atrocities such as "xenophobia towards the Aboriginal peoples" and "the enslavement of Black Canadians." They also revealed contemporary implications for marginalized young people, such as the ones I identified in previous sections of this book. Among other things, the Caravan pointed to "dropping out from school," "devastating mental health effects," and "employment and economic exclusion." Such reiterations are useful in helping young people to associate prejudice with specific situations that occur in society, reminding them that these problems unfold both at the macro level and in the micro dynamics of their daily lives. Students were taught that racism poisons their families and triggers an "ensuing lack of harmony and social cohesion." Adolescents could see that racial prejudice not only hurt its victims, it infects its perpetrators, fellow citizens and society as a whole. At this stage of the workshops, the Caravan insisted on the need to eradicate racial prejudice, stressing: "It is in order to avoid such ... consequences, we should equip ourselves with efficient tools to counter intolerance" (AJFAS n.d.b). This is a judicious decision because by then the young people will have grasped the meaning of prejudice, how it functions, and its adverse implications, and will therefore be sufficiently aware to defeat it. They were taught that pre-judging people is not a shortcoming on the part of the person who is stereotyped but a pejorative behaviour on the part of the actors and structures that feed it. Therefore, the struggle against prejudice is a collective responsibility, schools should teach about these problems and individual students should make good use of this education. The young people were advised to "take the time to verify whether the information received is true or false or complete or incomplete." It is evident that such precisions build skills that help to avoid jumping to unfounded conclusions and making uninformed decisions. It is noteworthy that the teaching materials stressed Canada's efforts to prohibit racism, notably the Policy and the Charter. The materials also pointed to community initiatives that sought to eliminate prejudice, portraying the Caravan itself as one of these activities. It was useful to draw the young people's attention to Canada's initiatives to fight racial prejudice, because this would have taught them that positive change was achieved and that such efforts should be extended because racial prejudice persists. It would also have taught them that others have assumed the responsibility of challenging racism and that young people can do the same. This approach would have allowed the young people to understand that existing policies require better implementation because of the short-comings I mentioned earlier. They could discern additional strategies through which they themselves, the school, their families, and our entire society could wipe out racial prejudice.

How did the Caravan convey this intricate curriculum to young people? The answer to this question lies in its pedagogy, which encompassed a variety of teaching tools such as interactive animation, PowerPoint presentations, and SMART Boards®. Furthermore, the Caravan used teaching techniques that encourage interaction, including lecturing, as well as individual and small- and large-group activities and discussions, ranging from role-playing and staging, to singing, painting, and writing on posters. Clearly, these methods proved to be a sound teaching philosophy that accommodates different styles of learning and facilitates understanding. The community organization that created the Caravan, the AJFAS, is cognizant of these pedagogical aspects, which is why it proclaimed that this set of techniques:

> favours personal development and helps youth from different origins to get closer to each other... express diverse convictions... help[s] to prepare youth to fight against prejudice... [teaches students] to work toward lessening their own prejudice and identify and challenge their own biases... [that] interaction with various racial and ethnic groups teaches us to base our judgement on lived experience not on pre-existing opinions... identify ways through which they can overcome prejudice on their own and in the school and the community... [and be aware of] the impacts [of racial prejudice] (AJFAS n.d.b).

The Caravan's interactive activities were meant to foster academic and social development, as well as cooperative learning. The Caravan echoed the precepts of critical multicultural education, according to which such techniques are crucial to anti-oppression education because they optimize active engagement with social problems (Baines 2011). These techniques are decisive because they help to develop critical thinking and assist learners in working through big concepts, such as prejudice. In this respect, the Caravan asked students to discuss the following questions: "What do I know about the other students in my class and how do I know that?" and "What do I know about my neighbours and how do I know that?" "What is an example of [racial] prejudice and what can I do when I witness it?" "How can it be prevented?" Based on these questions, the young people debated who embraces prejudicial ideas and for what reason. They also discussed questions about who benefits from the impacts of racial prejudice and who suffers, along with solutions that could be forged to reduce and eliminate prejudice. The techniques were also used to further students' awareness of related events in Alberta at that time. In particular, the Caravan shed light on the white supremacist organizations that were visibly active in Alberta. It created a dialogue about the organizations' purpose and activities, their rationale, impacts on specific groups of people and on society in general, and ways to refute them. Therefore, the Caravan adopted a constructive approach to the teaching and learning of racism and anti-racism. It illustrated CRT's tenet of the centrality of racism, pinpointing racism explicitly and helping students to grasp its origins, manifestations, and outcomes, and how to stop it.

The quotes about the Caravan also allude to the four meanings of multiculturalism: fact, policy, ideology, and practice (Fleras & Elliot 2002). The reference to "the diversity that characterizes a country as multicultural" directly echoes the fact of multiculturalism, which is diversity. Notions such as "to respect... multiculturalism... and the... cultural diversity of Canadian society" allude to the policy of multiculturalism because they are goals the policy seeks to achieve. The contentions about "the struggle against racism and discrimination" describe the ideology of critical multiculturalism, which challenges racism. The statements: "Alberta needs everybody to work for its development," corroborate the practice of multiculturalism, because they urge Albertans to build a successful, equitable future.

The Caravan's workshops conveyed multicultural ideals in a manner that made them accessible to students. They provided everyday examples of the diversity of the student population and their neighbourhoods, then brought to light the pluralism of cities, provinces, and Canadian society as a whole. Significantly, multiculturalism was incorporated into the workshops about racial prejudice following the sessions defining prejudice, its implications, and the need to eliminate it. This approach projected critical multiculturalism as a solution to racial prejudice. To this end, the Caravan explained the goals of the Policy to the young people by encouraging them to "learn to be interested in each other, to break the ice, to know each other better and to better appreciate the richness of Alberta's diversity."[19] But this did not project liberal multicultural education, which deracializes culture and depoliticizes it, because the Caravan simultaneously disproved the arguments that fuel racist beliefs and stressed that it deters the achievements of the multiculturalism slogans about social cohesion in a diverse society. The Caravan also alluded to the current education phase of multiculturalism, citizenship education. This is conveyed through the statements: "invite the young people to pledge to build a society where citizens of various backgrounds are able to succeed."[20] Thus, the Caravan related the need to educate future citizens to embrace ethics and morality. This stance does not resemble liberal multiculturalism, which distances culture from anti-racism, because the Caravan insisted that these objectives could not be achieved without eradicating racial prejudice. Furthermore, while students should appreciate diversity in the classroom and in society, they need to be sensitive to the injustice that permeates society, racial prejudice.

19.   Internal documents about the Caravan.
20.   Internal documents about the Caravan.

Therefore, the Caravan's emphasis on cultural exchange was associated with anti-racism.

Furthermore, the Caravan's workshops about racial prejudice emphasized identity, which we observe in assertions that the Caravan aimed to "help them [Black youth] find a sense of belonging in Albertan society" (AJFAS n.d.a, 5), and "the sense of belonging to this great nation, Canada" (Ndagije 2012b, 2).This standpoint revealed awareness of the important role school plays in identity formation. Although the Caravan's materials invoked identification with Canada and Alberta, they did not point to La Francophonie. A more thorough discussion about identity could have helped students to break down this concept and understand its relevance to social justice. However, the Caravan made significant indirect contributions to identity issues. The very implementation of the educational program in French-language schools is a negotiation of an inclusive identity that takes into consideration the diversity of schools and the entire Francophonie. The overall goals and practices of the Caravan suggest that it sought to construct an inclusive identity that refutes whiteness and white privilege to acknowledge racial and ethnic diversity as a key identity component. It alerted people to the danger that racial prejudice poses to social cohesion, and therefore to belongingness. Moreover, the Caravan equipped schools and young people with tools to help them to respect Francophone diversity. It aimed to negotiate identity in a manner that guarantees equitable access to education and other societal resources as well as inclusion in society. In a previous section, we expressed concerns that French-language schools jeopardize Black-African children's affiliation with La Francophonie, and in this context we see that the Caravan had the potential to empower Black youth to see themselves as genuine Francophones whose dreams will come true.

In the sections dedicated to language-based prejudice, the Caravan asserted that unfavourable generalizations about some languages serve to marginalize certain social groups and that, while these outcomes can involve any language and its speakers in the Canadian context, the linguicism targets French and Francophones. Then, the Caravan confirmed the aforementioned discrimination against Francophones, well as the historical struggle they have led to claim their rights. Arguably, this process would have reminded young people of the exclusion that Francophones endured and the courage they exhibited in protecting their rights. Though the Caravan's focus on La Francophonie per se was scant, it provided information that pertained to La Francophonie in a manner that would allow it to associate Francophone identity with racial prejudice. Does this mean that the Caravan overlooked linguicism towards La Francophonie? Not necessarily. One research participant who volunteered for the Caravan said: "If they [white Francophones] don't want to tackle racism, then we [Black-Africans] are going to do just that." The participant did not intend to minimize La Francophonie; on the contrary, they recognized its significance, demonstrated attachment to it, and even took action to ensure that it flourishes. What they suggested was that French-language schools place deserved emphasis on La Francophonie but ignore issues of race and racism. By implication, these schools replicate the "Franco-centric approach" (Labelle 2011)—the denial of racism—that furthers the exclusion of Black-African students. Thus, the Caravan recognized La Francophonie reasonably, while it filled important gaps concerning race, racism, and multiculturalism. It added much-needed anti-racist perspectives to La Francophonie in general and French-language schools in particular. Although adding knowledge about La Francophonie would not have been harmful in any way, the Caravan's strategy is judicious. This is because, from an equity perspective, we need to include what and who is excluded without dismissing what and who is included. The Caravan followed this rationale, which reveals that it applied CRT's tenet of the critique of liberalism that chooses equity over equality. The discourse of the mainstream Francophonie, including that of French-language schools, is seemingly liberal, denounces linguicism and claims rights without referring to structural inequities. In particular, the French-language school system does not afford race, racism, and multiculturalism its deserved status. Thus, the mainstream Francophonie conveys the premise of equality, which disguises Francophone racism, while the Caravan ascribed the premise of equity, which added what was missing in the mainstream Francophonie.

In the end, that the Caravan achieved such significant milestones as the development and systematic implementation of an anti-racist curriculum is an accomplishment in its own right. To better assess the achievements of the Caravan, the AJFAS evaluated it on an annual basis to determine its effectiveness, what was appreciated in the program and what was not, concerns that arose, and how to improve and sustain it. The students, teachers, and school administrators who took part in the Caravan evaluated it. The AJFAS hired independent consultants to conduct the evaluations, and these consultants developed questionnaires consisting of qualitative and quantitative questions pertaining to the various sections and topics of the workshops, i.e., prejudice, bullying in schools, and so on. For example, the section of the questionnaire that dealt with prejudice posed the following questions: "How well do you understand the meaning of prejudice? ... The causes of prejudice? ... The impacts of prejudice? [Which] actions can be taken to fight prejudice?" indicated their level of satisfaction or dissatisfaction with the topics on a scale from 1 to 5. These questions were followed by qualitative questions inviting participants to explain the rationale behind their responses to the quantitative questions. In addition, the questionnaire sought the participants' opinion on the teaching methods, the clarity of teaching, student participation, and the general atmosphere of the workshops. The students' evaluations of the Caravan were revealed in statements such as the following:

"The workshop taught me that we pre-judge people on a daily basis."

"Yesterday's presentation really made me aware that racism persists."

"I learned there is racism and what it means."

"Me, I don't like discrimination and racism. Now I understand that there is a lot of it ... because I myself do that sometimes."

"I know why racism happens [what causes it]."

"I understood that racism hurts people, it really hurts."

"I am against racism."

"The workshops made me think. Because of these workshops, I will think before I speak so that I don't say anything discriminatory."

"School is important ... It can eliminate prejudice."

"I didn't know that racism and discrimination are illegal."

"One thing I took away from the workshops is that there are laws in Canada that protect us from racism and discrimination ... We can use these laws [to halt racial prejudice]."

Clearly, the Caravan achieved its goal to educate young people about racism and anti-racism. As the students' statements reveal, they had not learned much, if anything at all, about racism before they participated in the Caravan. The Caravan helped them to question their inner conscious ness and the reason why racism is horrible. They reflected on their behaviour and challenged their past mistakes. They understood that schools are not neutral, but rather a contested terrain where inequitable power is reproduced and racism is entrenched in institutional practices, which hinders academic success. They acknowledged their individual responsibility to fight racism, as well as the collective responsibility of schools to eradicate it. Their appreciation of Canadian laws prohibiting racism, in this case the Charter, is also significant because it drew their attention to the connection between the Charter and anti-racism. As stated previously, the Charter does not allude to racism in La Francophonie specifically; therefore, it is important that the students understood that the Charter should be about anti-racism as much as it is about anti-Francophone linguicism. This can help them to associate racism with the concerns of La Francophonie, and anti-racism with the Francophone struggle for language rights. In addition, the students' evaluations of the Caravan alluded to multiculturalism in comments such as: "I like multiculturalism," "It [multiculturalism] makes our society better," and "I like it when I hang out with my friends and they tell me about other countries." Such statements reflect students' appreciation of the cultural diversity that characterizes their classrooms, schools, La Francophonie, and Canadian society as a whole. In addition to multiculturalism, the students commented on the Caravan's impact on identity. For example, one student wrote on a poster: "I am Canada. We are the Canada of tomorrow" (Ndagije 2012b, 2). It is significant that the young people made a connection between what they learned in the Caravan and Canadian identity. Although the Caravan did not explore identity thoroughly, these expressions affirm that the young people understood that racial prejudice hinders belongingness and that multiculturalism defines Canadian identity. Similarly, the teaching pedagogy and techniques proved to be useful, since the students displayed admiration for them in phrases such as "role-playing...because we could see the words in action." They also appreciated the variety of the tools utilized, including "the posters, PowerPoint presentations, films [because] they allowed me [them] to see pictures and real people. I [they] saw [that] people were hurt."

It is noteworthy that the young people are not the only ones who praised the Caravan, since their teachers and the school administrators, as well as the research participants who participated in the Caravan testified that it had inspired the students. According to the teachers and administrators:

> "The workshops are informative and educational, because the participants gained new information they didn't know before."

> "The workshops will probably lead our young people to understand that prejudice should not continue to unfold. Thank you!"

> "Good student awareness."

"It is good for our students to get used to learning and talking about these issues"

"Bravo! Keep up the excellent work. People need to hear [learn] about prejudice."

The teachers also admitted that the Caravan shed light on topics that students were not aware of, especially racism. Considering that these teachers themselves should have taught these topics, we infer that the Caravan assumed the responsibility that the school did not by raising young people's awareness of such pressing social issues. Similarly, the research participants were satisfied with the impact that the Caravan had on the young people. One participant who volunteered for the Caravan said that "a white student said something that was really striking . . . [the student's] parents had racist sentiments and didn't want . . . [the student] to mix with Blacks." The student stated that the "Caravan taught [them] that our skin colour doesn't decide [determine] who we are." The student concluded that "the Caravan showed [them] we should learn to live together peacefully" and "rid ourselves of racial prejudice." Such statements revealed that the Caravan equipped young people with emancipatory tools that assist in the pursuit of social justice. Thus, we surmise that the Caravan succeeded in achieving a fundamental goal of critical multicultural education, to "prepare students to critique, challenge and question the existing social order so that they can participate in the struggle for a more just world" (Gutstein 2010, 127). Further, it is significant that the milestones the Caravan achieved did not prevent the AJFAS from seeking additional improvements. Throughout, it paid close attention to the feedback that it received in the evaluations. This process revealed another efficient aspect of the Caravan. In general, program and curriculum evaluation serve to verify strengths and weaknesses to help make improvements (Frye & Hemmer 2012). In particular, critical multicultural education espouses these goals but stresses the need to ensure that all the parties involved are committed to social justice and that such outcomes align with equity (Carr & Kemmis 1986).

There is reason to believe that the AJFAS followed this pattern, since the evaluations were both "process-based" and "outcomes-based" (Carr & Kemmis 1986). The consultants analyzed the feedback that the students, teachers, and administrators provided in the questionnaires. The Caravan's team was equally interested in the positive feedback, such as the aforementioned comments, as well as the concerns raised about the program. The consultants weighed the comments against the Caravan's goals, and then made recommendations for improvement. The positive feedback helped to identify the content and techniques that deserved to be maintained, while the unfavourable feedback incited change. For example, students' comments such as "I don't agree that there is a lot of racism," and "I don't believe that many people are racist," drew attention to the possible internalization of the "Franco-centric approach" to race and racism (Labelle 2011). In response, the consultants suggested adding sections and materials about the denial of racism: what leads people to deny it, the problems that this standpoint triggers, and how to counter the denial of racism. The consultants and the Caravan's team also took teachers' evaluations of the Caravan seriously. Comments such as "the workshops are too long for the students" led the consultants to suggest reducing the length of the workshops. Feedback such as "some of the vocabulary is too complicated for the students" resulted in proposals to modify teaching materials and maximize role-playing in order to introduce various concepts. The AJFAS took the feedback and recommendations into consideration; it discussed them at its regular meetings to assess the progress of the Caravan. Consequently, it incorporated the constructive comments in both the curriculum and the training it offered to the Caravan's instructors on a regular basis. In the process, the Caravan's team paid close attention to the outcomes that were achieved with regard to racism, anti-racism, and multiculturalism. The team also reflected on the relevance of the Caravan's teaching materials and pedagogy and sought further involvement on the part of schools.

The schools eventually understood the benefits of the Caravan, many schools in Alberta ending up hosting it. In its seven years of existence, the Caravan moved across the province, covering a large number of schools. In so doing, it truly became what it was called to be: "the Caravan." It brought together a group of people, instructors, and volunteers, who travelled, interacted with students and teachers, co-constructing knowledge with students, and brought hope to alleviate the pain that many endured. Nevertheless, it is important to state that the introduction of the Caravan in schools was not an easy task, requiring significant efforts on the part of the AJFAS. The AJFAS contacted schools, explained the purpose of the Caravan and persuaded them to host it. This process did not go unchallenged because, as participants put it, some schools resented the term "racism" in the Caravan's name under the pretext that "hosting it [the Caravan] would mean that there is racism in the schools." The AJFAS did not have the power to oblige the schools to accept the name of the program as it was; therefore, they respected that condition and omitted the term "racism" from the name of the program, re-branding it "La caravane contre la discrimination."[21]

It bears noting that we conducted the fieldwork during the peak years of the Caravan and, in the interviews, the participants kept referring to the educational program as "La caravane contre le racisme et la discrimination" long after the word racism was removed. The participants were unhappy with the schools' standpoint, which they illustrated in contentions such as "this is absurd" and "what a shame!" The participants' insistence on using the word racism in their reference to the Caravan is a discursive strategy: they countered Francophone racism by continuing to use the word. The participants' standpoint illustrates CRT's disavowal of the denial of racism and the need to remedy this problem by naming racism explicitly. Therefore, the French-language schools' approach to the Caravan merits close attention. We have before us publicly funded schools that refute the reality of racism, whereas they should be teaching about and fighting against racism in the first place. French-language schools are intended to maintain Francophone identity and culture, but they were unwilling to confront a factor that impacts the identity of Black-African Francophones. The Caravan presented the schools with a historic opportunity to improve their shortcomings, yet the schools worried about a word in the name of the program instead of focusing on how to fight racism that is inherent in their schools. How did the French-language schools get away with this? Because of the white privilege they enjoy, they are autonomous Francophone institutions governed by white Francophones who can act as they please even when this means undermining the concerns of Black-African Francophones and social justice in general. We also note that the federal government is complicit because, as the main funder of the Caravan it could—and should—have imposed guidelines on the schools, such as agreeing to host the Caravan without changing its name. At the same time, the government imposed numerus conditions on the AJFAS, first in order to fund the Caravan, then to continue to fund it. For example, although the AJFAS appreciated the aforementioned evaluations, they were one of the many criteria that the AJFAS had to comply with to ensure the continuity of the Caravan's funding, while the schools had decision-making freedom. Time and again, we see that the federal government makes concessions to white Francophones that strengthen white privilege. This factor is further evidence of our contentions about the relations between Anglophones and Francophones, that on many occasions they collaborate,

---

21.   The Caravan against Discrimination.

especially when it comes to racism towards Blacks. French-language schools only welcomed the Caravan after the term racism was deleted from its name. In this respect, the AJFAS stated:

> During the school year (September to June) the Caravan ... [was implemented] in the following regions:
>
> Edmonton and surroundings: Sherwood Park, Leduc, St-Albert and Legal
>
> The North-West region: Grande Prairie and Peace River
>
> The North-East region: St-Paul, Bonnyville, Cold Lake, Plamondon and Fort McMurray ... 10 cities in Southern Alberta: Calgary and surroundings: Airdrie, Okotoks. Banff and Jasper, Medicine Hat, Lethbridge, Cochrane, Red Deer, Brooks (AJFAS n.d.b).

Additionally, the newsletter *Écho de la Caravane* documented that the Caravan was hosted in approximately 40 to 50 schools across Alberta every year (Ndagije 2012a). The Caravan was first implemented in French-language schools in Alberta, and was then extended to the province of Saskatchewan[22] when the AJFAS was invited to introduce the Caravan to schools in Regina and Saskatoon. The expansion of the Caravan is another factor that speaks to its success and popularity because it reveals interest in the program. That appreciation was well deserved because, in addition to the aforementioned benefits, the Caravan created a productive partnership between the school and the community. It is the kind of "[s]chool-community partnerships [that] have shown promise as an educational reform effort" (Valli et al. 2018, 31). As critical multicultural education holds, such partnerships pave the way for educational transformation because they assemble community groups, families, schools, businesses, etc., to sensitize the school to community needs. They enhance and support schools, struggling community groups, and neighbourhoods. The community, in this case the AJFAS, initiated a dialogue with the schools and launched the Caravan, taking ownership of its solution in support of social justice. The Caravan achieved successful school-community partnership inasmuch as it contributed "curriculum connected to real world experiences," "cross generation learning," and "locals designing solutions to local problems" (O'Keefe 2011) and, I would add, skill sharing. Moreover, the partnership afforded young people an opportunity to articulate what they wanted their school

---

22.   This analysis focuses on the Caravan in Alberta; its work in Saskatchewan is beyond the scope of this book.

and community to do, what matters to them, and how they could help their peers, the community, and society as a whole to fight racism. These repercussions had the potential to benefit La Francophonie in Alberta because of the knowledge that they disseminated about anti-racism and multiculturalism. The Caravan had even more value because, as a research participant maintained, "it applied the objectives of the Charter and Canada's Action Plan about [against] Racism." Although these provisions did not result in financial or logistical support, the Caravan helped achieve their goals, making larger societal contributions.

The Caravan continued to produce positive outcomes, and the AJFAS planned to expand its scope to add more themes and teaching pedagogies. In particular, it sought to elaborate on immigration issues to help young people better appreciate the advantages of immigration and the challenges that immigrants face. In essence, the Caravan referred to immigration briefly in the workshops about multiculturalism; therefore, its plan to expand on immigration was constructive, since this topic requires more thorough investigation. It is fair to acknowledge that the Caravan did not have the scope or resources to build an all-encompassing curriculum. However, the intention to broaden the content of the Caravan was progress, since it could have eventually examined the topics missing from its curriculum, such as immigration and identity in the Francophone context, in greater depth. Unfortunately, the AJFAS did not get the chance to fill these gaps and make additional improvements. In 2013 the federal government terminated the Caravan's budget entirely, which ended the program that year. The AJFAS announced this news at its 2013 Annual General Assembly as follows:

> Dear members: I want to inform you that we started the 2013-2014 fiscal year with sad news. In fact, we lost our main funding with the Ministry of Citizenship and Immigration of Canada [now Immigration, Refugees and Citizenship Canada]. The federal program that funded the Caravan . . . was abolished, and we had to lay off all our employees [who participated in the Caravan] and shut down our Calgary office. We, however, continue to make significant efforts to revitalize all our activities and diversify our revenue sources (Mulumba 2013, 3).

At that time, the Conservative government, led by Stephen Harper, reduced or eliminated social programs, including the funding allocated to anti-racist initiatives such as the Caravan. The AJFAS did all it could to salvage the Caravan; it publicly protested against the budget cuts, it tried to have the Caravan's funding reinstated, and so on. When that did not materialize, it put an end to the Caravan. It terminated all the Caravan staff's contracts, and closed the offices that oversaw the Caravan in Calgary and Grand Prairie. If the AJFAS did not have the power and resources to salvage the Caravan, what about the rest of the mainstream Francophonie? French-language schools, including those that hosted the Caravan, did not make any effort to maintain the Caravan. This reminds us that schools were ambivalent about the Caravan since they are by far more resourced and funded than the AJFAS and are better placed to request and receive funding. They could have provided the Caravan with financial support, or at least sought funding to maintain it. The French-language school boards are equally well funded, and could have afforded at least some financing to allow the Caravan to continue to function. In addition, they could have taken action such as claiming funding for the Caravan as an important Francophone educational initiative. Schools and school boards were in dire need of the Caravan, yet their action was non-action, a standpoint illustrating CRT's tenet of contradiction-closing cases. They supported the Caravan but not entirely; they ignored it but not completely. The government acted similarly: on the one hand, it funded the program; the Alberta Francophone Secretariat offered financial support for one year, and the Ministry of Immigration and Citizenship funded it from 2006 to 2013. Although this support was part of the government's responsibility towards La Francophonie, it was an important recognition of the relevance of race, racism, and multiculturalism to La Francophonie. On the other hand, the government contradicted itself by terminating the Caravan when it was most needed.

The schools and the mainstream Francophonie remained silent about racism. In particular, the ACFA did not do what it usually does when Francophones' rights have been violated. It did not issue a press release to condemn the defunding and ensuing termination of the Caravan, let alone sponsor the issue legally and financially as it did the aforementioned Caron Case that it took all the way up to the Supreme Court of Canada. Arguably, the ACFA did not see, or chose not to see, the close relationship between the Caravan and Francophone rights. Similarly, neither regional ACFA contested the budget cuts, despite the fact that the program was hosted in cities that fall under their auspices. The only mainstream Francophone institution that has shed light on the termination of the Caravan was the French CBC. In so doing, it corrected some of the aforementioned short-comings regarding the Francophone media, since it at least provided a space to protest the defunding of the Caravan. Although that action was meaningful, it was not powerful enough to salvage the Caravan.

Nevertheless, the Caravan remains a crucial educational program, for it served to construct an inclusive Francophone identity encompassing racial and ethnic diversity. It negotiated this identity by refuting racism and enhancing multiculturalism. The reason I included the Caravan as a case study in this book is that, in addition to the emphasis that the research participants placed on it and its relevance to the analysis, I do not wish for it to fade from memory. Like any historic event, it deserves to be documented, since it epitomizes Black-African Francophone agency and commitment to social justice when many did not assume that responsibility. It showed us constructive ways to counter Francophone identity exclusion and develop future programs. Nonetheless, in order to better analyze how the Caravan helps us to construct and negotiate identities in more inclusive ways, we need to situate it in the context of the multiple affiliations that the research participants adhered to, in this case, Black-African identity.

CHAPTER 5

THE CONSTRUCTION AND NEGOTIATION OF BLACK-AFRICAN IDENTITY

"I am because we are."

An adage from the Xhosa people of South Africa.

All the research participants expressed a Black-African identity encompassing distinctive similarities and a few differences.[1] The resemblance boils down to the two aforementioned aspects that characterize the construction and negotiation of Black identity: 1) anti-Black racism that annihilates Black identity, and 2) fighting anti-Black racism to improve the well-being of Blacks. The participants explained the adverse implications that anti-Black racism causes to Black identity in statements such as the following:

> Participant: Well, I am Black, I look Black. When people see me, they see Black[ness]. It is as if my appearance tells everything about me. The "everything" is not good ... it is all the negative things [stereotypes] about the Black colour.

> Participant: Our race has a big impact on us. The way they [whites] see us, it is as if we didn't exist before [as if] we do not have a history ... as if we don't matter.

---

1. I do not examine the identity differences in this book because they extend beyond the scope of the analysis. The similarities suit the study's analysis of the collective Black-African identity.

The participants alluded to the obliteration of Black identity through the means of anti-Black racism, and Frantz Fanon's seminal analysis of Black identity in *Black Skin, White Masks* (1967) allows us to better understand this problematic. Fanon (1967) insists that identity imposition determines the conditions in which Blacks exist. That Black identity has been alienated, and this exclusion is realized through two interrelated processes that are at the heart of the European white supremacist colonial project. These are: 1) the objectification of Black subjectivity, and 2) the denial of Black history. Significantly, both of these aspects are portrayed in the participants' statements. With regard to objectification, Fanon teaches that the hegemony of the European culture objectified Blackness from the outset; it infiltrated the colour Black and fixated it permanently in the eyes of the oppressor. It negates Blackness, vilifies it, and turns it into an object, a racial object. It is noteworthy that the participants expressed the objectification of Blackness in relation to their "appearance" in the above quotes, and this is because Fanon conceptualizes this process in a similar manner. In *Black Skin, White Masks* (Fanon 1967), the narrator, who could be Fanon himself or any other Black person, emphasizes that their "appearance" is detrimental to their existence. The narrator says: "I am overdetermined from without . . . . I am the slave of my . . . own appearance" (116). Blacks are reduced to their "appearance"—skin colour, physical features, hair, facial traits. They are fixated, caught in a racial situation that nullifies their subjectivity. In Fanon's words, "it is the moment of 'being for others'" (109), when Black inferiority is determined by the oppressor. Fanon's narrator states: "I found that I was an object in the midst of other objects" (109). This inferiority is embedded in the language of racial identification, all the previously stated negative stereotypes that equate Blackness with evil and backwardness. The participants were also objectified since, as they say, they felt that they were considered objects that "don't matter." Therefore, the concept of race is integral to Black identity formation. It holds crucial meaning for the participants, as it did for Fanon's narrator. Because the participants are phenotypically identifiable as Black, they are subjected to the pejorative connotations that are imposed on the colour Black. We are reminded of CRT's tenet of the saliency of race as a social construct. In this context, the visibility of the "appearance" of Blacks is not inherent in their existence but in the meanings that dominant groups attach to them to negate Black subjectivity. The participants were aware that white supremacy's negative construction of Blackness aimed to demean them; it marked their objectification as it did for Fanon's narrator. It is anti-Black racism that lumps all Blacks into one homogeneous racial category—Black—to facilitate the erasure of Black identity.

In regard to the denial of Black history, Fanon (1967) epitomizes it in the words of the narrator when the narrator was told: "Too late. Everything is anticipated, thought out, demonstrated" (121). Fanon refers to the time when the Western world was still questioning the very existence of Black history. White supremacy brushed aside Black history and the past accomplishments of Blacks to erode Black identity. Why did colonialism seek to annihilate Black identity by eradicating Black history? This goes to the close relationship between identity and history. In order for identity to foster belongingness, its construction and negotiation require continuity (versus rupture). It is for this reason that Friedman (1992) holds that the sense making that construes identity:

> does not occur in a vacuum, but in a world already defined… The construction of a past in such terms is a project that selectively organizes events in a relation of continuity with a contemporary subject, thereby creating an appropriated representation of a life leading up to the present, that is, a life history fashioned in the act of self-definition. Identity, here, is decisively a question of empowerment. The people without history in this view are the people who have been prevented from identifying themselves for others (837).

Social actors would once have belonged to a world on which they drew to make sense of their existence. People's history is the basis of a collective memory that provides them with a sense of identity continuation. Conversely, the denial of history ruptures identity and creates insecurity that culminates in a situation of "not knowing where one came from," and "not knowing where one is heading." By implication, the people in question do not know "who they are." Therefore, the colonial project purposely aimed to deprive Blacks of the empowerment and agency that self-definition would have afforded them. Rather, the Western world imposed an ahistorical perception of Blackness, leaving Blacks without, to use Jennifer Kelly's (2001) words, "identity sources" to rely on. The purpose is to make Blacks believe that they are void of a history of their own making and that they are solely the objects of white domination throughout time. Understandably, in the above quotes, the participants pointed to the denial of Black history: "as if we didn't exist before [as if] we do not have a history." For the participants, the denial of Black history is a crucial problem that fragments Black identity, making it almost non-existent. Thus, colonialism used the objectification of Blackness and the denial of Black history to erase Black identity, paving the way for the anti-Black racism that has plagued Blacks across the diaspora. The participants are aware that these patterns of anti-Black racism—objectification and the denial of Black history—are pervasive and that they afflict Blacks across place, a factor that they illustrated as follows:

> We have been cornered, we still are... everywhere. We suffered for a long time. For a very long time ... slavery, colonialism. And now all these problems.... In our countries, in Africa, we were not always in peace because of the conflicts. We also suffered in Europe [i.e., in France]. We thought we would be better off in Canada. We have been here [in Canada] for a long time now, and we lived in many places [Quebec and other provinces]. They [whites] still consider us... outsiders. They don't care [if] we are newcomers or not, whether our children are born in Canada or not. It [racism] is just something against the Black body.

The participants recognized the collective position of Blacks worldwide as one of lasting racial oppression that reconfigured the participants' lives "everywhere" they settled, in this case, in African countries, France, and Canada. They spoke to the damage that Europeans caused Blacks in the course of slavery, colonialism, and neocolonialism. The transatlantic slave trade displaced millions of Blacks and tore them from their motherland. For example, Europeans objectified Blackness in Africa when colonial rule resorted to self-serving policies and practices in the course of the "scramble for Africa" and in the drawing of the borders of the African countries, among other things. That subjugation disenfranchised Blacks in general and ravaged the African continent in particular. It served to "depopulate Africa and dispossess it of its rich resources," which contributed to impoverishment. It separated Blacks geographically and socially so as to dilute their understanding of their collective identity. In discussing these historical problems today, the participants explained that that history of domination had not ended, since the ramifications of slavery and lingering colonial legacy are reproduced in the contemporary era in the form of neocolonialism.

In Africa, the participants suffered the ongoing social and political upheaval and conflicts that ravage many regions on the continent. The participants produced a politicized anti-colonial discourse, positing that this turmoil occurs under the heel of neocolonialism. That neocolonialism functions in clandestine, more subtle ways than the direct occupation of colonialism. Whether it is through "the support Western countries provide to dictatorships" or "when they [Western countries] equip warring groups with weapons to fuel conflict," neocolonialism intervenes to disrupt stability in Africa. The participants alluded to inequitable global policies, such as "those of the International Monetary Fund and the World Bank," which cripple "African countries with Western debts and inflation." Such provisions preclude Africa from the power of globalization, which contributes to rising poverty and underdevelopment. The denial of Black history was illustrated in these processes through slavery and colonialism, which associated history with colonial domination rather than anything created by Africans themselves. It views Africans as objects, not subjects of history. The participants dwelled on the ensuing instability in Africa because it shaped their lives in many ways. Not only does it afflict their countries, communities, and families, it pushed them—and many Africans—to immigrate to the West in search of better opportunities. There, the participants suffered another facet of neocolonialism, the harsh reality of being Black in a predominantly white Western society.

Fanon (1967) suggests that in these societies anti-Black racism means that Blacks are in a subordinate position, a direct encounter with white supremacy. Fanon theorizes that white supremacy makes racialized existence a "facticity" for the Black, a common sense and an all-encompassing reality that permeates Blacks' lives. In these societies, anti-Black racism erases Black identity directly through the objectification of Blackness and the denial of Black history. According to Fanon, these societies objectify Blackness by negating the Black existence in all facets of social life, and this discrimination occurs constantly. Racist situations and voices intervene in the everydayness of Blacks and generate an alienated racial existence. Fanon (1967) depicts this plight in the narrator's confession that the white supremacist society "demanded of me that I behave like a [B]lack man" (94). Blacks were made objects, construed with pejorative meanings to hold them in place, as one would hold any object, confining them to the lowest rungs of society. The participants suffered this objectification in France, feeling that they were treated as if "they did not matter," as if they were objects. The participants also experienced the denial of Black history. The aforementioned "Franco-centric approach" to racism (Labelle 2011) means that in France, Black history lacks recognition, for it does not receive formal acknowledgement in political discourse, the school curriculum or any other public arena. The objectification of Blackness and the denial of Black history facilitated the participants' oppression. The "material conditions of their existence," to use Fanon's (1967) words, were evidence of anti-Black racism. They were not only unemployed and underemployed; they were unceasingly denied belongingness. As Montague (2013) points out, in France, Blacks and North Africans are policed, controlled, asked to produce identity papers and detained if they fail to do so. In essence, racism in the form of the policing of Blacks is an integral aspect of France's pop culture. Having myself lived and studied in France, I have witnessed these acts of racism. I was always sure to carry my identity cards to avoid the adverse consequences of policing. In the end, this marginalization created an identity dilemma for the participants, making it clear to them that they were not considered French. Yet they could not embrace a Black-African identity because of the aforementioned silence about racism through which France made even the collection of race-based data illegal. Thus, society and politics do not approve of any identity other than French. These dynamics made the participants realize that France's reputation for being a country of human rights is a more of a myth than a fact. Consequently, they decided to immigrate to Canada in the hope that it stands by its reputation of being open to immigrants from all backgrounds. Indeed, the participants soon discovered that Canada does welcome immigrants but is more open to people from some backgrounds than others.

The participants' move to Canada meant a continuation of the anti-Black racism that they experienced in France. As in France, in Canada they endured both the objectification of Blackness and the denial of Black history. They were objectified inasmuch as they were rendered invisible and irrelevant, second-class citizens at best. As we saw in the previous chapters, they did not have a fair chance in Canada, either in Quebec or in other Canadian provinces such as Alberta. They understood that, by virtue of being Black or of African descent, they are automatically relegated to a lower social status, that of an object rather than a subject. When it comes to the denial of Black history in Canada, it deserves further elaboration because it is a fundamental facet of the anti-Black racism that annihilates Black identity. According to one participant:

> One [white/Francophone/Canadian] ignores Black history, it is as if we arrived in Canada yesterday. My children are born here, they do not learn about Black history in school. The other kids [who are not Black] don't know a thing about slavery [of Blacks in Canada], a lot of adults do not know about it [Black history/slavery] either.

Admittedly, Canada has officially recognizes February as Black History Month (BHM) and, in so doing, exhibits an important acknowledgement of Black Canadians. However, this gesture has been more discursive than actual, since it does not translate into specific anti-Black racism initiatives. It does not allow Black Canadians to prosper. In essence, in spite of this recognition, Black history continues to be denied in subtle ways that contribute to the continued marginalization of Blacks. For example, Black history is denied through the construction of all Black Canadians as new-comers, immigrants, and outsiders, regardless of how long they or their ancestors have been part of Canadian society. The participants related that, though they are first-generation immigrants, they "have been... [in Canada] for a long time." However, the length of time does not reduce the amount of anti-Black racism directed toward them. Not only does it hinder their integration into La Francophonie and Canadian society, it infects their Canadian-born children. For the participants, "It is just some-thing [racism] against the Black body," regardless of Blacks' place of birth, nationality, education, occupation or how long they or their ancestors have been part of Canadian society. This is because "racism cannot tell one [B]lack from another, a citizen from an immigrant, an immigrant from a refugee" (Lloyd 2001, 73). As I stated previously, Black Francophones in general are not considered part of the French-speaking population who are a "founding people" of Canada. The exclusion of Black Canadians from the master narratives about Canada's founding is a denial of Black history because it projects Blacks as being ahistorical, "late arrivals" (Razack 2007), unwelcome guests of the nation. They are therefore considered "ethnics," immigrants who have no roots in Canada. Furthermore, Black Canadian history is denied through its absence in the curriculum, the media, and other forums of education. In the specific case of La Francophonie, the mainstream does not generally acknowledge BHM. For example, the ACFA, which announces all the important events publicly in its capacity as the spokesperson for La Francophonie, does not mention BHM. It does not issue press releases to stress the significance of the occa-sion as it does other crucial events. Few French-language schools celebrate BHM; this is done through the efforts of Black-African organizations, such as the AJFAS. It is important to note that one mainstream media outlet, the French CBC, recognizes BHM and hosts programs about it. Though such initiatives are important inasmuch as they remind people of the occasion, they do not reestablish Black history. This is because they are conducted in the context of the under-representation of Black-Africans in the mainstream Francophone media. They do not produce the mean-ingful representation that acknowledges the historical contributions that Blacks made to the building of Canada.

Participants mentioned a specific incident that indicates that the mainstream Francophonie distances itself from BHM. One participant stated that a group of Black-African Francophones including the partici-pant decided to celebrate BHM and asked a mainstream Francophone organization to support their initiative, to partner with them or offer them logistical or financial support. According to the participant, the mainstream organization refused to do that, contending that BHM is not related to La Francophonie. For the participant, that response was shocking because they believed that BHM is of the utmost relevance to La Francophonie. In addition, the mandate of that organization in particular was to promote key events that concern La Francophonie. Thus, the organization's response was a denial of Black history in general and the long-standing contributions that Blacks have made to La Francophonie in particular. It is also a rejection of the subjugation and oppression that Blacks endured in Canada at the hands of white Francophones in the course of slavery, colonialism, and the ensuing racism. It indicates an escape from the responsibility and accountability for the atrocities that white Francophones committed against Black Canadians. White Francophones participated actively in the enslavement of Blacks in French Canada and their oppression in the course of colonialism and with various types of racism. In Canada as in France, the objectification of Blackness and the denial of Black history, to use Fanon's wording, paved the way for lingering anti-Black racism that exacerbated Black-African identity alienation for the participants. This racism was apparent in the types of racial oppression that the participants faced. I noted that white racial attitudes, systematic policies, stereotypes, and rhetoric permeate Black lives. Luckily, the participants' awareness of the erasure of Black identity through objectification and the disavowal of Black history did not translate into defeat and powerlessness. On the contrary, it gave rise to a strong determination, for the participants did not fall into the trap of marginalization. They capitalized on their agency to achieve the second aspect that characterizes the construction and negotiation of the identity: fighting the identity imposition with which anti-Black racism taints Black identity.

Fanon theorizes that Blacks refute identity imposition by subverting objectification into subjectivity, redefining the Black identity, and restoring Black history. The participants also engaged in these three processes, adding specific strategies. Fanon (1967) opines that, because objectification is an absolute limit to Black existence, Blacks must destroy it in order to live at all. To this end, Blacks denounce objectification; they turn the object into a new subject, "a new man" in Fanon's words, and redefine Black identity in their own terms. In *Black Skin, White Masks* (Fanon 1967), the narrator opposes objectification when their self-awareness about their alienated racialized condition in a white supremacist society empowers them to break "this vicious circle [of domination] that throws me back at myself" (217). The narrator "explodes" their objectification and simultaneously reinterprets Black identity:

> I was denied the slightest recognition. I resolved, since it was impossible to get away from an *inborn* [innate] *complex*, to assert myself as a BLACK MAN. Since the Other hesitated to recognize me, there remained only one solution: to make myself known (Fanon 1967, 115).
>
> [I] made up my mind to utter my Negro cry [shout my Blackness] (101).
>
> My cry . . . : I am a Negro, I am a Negro, I am a Negro (138).

The narrator counters objectification by opposing the ideological and material power of white supremacy. They affirm their Black identity, and that self-emancipation empowers the narrator to turn the hegemonic racial relationship inside out. They restructure the dominant social order, "shouting" their Black identity, making it crystal clear and insisting on shaping their own existence. The participants followed the same path; they repudiated objectification when they determined "enough is enough" and decided to "do something about [identity alienation]." Much like Fanon's narrator, the participants also turned Black objectification into subjectivity. To this end, they asserted their Black identity, which they declared in phrases such as: "I am Black . . . being Black in the way I see it is an important aspect of my identity." In this regard, Fanon ascertained that subjects, in this case Blacks, have the capacity to determine their own destiny; they recreate meanings about their identity, and this conscious self-identification challenges the pejorative images that the oppressor imposes on the marginalized Black identity. Then, both the narrator and participants reestablished Black history.

Interestingly, both resorted to the same "identity sources" (Kelly 2001) to restore Black history: the Black diasporic intellectual and political thought, Negritude. As a philosophy and framework of critique and literary theory that Black Francophone philosophers, intellectuals, writers, and politicians developed during the 1930s to assert their Black identity, Negritude does indeed deserve independent volumes to study and appreciate. However, in this context I focus on Negritude's relevance to the participants' identity discourse, in particular in relation to the affirmation of Black history. It is noteworthy that Negritude developed during European colonialism of the African continent, which, as we noted earlier, denied the existence of a Black history. The founders of Negritude, Léopold Sédar Senghor (the first President of Senegal), the Martinican poet Aimé Césaire, and Léon Damas, the poet and politician of French Guiana, did much to reestablish the terrain of Black history (Césaire 1939; Damas 1937; Senghor 1945).

These philosophers substantiate that there has been a massive African history that predates antiquity. Notable civilizations, states and societies, including but not limited to the Mali Empire, the Ghana Empire, the Nubian Kingdoms of Sudan, the Aksum Empire of Ethiopia, and the Great medieval Zimbabwe, have made their mark on African history and human history as a whole. These and other powerful empires built sprawling cities and crafted architectural monuments that still stand today, and produced the world's oldest and largest collection of ancient writings. Not only did they master geometry, they controlled trade routes and smelted iron, among other scientific and technological achievements. Other Negritude thinkers assert Black history by denouncing the colonial bias inherent in the "scientific" research of European archaeologists, which understates the extent and possibility of Black civilization. Europeans associate these civilizations with people who are not Black; for example, they claim that the creators of pharaonic civilization in Egypt were not Black but lighter-skinned Egyptians. In particular, Cheikh Anta Diop refutes this bias in *The African Origin of Civilization: Myth or Reality* (1967). Diop provides archaeological and anthropological evidence that authenticates that the Pharaohs of Egypt were of Negroid origin. Overall, Negritude ascertains the independent nature, value, quality, and validity of Black history and the Negro-African cultural heritage. In so doing, it upholds an identity for Black people around the world that is of their own creation, and goes on to emphasize the need for people of African descent worldwide to embrace this identity in order to free themselves from the dehumanizing clutch of European colonialism. As such, Negritude responds to the alienated position of Blacks in history and, therefore, has been fundamental to the affirmation of Black identity. It is not surprising that Negritude has inspired many Black thinkers, including Frantz Fanon. Fanon was a student of Aimé Césaire, who taught him the philosophy. In particular, Fanon embraced Negritude's approach to Black history, an appreciation that we note in the trope of Fanon's narrator when they glory:

I took up my Negritude (Fanon 1967, 138).

I made my most remarkable discovery. Properly speaking, this discovery was a rediscovery. I rummaged frenetically through all the antiquity of the [B]lack man. What I found there took away my breath . . . all of that, exhumed from the past, spread with its inside out made it possible for me to find a valid historic place. The white man was wrong, I was not a primitive, not even a half-man. I belonged to a race that had already been working in gold and silver two thousand years ago (130).

From the opposite end of the white world Negro sculpture! I began to flush with pride (123).

I was no longer a zero [nonentity] (129).

For Fanon, Negritude provides Blackness with "historicity," the concrete conditions of human existence and the conscious will to change them. It counters the "false history" that white supremacy imposed on Black heritage. Negritude's restoration of Black history became a foundation of Black existence that European colonialism had combatted. Given the relationship between history and identity, we note that Negritude's recovery of the past provides a veracity that ensures the continuity of the Black subject in the contemporary world. It allows Blacks to claim the past and alter the present so that they can shape the future. Understandably, Negritude inspired the research participants as it did for Fanon, for they drew on it to recover Black history. One participant maintained:

> I still read the writings of [Leopold Sédar] Senghor and still get a new understanding about it, especially about Negritude. He [Senghor] and his brothers, [Aimé] Césaire and the other ones . . . who are Francophone. It intrigues me . . . . The history, you know, all the achievements, of our ancestors. We honour that . . . It inspired our heroes, the independence of our [African] countries. I find it relevant to our life today.

For the participants, it is significant that the founders of Negritude joined together through the French language to vindicate the richness of Black history and culture, producing rich knowledge in French. Negritude developed an alternative approach to global humanity at a time when white French intellectuals were recognized as the legitimate voice of French-language intellectualism. Enlightenment was associated with whiteness, which precluded Blacks from the realm of knowledge. Therefore, for the participants, Negritude is in its own right a dignified source of Black identity. As contemporary Black subjects, the participants were inspired by Negritude to praise the grand accomplishments of their ancestors. They considered Negritude an inspiration for the African anti-colonial struggle and independence heroes, and this is because Negritude is one of the philosophies that impacted the Black liberatory movements. In particular, Negritude influenced the anti-colonial revolutions because it made a huge impact on how the colonized viewed themselves. It dignified Black history and identity, disavowed the European colonialism of Africa and considered it a violation of Africans' right to self-determination. Therefore, Negritude nourishes the tenacity of the colonized and pushes them to free themselves from the bondage of colonialism. Not only did Negritude impact Blacks in the past, as the participants put it, it continues to be "relevant to our life today." We saw that Negritude empowered Fanon's narrator to redefine Black identity by associating it with a glorious history, and the following statements reveal that it also enabled the participants to reinterpret their Black-African identity:

> Participant: We want to describe our identity as we ourselves see it. We are Africans, Black. Africa is my history, our place of birth... the land of my ancestors. The education and values I earned there. The respect, caring about people, the community, sharing. All of that.

> Participant: [Being] Black African is a *pride*. You know, all the *glory*, and we don't forget the suffering... their struggle [emphasis in the original].

> Participant: My Black identity means to me... the culture. The values. The music, the rhythm, rhymes... the food, and dress... make you feel you are someone.

> Participant: I feel good about my people [Blacks]. I care about Black Francophones, [and] the other Blacks here in Canada, back in Africa. We don't forget all Blacks and Africans in [other] places.... There are Blacks in Brazil, I met many in Europe.

The participants' keenness to construct their identity on their own terms divulges the power of self-identification that Fanon (1967) points out. The participants found emancipatory meanings in their identity and belong-ingness. The emphasis that they placed on "pride" and "glory" to describe Black-African identity indicates that their power and agency are not reac-tionary, in response to white supremacy, but actionary, and thus revolu-tionary. They are meant to serve the Black subject. The participants gave dignity to Blackness in a manner that consolidated their image of them-selves as Black and, as Bambrick (2015) put it, created positive "new and liberating notions of [themselves]." They redefined Black identity, replacing negative stereotypical generalizations about Blacks with emancipatory meanings. As the above quotes reveal, the Black-African identity that the participants constructed is multidimensional because it draws on history, descent, and cultural heritage. Once again, we observe the close relationship between history and identity because historical knowledge helped the participants to find both "where they came from" and "who they are." Furthermore, heritage, or cultural background, including expressive traditions, food, art, and music are important symbols underlying Black-African identity. As the participants' quotes illustrate, these cultural facets are embedded in "values," a system of "caring" for one another. It is noteworthy that, in general, values anchor social groups because they hold them together and allow them to grow and prosper. In particular, values are important to belongingness because they are the habitus (Bourdieu 1991) that informs people's beliefs and behaviour and shape their vision. The participants stressed a core value that constitutes the essence of their identity: "caring for one another." This ethos projects an attachment to the collectivity to which they belong. It entrenches a collective identity, which they also ascertained through the use of the collective pronouns "we," "our," and "us." Not only do the participants "care" about Black-African Francophones in Alberta, they feel an attachment to Blacks in Canada and other parts of the world. Indeed, their affinity with Blacks other than themselves reflects the Xhosa proverb at the beginning of this chapter "I am because we are." It projects an African philosophical approach to identity signifying a collective paradigm, whereby one's identity is tied to a body larger than the self. In order to understand the self, one must establish a communal affiliation with the community to which one belongs. The community protects its members and, in turn, these actors place themselves in a relationship of accountability to the other members of the collective. As such, the self is *not* the alterity and dichotomy of the other; the self *is* the other, to the extent that there is no self *and* other. There is a larger self : the community. This alternative view to human belonging is entrenched in Negritude's theorizing, for example, in Senghor's (1964) conceptualization of African traditionalism. Although the participants did not explicitly identify this facet of Negritude as a framework for their identification, it is embedded in their identity discourse. The values that they iterated are engraved in the African systems of knowledge that our communities equip us with in the course of our social upbringing. They enhance cohesion and continuity and are therefore crucial to identity.

The participants specifically stressed a collective identity, the larger self that is the community. They prioritized a collective identity because they believe that it is the pillar that unites them against the backdrop of anti-Black racism. Black-African identity became synonymous with unity in the participants' discourse and, once again, they turned to Negritude to explain this perspective :

Participant : Negritude resonated with me. I am increasingly interested in the works of Sénghor ... the messages he and the others [philosophers of Negritude] sent to Africans ... they are strong [powerful]. Their call for African unity, for Africans to unite ... you know. Unity is everything [important].

Participant: Movements like Negritude and Pan-Africanism held us together at a difficult time, they united us. They will hold us together now. We need that today, in Africa ... in Canada. We need this unity.

In this case, the participants articulated their admiration of Negritude as a worldwide philosophy and political movement that aims to unify all people of African ancestry in order to emancipate the Black race. This contention echoes an overarching tenet of Negritude that views continental Africans and all people of African heritage as belonging to a single race, the Black race. This commonality creates the basis for unity that could connect all African nations and peoples around the world (Mark 2008). The participants held that they, and all Blacks, need such unity to free themselves from the chains of European colonialism. They stressed that, not only is this unity useful to Black-Africans, it is not new, since Blacks have historically fostered unity. This counters the stereotypes that project Blacks as being unable to work together, contending that disputes among Blacks are "a chronic" problem (Chioneso 2008). Others emphasized both historical "divisions in the Black Community" (Bullock 2011, 83) and contemporary "hegemonic practices of group separateness. The gap ... that has emerged among Blacks" (Storr 2009, 665). The participants rightly acknowledged the existence of tensions among Blacks but urge us to examine the discourse with vigilance in order to distinguish the facts from the racist stereotypes that objectify Blackness. In this regard, tensions are not peculiar to Blacks but are rather general social problems. It is evident that no social group or community is immune to conflict, since conflict extends to all social groups both in and outside Canada. It is also clear that conflict surfaces between white colonial powers, such as French Canadians and British Canadians. But, as stated earlier, although these people have been involved in a long-standing conflict, they overcome their differences to annihilate Blacks. Not only did they support their shared imperial agenda against Blacks during slavery and colonialism, they reproduced these tactics through neocolonialism to oppress Blacks worldwide. This is the global anti-Black racism we observed through the participants' experiences in Africa, France, and Canada.

Therefore, projecting Black communities as dysfunctional because of conflict is a generalized racist stereotype that should be deconstructed. What is important is to mitigate conflict, prevent it from being reproduced, and minimize its adverse impacts. Many groups overcome disputes to protect their shared interests, and Blacks can do the same. However, it is important to acknowledge that the tensions between Blacks are more intricate because they have been manipulated by numerous external forces that have vested benefits in polarizing Blacks. These conflicts are not impossible to solve, but this requires a concerted effort. That is why the participants stressed the need for unity and highlighted numerous moments of solidarity among Blacks. Thus, they echoed another thinker of Negritude, Cheikh Anta Diop, who, in *L'Unité culturelle de l'Afrique noire*[2] (1963), affirmed the shared cultural coherence and continuity across African peoples in Africa before colonialism. This unity was more important than the different ethnic groups, languages, and cultures that developed over time. It was therefore important for the participants to name specific coalitions representing strong consensus not only in Africa, but within the Black diaspora. These include the anticolonial movements in Africa and the civil rights movement in the US. Their admiration was evident in phrases such as "that period of history, the movements for African independence … teaches us a lot" and "I got interested in the civil rights [movement] since I was young. The speeches of the king [Martin Luther King Jr.] resonated." For the participants, the anticolonial movements ignited unity among Africans because it consolidated their efforts to dismantle colonialism. Similarly, the civil rights movement is exemplary of unity between Blacks because a Black coalition succeeded in redefining the place of African Americans in the US constitutional order and race relations in the country as a whole. The participants are intrigued by Black liberatory social movements because they show cooperation between ethnically diverse groups of Blacks and created significant political and social change. Thus, the participants drew on both the philosophies of the Black diaspora, in this case, Negritude and Pan-Africanism. This is not a coincidence, since it demonstrates connections and unity between schools of thought and social movements. These relationships can be found at many levels; for example, Negritude inspired various generations of Black thinkers. As stated previously, it motivated Fanon, and it also influenced Pan-Africanist leaders, such as Patrice Lumumba. In turn Pan-Africanism sparked the civil rights movement in the US. This is because Martin Luther King Jr. admired Pan-Africanism's founder, Marcus Garvey, something he stressed on many occasions, notably during his visit to Jamaica in 1955. On that occasion, he praised Garvey unequivocally:

---

2.   The Cultural Unity of Black Africa.

[I]n Jamaica I feel like a human being . . . . [Marcus Garvey] was the first man of color to lead and develop a mass movement. He was the first man on a mass scale and level to give millions of Negroes a sense of dignity and destiny. And make the Negro feel he was somebody (King, in Garvey 2016).

King's endorsement of Garvey also signals connections between Negritude, Pan-Africanism, and the civil rights movement, as well as the anticolonial struggle on the African continent. Although some may think that the civil rights movement in the US and the anticolonial movement in Africa are separate and distinct, but in reality they overlapped and nourished each other. There has been a long-standing collaboration between civil rights figures, such as Martin Delany and Henry McNeal Turner, and African anticolonialist leaders that dates back to the 19th century. More recent interactions occurred between Malcolm X, another strong advocate of Pan-Africanism, and African leaders (Clark 1991). These and other contacts between the leaders and the peoples involved helped to spread the ethos of the civil rights movement to Africa. Similarly, US civil rights leaders found inspiration in the African anticolonial struggle and its heroes, such Kwame Nkrumah. African leaders fought racism against African Americans and challenged colonial intervention in Africa. For example, they openly contested Apartheid in South Africa. It bears noting that the ties between Black philosophies and movements include additional historical and contemporary connections. For example, Garvey's philosophy-activism ignited Black South Africans' struggle against Apartheid, and both the civil rights movement and the anticolonial struggle inspired Black Brazilians' struggle against racial inequality in Brazil. There are other global connections that prove unity among Blacks worldwide. For example, I previously noted that Black pioneers in Alberta replicated Garvey's Universal Negro Improvement Association, which indicates that Garvey's thinking also inspired the Black struggle in Canada. These are moments of solidarity that provided continuity in the diasporic Black struggle at different times and places in history. What the participants want us to learn from these ties is that Blacks have joined forces throughout history. They recall these legacies and stress the need to capitalize on them, reproduce them, and adapt them to the specific locations where Blacks find themselves in the contemporary world, including in Alberta. Thus, the participants captured the essence of Negritude, which asserts that what brings Blacks together is stronger than what divides them. They are aware that stereotypes about the tensions between Blacks overshadow the unity they have forged many times. These contentions remind us of the importance of history to identity, since the participants reiterated them to prove both the need for and possibility of Black unity. In so doing, they "reversed the colonial gaze," to use Fanon's (1967) wording. Their consideration of Black unity through the insights of Negritude sparked renewed interest in this philosophy and its relevance to 21st-century issues. The intellectual and political philosophy of the African diaspora, i.e., Negritude, speaks to the participants' "life today," since the participants drew on it to underscore the advantages that unity will bring to Black-African Francophones in Alberta. In short, for the participants, to be Black-African means to embrace a collective identity that they believe uplift the Black race.

To recapitulate, anti-Black racism disparages Black identity through objectification and the denial of Black history. This construction is negotiated in racist practices that Black-African Francophones suffer in all spheres of society. But these actors counter that alienation, transforming their objectification into subjectivity by refuting the disenfranchisement imposed on them, redefining Black-African identity in their own terms, and revitalizing Black history. Significantly, they negotiated these meanings in praxis that encompassed many facets, including the commemoration of Black History Month.

CELEBRATING BLACK HISTORY MONTH IN FRENCH

Like all social actors, Black-African Francophones engage in organized patterns of relations and create structures that lead them to establish a multitude of associations and organizations. Examples of these are the AJFAS, the Portail de l'immigrant association[3] (PIA) in Calgary, and the Association multiculturelle francophone de Brooks.[4] There are also organizations associated with specific countries, such the Association sénégalaise de Calgary[5] and the Association Camerounaise d'Edmonton.[6] Arguably, these groups construct and negotiate an inclusive Black-African Francophone identity that aligns with the one the participants formed. Most of the research participants took part in these organizations and co-founded some of them. Of the wide array of initiatives, I will analyze those that concern Black History Month (BHM) in French because they are of utmost relevance to the preceding analysis.

---

3.   Immigration Portal Association.
4.   Brooks Multicultural Francophone Association.
5.   The Senegalese Association of Calgary.
6.   Cameroonian Association of Edmonton.

A few Black-African Francophone organizations, such as the AJFAS and the PIA, commemorate BHM in French on an annual basis. The participants display their admiration for BHM events for a number of reasons. Significantly, the events implement Negritude's approach to reestablishing Black history. Not only do they stress the veracity of Black history in general, they reintroduce the forgotten Black history in Canada and assert its relevance to La Francophonie. One celebration screened a documentary about the Haitian Revolution and the heroism of Toussaint L'Ouverture. It, and the ensuing discussion, showcased long-established Black history. They centred on Black history in relation to the International Francophonie, showing that the French revolution is not the only revolutionary symbol of La Francophonie as it is often understood. Another BHM event focused specifically on Black Francophone history in Canada, honoring Mathieu Da Costa and claiming him as an icon of French-Canadian nationhood. A panel in which two research participants took part shed light on the enslavement of Blacks in Canada, insisting that slavery was a legal instrument that supported the colonial economy in Canada. That slavery wounded Black Canadians and continues to harm them in the present through the ensuing anti-Black racism. Yet another activity emphasized the bravery that the Black Pioneers of Alberta showed in the face of the horrific racism that they endured. That the Pioneers helped to develop the province—Alberta—in which citizens take pride today. Much like Negritude, the organizations, including the participants, reinstated Black history. They substantiated the longevity of Black history in Canada and posited that this history is an integral part of Canada's history. The reference to the enslavement of Blacks in Canada and the pain it inflicted on them reminds Canadians of this atrocity, since many continue to ignore it. It also opens the door for the accountability and reparations for slavery that we—Blacks—owe Canada.

The celebrations of BHM echo our previous affirmation about the continuation and connections within Black history. They present Black history as a continuum that feeds into Black-African Francophones' lives today. In addition, they mirror the relationship between history and identity, depicting Black history as a source of dignity to enhance the identity of Alberta's Black-Africans. Significantly, the BHM events make reference to multiculturalism. In a previous section, I posited that Francophones deny multiculturalism, and in this context I state that Black-African Francophones counter this denial in strategies they use during BHM events. This can be seen in statements such as "We celebrate Black history because we deserve a place at the heart of the multicultural mosaic." I have already addressed the impacts of multiculturalism on Black Canadians in general, and at this juncture I focus on its connection to Black history in La Francophonie. Multiculturalism could—and should—promote Black history in this sphere, but this is not the case. As previously stated, Black history is far from being normalized in the French-language school curriculum, for example. This shortcoming extends to the celebration of BHM in La Francophonie. Once again, because the Multiculturalism Policy (the Policy) does not treat Blacks as a separate designated group, it overlooks the linguistic diversity within the category of Blackness, which means that it does not afford Black Francophones the attention they deserve. Thus, it does not provide significant support for the issues of Black history in La Francophonie. It could be argued that these issues should be addressed by the *Official Languages Act* (OLA). However, the OLA ignores Black issues that concern La Francophonie, including Black history. Similarly, the strategic nationalism of Francophones does not emphasize Black history, which also hinders the recognition of BHM in La Francophonie. Although the participants and the celebrations in general did not allude to Canada's Action Plan against Racism (the Plan), we argue that the Plan could have facilitated the inclusion of Black history in La Francophonie. However, this did not materialize.

The participants and their counterparts volunteered to take an initiative that should have been backed by mainstream Francophone organizations and the government. Although they did not receive this support, their celebration of BHM in La Francophonie is a powerful strategy that serves to construct and negotiate the collective Black-African identity. Their action illustrate CRT's concept of "political struggle," since they created a coalition that endeavoured to achieve justice. It is significant inasmuch as it made the participants "feel liberated," that "a major, shared goal was accomplished." That "it [was] a step towards achieving even bigger aims" because "we are here to stay." The participants' negotiation of Black-African identity added to their efforts to construct and negotiate Francophone and Canadian identities, teaching us how to overcome multiple identity exclusions.

CHAPTER 6
CONCLUSION

> "[The] Negro . . . simply wishes to make it possible for a man to be both a Negro and an American without being cursed and spit upon by his fellows, without having the doors of opportunity closed roughly in his face." Du Bois (1961, 16-17).

While the participants constructed multiple identities—Canadian, Francophone, and Black-African affiliations, they endured multiple jeopardy that they countered with multiple negotiations in order to enhance their inclusion in La Francophonie and Canadian polity. In so doing, they illuminated strategies that offer hope for a just future. They were excluded from Canadian identity because, as CRT's race theorists would argue, the forces of domination construct this identity in a manner that proves the centrality of race and racism. Race continues to matter as a social construct, reinforcing white privilege and white supremacy, which in turn reproduce anti-Black racism. This racism illustrates the negotiation of the dominant Canadian identity, since it results in the marginalization of Black-African Francophones in pan-Canadian institutions and society. To address this plight, the participants reconstructed Canadian identity in a more inclusive way in which they asserted racial, ethnic, and linguistic diversity. They negotiated this affiliation by taking on the duties of citizenship, such as voting, political activism by taking part in anti-racism protests, and relations they built with people from various backgrounds. Their antiracism constitutes what CRT considers an "individual-ideological nexus" (Fleras 2014, 224). Their efforts were supported by the civil society, Calgary Anti-racist Action (CAA), which assumes the collective responsibility that anti-racism requires. Both the participants and the CAA founded an "action-oriented strategy" (Dei 1996, 252) and a "political struggle" that CRT recommends in order to bring about social justice. While these actors took action to renegotiate Canadian identity, others, particularly law enforcement, did not. This shortcoming goes to the intricacies of Canadian policies, in this case the Charter, the Multiculturalism Policy (the Policy), and the *Employment Equity Act* (EEA). The Charter prohibits race-based discrimination, but its flawed perception of freedom of expression does not condemn white supremacy as a violation of racial rights. The Policy denounces racism, but its current phase, civic multiculturalism, does not effectively counter racism. The EEA is no different, since it did not improve Blacks' inclusion. Critical multiculturalism's (CM) tenet of "the critique of liberalism" allows us to assert that these laws function within an equality paradigm that does not confront racism effectively.

Both similar and additional trends shape Francophone identity, from which the participants felt alienated, since the dominant construction of this identity replicates the master narratives of white French Canadians as a "founding people" of Canada. Francophones have historically employed strategic nationalism to denounce the linguicism that has afflicted them. Nonetheless, they reproduce the oppression that they endured, refuting linguicism without taking into consideration the racism that afflicts Black-African Francophones. The inequitable distribution of resources among Francophones is a discriminatory negotiation of Francophone identity; it pushes Black-Africans outside the spaces of belongingness. It illustrates CM's approach to language that perceives it as a factor that generates linguicism against Francophones, while it reminds us that racialized linguicism produce multiple exclusions for Black-African Francophones. This is because they suffer the racialization of accent and exclusion in the labour market regardless of their fluency and accent in English and French. Overall, the under-representation of these actors in the mainstream Francophonie, the rejection of multiculturalism, and the "Franco-centric approach" to race and racism (Labelle 2011) propagate anti-Black racism in La Francophonie. These dynamics illustrate CRT's contentions about the danger of the denial of racism but, again, the participants' resilience pushed them to improve their plight. They reconstructed Francophone identity in an inclusive fashion that envelops the changing demographics of La Francophonie. Their negotiation of this identity demonstrates the relevance of race, racism and anti-racism, and multiculturalism to La Francophonie.

In particular, the Caravan applied CRT's suggestion concerning the need for educational reform in order to instill social justice. It also extended critical multicultural education's suggestions of how such reforms can be put in place. Curriculum development, explicitly naming power inequities such as racism, incorporating diversity at all educational levels, and intersecting culture with anti-racism are useful ways to ensure the success of such a reform. Other actors supported the construction and negotiation of an inclusive Francophone identity, including the few researchers who bring race and anti-racism to La Francophonie (Carlson Berg 2012; Huot 2017; Madibbo, 2014; Maillé 2015; Mianda, 2021; Sall 2021; Veronis 2012), and the French-language schools that hosted the Caravan and the governments that funded it, albeit in an ambivalent manner. Shortcomings were illustrated in the lack of support for the Caravan on the part of the mainstream Francophonie and of anti-racism in the OLA. The OLA ensured the development of the Francophone space but did not result in provisions or programs that enforce equity and anti-racism in La Francophonie. Like the Charter and the Policy, the OLA projects CRT's precept about the "contradiction-closing cases," because the legislation seems to be inclusive but does not improve the plight of Blacks in any substantial manner. If we do not examine such "contradiction-closing cases" with caution we cannot improve them in order to achieve justice. Rather, we will continue to believe that change is occurring while it remains confined to minor achievements. Thus, we see that the OLA generated differential racialization, to use CRT's wording, in La Francophonie that advantages white Francophones while it disenfranchises Black-Africans. The Charter and the EEA have also generated differential racialization among visible minorities that improved the situation for some of these minorities but does not allow Blacks to advance in society. The dilemma that makes Black Canadians one of the most educated yet most marginalized groups in Canada renders Black-African Francophones even more discriminated against because of their multiple minority status.

When it comes to Black-African identity, CRT's emphasis on the utility of the theorizing and the voices of people of African descent allows us to corroborate that the participants were jeopardized by the negative construction of this identity. Blackness was objectified, and Black history was erased (Fanon 1967), and the negotiation of this identity exclusion rendered the participants invisible, second-class citizens at best, regardless of their place of birth, level and country of education, time of settlement in Canada, and so on. Black intellectual and political thought, in this case Negritude, also allows us to decipher the participants' reconstruction of Black-African identity by turning objectification into subjectivity, giving identity new meanings, and reestablishing Black history. The new Black-African identity was negotiated through practices such as the celebration of Black History Month in French. This action projected CRT's perception of antiracism as an "infrastructural nexus" (Fleras 2014, 224). This is because the events were commemorated by the participants and Black-African Francophone organizations that advocate for the language and racial rights of Black-African Francophones. Thus, we note that the multiple identity exclusion endured by the participants mirrored critical multiculturalism's conceptualization of identity as both a means of domination and a tool of emancipation. Multiple identity exclusion was fueled by the Eurocentric binary approach to identity (Shohat & Stam 2013), as the images that dehumanized Blacks in the course of slavery and European colonialism continue to permeate contemporary constructions of these identities. As such, Black-African Francophones are distanced from the dominant constructions of Canadian and Francophone identities, which also imposes pejorative connotations on Black identity. Multiple identity jeopardy was caused by racism and racialized linguicism, and generated adverse impacts, for as Nabors (2012) asserts, the outcomes of marginalization are "compounded for people with multiple minority identities" (29). Multiple oppression generates multiple problems (Olaoye 2012), and for Black-African Francophones, these outcomes include identity alienation, disenfranchisement, poverty, and mental distress.

I extended the two theories, CRT and CM, further in this analysis. I added that the two theories complement each other because CRT explores race and racism in depth, while CM investigates language and identity more thoroughly. CRT illuminates the issue of legal reforms, and CM expands on educational reform. In addition, I brought new conceptions to both theories. I put forth the African traditionalism approach to identity (Senghor 1964) which is embedded in the Xhosa proverb "I am because we are," to corroborate a collective identity. This also allowed me to contribute to CM, because this perspective on identity is a viable solution to the Eurocentric self/other identity binary that critical multiculturalists problematize (Shohat & Stam 2013). It erases binaries to stress oneness. In addition, I added the concept of "racialized linguicism" to critical multiculturalism's perspective on language, and the fact that language collides with race to target speakers of specific languages because of their skin colour. Furthermore, I merged CRT's critique of liberalism and CM's critique of liberal multiculturalism to suggest an intersection between liberal multiculturalism and critical multiculturalism ideologies. These

ideologies should not be perceived as opposing binaries but as complementary ideals. The liberal trend of multiculturalism sheds light on
citizenship, which is important for the understanding and practice of
collective identity. Critical multiculturalism stresses equity and antiracism,
which are crucial to any identity. This leads me to suggest a critical civic
multicultural ideology that will be illustrated through a critical civic multicultural policy. The policy should take the form of a civic critical
multiculturalism phase, which I suggest as a fourth phase of multiculturalism in Canada. This is because the equity phase of multiculturalism
should be reintroduced, since equity is not a short-term exercise to be
abandoned without thorough application. It is a social justice project that
requires sufficient time and resources to achieve the desired transformation.
However, given the importance of citizenship to the building of a collective
identity, it would be useful to merge civic multiculturalism with equity.
Accordingly, the proposed ideology, policy, and practice would result in
critical civic multicultural education.

It is clear that the theory I drew on corresponds to the methodology
I utilized, which is the qualitative research tradition (Berg & Lune 2012).
Like the theory, this methodology was in line with the critical perspective
because it allowed me to centre the "experiential knowledge" of marginalized groups, in this case Black-African Francophones, and the voices of
their intellectuals, Fanon (1967) and Negritude's philosophers (Senghor
1967), in order to redress inequities of power. Both theory and methodology
were useful in that, in line with the critical tradition, they enabled me to
analyze injustices and oppressive regimes of knowledge and make recommendations for policy and research in order to achieve our cherished goal
of justice. Situating this methodology in the context of critical ethnography
proves to be useful inasmuch as its emphasis on the need to "challenge
institutions, regimes of knowledge, and social practices that limit choices,
constrain meaning, and denigrate identities and communities" (Madison
2012, 6) led me to conduct this study in order to battle oppression and
instill equity and justice.

To date, Canada and Canadians have not achieved the comprehensive
anti-racism framework that both CRT and CM envisioned. We recall that
CRT called for "an action-oriented strategy" (Dei 1996, 252) and an
"individual-institutional-ideological-infrastructural nexus" (Fleras 2014,
224) that includes legal and educational reform. The above discussion
shows that the participants and other actors met some of these criteria,
materializing a relatively small level of "an action-oriented political
strategy" and an "individual...-ideological-infrastructural nexus," What

is missing is an "institutional nexus" and a larger scope of the "action-oriented political strategy" and "individual . . .-ideological-infrastructural nexus" on the part of all actors. Every Black-African Francophone, La Francophonie as a whole, and the state need to assume their collective responsibility to apply the missing aspects to achieve the shared goal of emancipation. Thus, legal reforms are needed, and they should first consider Black Canadians a separate designated group. This status will make it possible to identify the magnitude of anti-Black racism and how to fight it effectively, and provide funding and programs to achieve this objective. This entails naming Black Canadians a designated group in the existing legislation, including the Policy, the OLA, the Charter, and the EEA. These policies should acknowledge the diversity of Blacks, including the linguistic diversity that culminated in the existence of Black Francophones. Thus, Canadian laws will recognize the intersection of linguistic duality with anti-racism.

The revised legislation should result in an action plan, or action plans, to counter anti-Black racism and be backed by provisions and resources similar to the ones the OLA grants. In particular, it will be beneficial to assign an Anti-racism Commissioner equivalent to the Commissioner of Official Languages, and to create an Office of the Anti-racism Commissioner equivalent to the Office of the Commissioner of Official Languages. At the same time, it will be important to establish a Standing Senate Committee on Anti-racism equivalent to the Standing Senate Committee on Official Languages. These provisions will counter racism in general while targeting anti-Black racism in particular. Accurate and precise follow-up measures will be extremely important to ensure the application of the new and revised laws. Proper practice of these provisions will represent an equitable negotiation of an inclusive Canadian identity.

La Francophonie should be more prone to justice. Nothing justifies the lack of equity policies in the Francophone space; therefore, such policies should be put in place to redistribute resources among Francophones. Francophone activism and the associated strategic nationalism should become a "political strategy," as CRT puts it, to fight linguicism intersected with racism and stand for the rights of all Francophones, including Black-Africans. It will also be imperative to stress race, racism, anti-racism, and multiculturalism in the mainstream Francophone discourse. The emerging scant but important scholarship examining these issues in La Francophonie is an important starting point that deserves to be extended to enhance equity in this space. The French-language education system will benefit from the kind of educational reform that critical multiculturalism supports.

The Caravan is a good example of such reform; it should be reinstituted with a broader scope and institutionalized as a long-term program carried out in partnership between schools and the community. This also means that the French-language school system will be transformed to reflect the diversity of Francophones at all levels. These initiatives will help construct and negotiate an inclusive Francophone identity.

There is a dire need for a Black-African Francophone political organization in Alberta. Following CRT's recommendation about the need to foster "a political struggle," a coalition among Black-African Francophones will help improve their status. It could lobby and claim rights on their behalf. Although mainstream Francophone organizations, especially the Association Canadienne-française de l'Alberta, should be the spokesperson for all Francophones, a Black-African Francophone coalition could ensure that their issues are on the agenda. The revised and new legislation should assist in the building of the coalition, which will allow it to become a united front that will enhance the development of Black-Africans. In addition, there is a need for a similar coalition at the national level that resembles the Fédération des communautés francophones et acadienne du Canada. This Federation should represent all Francophones, including Black-Africans, but the suggested coalition will complement the Federation's work, since it will oversee Black-African Francophones' issues at the national level.

Moreover, legislators should draw the line between freedom of speech and racial hatred to halt white supremacy and hold its promoters accountable. Put together, the suggested legal and educational reforms will enhance the "institutional and infrastructural nexus," but these policy recommendations will need to be accompanied by an "ideological nexus." Given the educational benefits of anti-racism at these levels, they will help reduce racism. Furthermore, these trends will include the thinking and rethinking of identity in the 21st century. In particular, they will show how to counter multiple identity marginalization. The participants showed that the construction of multiple minority identities is negotiated in discursive and practical ways. It requires redefining identities in inclusive ways and taking action to instill social justice, and perceiving multiple identities as being complementary in a manner that echoes Du Bois' (1961) quote at the beginning of this chapter. In the process, the "experiential knowledge" of the marginalized, to use CRT's wording, is empowering. Nevertheless, the construction and negotiation of multiple identity exclusion is daunting because it necessitates multiple efforts at multiple levels, which is why additional actors must intervene. Luckily, the civil society—Calgary

Anti-racist Action—and some levels of governments assumed their antiracist responsibility, but many shortcomings prevail. This is why the above recommendations are important to counter identity imposition and perceive multiple identities not as competing binaries but as complementary aggregates. This approach to identity helps to reconstruct Canadian and Francophone identities in a manner that entrenches Blackness as an integral part of these affiliations. The proposed model will automatically correct the objectification of Blackness and the denial of Black history, since Blackness will no longer be projected as the antithesis of Canadian-ness and Francophone-ness. In addition, the reforms would culminate in the inclusion of Black Canadians, including Black-African Francophones, in society. Black history will be acknowledged and taught properly; thus, Black identity will be reconstructed and negotiated equitably.

Further, it will be useful to conduct comparative research to illuminate these recommendations and identify specific programs and procedures to apply them. It will also be useful to contrast the construction and negotiation of Francophone identity among white, Black, and other racialized Francophones. This endeavour will provide more information about the nature of "differential racialization" in La Francophonie and how to improve it. Studying the first, second, and third+ generations of Black-African Francophone immigrants will bring to light whether these people are making progress in La Francophonie and Canadian society and what lessons can be drawn from the findings. Correlating the trajectories of Africans and other Black Francophones, i.e., Caribbean people such as Haitians, will allow for a more thorough investigation of anti-Black racism and help eradicate it. Moreover, it will be beneficial to extend these topics to the construction and negotiation of Canadian identity to learn how to make it more inclusive of all parties involved. These studies will bring to light additional ways in which Blackness is constructed and can be equitably renegotiated. In the process, we will challenge and repair the mistakes of the past and present. The founding of Canada will no longer be a historical matter or the property of two specific groups. It will be a collective project mounted by the numerous groups that have made Canada and La Francophonie what they are today. Strategic nationalism will be truly strategic because it will serve the interests of all citizens. The building of Canada will turn to the future, as Ryan (2010) put it, "if the nation is a community based upon the idea of a shared history, it is also based upon the idea of a shared future" (128). The participants agreed, contending that "It is the future that matters." Let us work together to build this shared future.

REFERENCES

Abu-Laban, Yasmin, and Christina Gabriel. *Selling Diversity : Immigration, Multiculturalism, Employment Equity, and Globalization.* Peterborough & New York, Broadview Press, 2002.

ACFA (Association canadienne-française de l'Alberta). "ACFA," 2016, https://acfa.ab.ca/index-main/

——. "Association canadienne-française de l'Alberta (ACFA)," 2015, http://www.ameriquefrancaise.org/fr/article-568/Association_canadienne-%20fran%C3%A7aise_de_l%E2%80%99Alberta_(ACFA).html#.X_DBHY-cFdd

ACFA Régional de Calgary. *Répertoire des ressources francophones de Calgary et ses environs,* Calgary, ACFA, 2009.

Africa Centre. "Welcome to Africa Centre," n.d., https://www.africacentre.ca/.

AJFAS (Alliance Jeunesse-Famille de l'Alberta Society). "Mission," *Alliance Jeunesse-Famille de l'Alberta Society : Nos programmes et services,* Edmonton, AJFAS, n.d.a.

——. "Overview." *Alliance Jeunesse-Famille de l'Alberta Society : Nos programmes et services.* Edmonton, AJFAS, n.d.b.

——. "The Caravan." *Alliance Jeunesse-Famille de l'Alberta Society : Nos programmes et services,* Edmonton, AJFAS, n.d.c.

——. "Mission statement." *Alliance Jeunesse-Famille de l'Alberta Society,* n.d.d, http://www.ajfas.ca/caravane

Akrofi-Obeng, Animwaa. *African Immigrants' Entrepreneurship in Canada, Challenges and Effects : A Case Study of African Immigrants Residing in Calgary,* MA thesis, Calgary, University of Calgary, 2015.

Alberta Government. "Statistics," 2017a, http://www.culturetourism.alberta.ca/francophone-secretariat/english/facts-and-statistics/

——. "Culture and Tourism," 2017b, https://www.alberta.ca/francophone-secretariat.aspx.

————. *French Policy*, n.d., https://open.alberta.ca/dataset/9818af69-7a54-43af-9d91-f899745d864c/resource/fbc613c8-aa52-4669-a3f9-80192a0a1283/download/french-policy-english.pdf.

Alberta, Land of Opportunity. "The Petition," 2001, https://www.collectionscanada.gc.ca/eppp-archive/100/200/301/ic/can_digital_collections/pasttopresent/opportunity/petition.html.

Alberta's Black Pioneer Heritage. "The Settlement of Oklahoma Blacks in Western Canada: The Canadian Response," n.d.a, http://www.albertasource.ca/blackpioneers/history/articles/response.html

————. "Discrimination," n.d.b, http://www.albertasource.ca/blackpioneers/history/1907-1912/discrimination.html

Allahdini, Seema. *The Colour of Poverty: Understanding Racialized Poverty in Canada through Colonialism*, MA thesis, Wilfrid Laurier University, 2014.

Angry French Guy. "Pure Laine is an English Word." https://angryfrenchguy.com/2009/01/11/pure-laine-is-an-english-word/

Annuaire (des entreprises, des professionnels et des organismes francophones de l'Alberta). Edmonton, Association Canadiennes-française de l'Alberta, 2016.

Appleblatt, Anthony. "J. J. Maloney and the Ku Klux Klan." *The Chelsea Journal*, vol. 2, no. 1, 1976, pp. 45-48.

Baber, Zaheer. "The role of place and metaphor in racial exclusion: South Africa's beaches as sites of shifting racialization." *Sociology*, vol. 38, no. 4, 2004, pp. 701-178.

Babiak, Todd. "Hate-crime incidents unlikely to build neo-Nazi popularity." *Edmonton Journal*, 12 March, 2011, http://www.pressreader.com/canada/edmonton-journal/20110312/289145789547280.

Baergen, William. *The Ku Klux Klan in Central Alberta*. Red Deer, Central Alberta Historical Society, 2000.

Baffoe, Michael. "The Social Reconstruction of "home" among African immigrants in Canada." *Canadian Ethnic Studies*, vol. 41-42, no. 3-1, 2009-2010, pp. 157-173.

Baines, Donna (ed.). *Doing Anti-oppressive Practice: Social Justice Social Work*. Black Point, Fernwood Publishing, 2011.

Balibar, Étienne. *Race, nation, classe: les identités ambiguës*. Paris, La Découverte, 1988.

Bambrick, Gail. "Black Identity and America's Lingering Racism." *Tufts Now*, 20 February, 2015, http://now.tufts.edu/articles/black-identity-and-america-s-lingering-racism.

Banks, Cherry, and James Banks. *Multicultural Education: Issues and Perspectives*. Hoboken, John Wiley & Sons, 2010.

Banks, James. *Diversity and Citizenship Education: Global Perspectives.* Hoboken, John Wiley & Sons, 2006.

Banton, Michael. *Racial Theories.* Cambridge, Cambridge University Press, 1987.

Bar-Tal, Daniel, and Yona Teichman. *Stereotypes and Prejudice in Conflict: Representations of Arabs in Israeli-Jewish Society.* Cambridge, Cambridge University Press, 2005.

Berg, Bruce, and Howard Lune. *Qualitative Research Methods for the Social Sciences.* Don Mills, Pearson, 2012.

Berns-McGown, Rima. *"I am Canadian," Challenging Stereotypes about Young Somali Canadians.* Policy Paper no. 38, Montreal, Institute for Research on Public Policy, 2013.

Bhabha, Homi. *The Location of Culture.* London & New York, Routledge, 1994.

Biles, John, Burstein Meyer, and James Frideres. *Immigration and Integration in Canada in the Twenty-first Century.* Kingston, Queen's School of Policy Studies, 2008.

Bissoondath, Neil. *Selling Illusions: The Cult of Multiculturalism in Canada.* Toronto, Penguin Canada, 1994.

Bourdieu, Pierre. *Language and Symbolic Power.* Cambridge, Harvard University Press, 1991.

——. "The forms of capital." In John Richardson (ed.). *Handbook of Theory and Research for the Sociology of Education.* New York: Greenwood, 1986, pp. 241-58.

Boyko, John. *Last Steps to Freedom: The Evolution of Canadian Racism.* Toronto, J. Gordon Shillingford, 1998.

Breton, Raymond. *Ethnic Relations in Canada: Institutional Dynamics.* Montreal and Kingston, McGill-Queen's University Press, 2005.

Bristow, Peggy (ed.). *We're Rooted Here and They Can't Pull Us Up: Essays in African Canadian Women's History.* Buffalo and Toronto, University of Toronto Press, 1994.

Brown, Kathleen. "Leadership for Social Justice and Equity: Weaving Transformative Framework and Pedagogy." *Educational Administration Quarterly*, vol. 40, 2004, pp. 77-108.

Bullock, Cathy. "'Freedom Is a Job for All of Us': The Arkansas State Press and Divisions in the Black Community During the 1957-59 School Crisis." *The Howard Journal of Communications*, vol. 22, 2011, pp. 83-100.

Caidi, Nadia, Danielle Allard, and Lisa Quirke. "The Information Practices of Immigrants." *Annual Review of Information Science and Technology* (ARIST), vol. 44, 2010, pp. 493-531.

Canadafirst.net. "Canada First Immigration Reform Committee," 2018a, http://canadafirst.nfshost.com/?page_id=27.

——. "The Myths of Immigration," 2018b, http://canadafirst.nfshost.com/commentary.html.

CanadianContent. "'Deemed Unsuitable': Black Pioneers in Western Canada," 2000-2019, http://forums.canadiancontent.net/showthread.php?t=56945.

Canadian Heritage. *Rapport Annuel sur les langues officielles, 2015-2016.* Ottawa, Government of Canada, 2017.

——. *A Canada for all: Canada's Action Plan Against Racism.* Ottawa, Canadian Heritage, 2005.

Canadian Museum of Immigration. "Immigration Act Amendment, 1919," 2017, https://www.pier21.ca/research/immigration-history/immigration-act-amendment-1919.

Canadian Press. "UN report on Canada to address anti-Black racism." 24 September, 2017, https://www.thestar.com/news/canada/2017/09/24/un-report-on-canada-to-address-anti-black-racism.html.

Carlson Berg, Laurie, (ed.). *La francophonie canadienne dans toutes ses couleurs et le défi de l'inclusion scolaire.* Laval, Presses de l'Université Laval, 2014.

——. "Parlons de la francophonie dans toutes ses couleurs : Un projet recherche-action en sciences humaines." *Canadian Issues*, Fall, 2012, pp. 51-54.

——. "Un regard critique sur les initiatives d'éducation inclusive des élèves immigrants en milieu scolaire fransaskois." *Francophonies d'Amérique*, vol. 32, no. 1, 2011, pp. 65-86.

Carr, Wilfred, and Stephen Kemmis. *Becoming Critical: education, knowledge and action research.* London and Philadelphia, The Palmer Press, 1986.

CBC News. "Morgan Thompson ID'd as man shot by police in downtown alley," 22 March, 2015, https://www.cbc.ca/news/canada/calgary/morgan-thompson-id-d-as-man-shot-by-police-in-downtown-alley-1.3005082.

CDEA (Le Conseil de développement économique de l'Alberta), 2010, https://www.lecdea.ca/en/areas-of-focus/canadian-francophone-economic-space/.

Césaire, Aimé. *Cahier d'un retour au pays natal.* Paris, Volontés, 1939.

Charest, Antoine. "Qu'est-ce que l'interculturalisme?" La Presse, 2019, https://www.lapresse.ca/debats/opinions/2019-08-16/qu-est-ce-que-l-interculturalisme.

Chioneso, Nkechinyelum. "(Re)Expressions of African/Caribbean Cultural Roots in Canada." *Journal of Black Studies*, vol. 39, no. 1, 2008, pp. 69-84.

Chong, Dennis, and Reuel Rogers. "Racial Solidarity and Political Participation." *Political Behavior*, vol. 27, no. 4, 2005, pp. 347-374.

Christopher Anderson, and Jerome Black. "The Political Integration of Newcomers, Minorities, and the Canadian-Born Perspectives on Naturalization, Participation, and Representation." In John Biles, Meyer Burstein, and Tom

Aiken (eds.). *Immigration and Integration in Canada in the Twenty-first Century.* Kingston, Queen's School of Policy Studies, 2008, pp. 45-76.

Citizenship and Immigration Canada. *Evaluation of Canada's Action Plan Against Racism*, 2010, file:///C:/Users/amadibbo/Desktop/Book%20all/Book%20 actual%20analysis/Identity%20book%20identity%20analysis/Plan%20 Against%20Racism%20Evaluation%20PDF%20.pdf.

.Citrin, Jack, and David Sears. "Balancing National and Ethnic Identities: The Psychology of E Pluribus Unum." In Rawi Abdelal, Yoshiko Herrera, Johnston Johnston, and Rose McDermott. *Measuring Identity: A Guide for Social Scientists.* Cambridge, Cambridge University Press, 2009, pp. 45-174.

Clark, Steve (ed.). *Malcolm X Talks to Young People: Speeches in the United States, Britain, and Africa.* New York, Pathfinder Press, 1991.

Clarke, George Elliott. *Odyssey's Home: Mapping African-Canadian Literature.* Toronto, University of Toronto Press, 2002.

Coburn, Elaine. *More Will Sing Their Way to Freedom: Indigenous Resistance and Resurgence.* Halifax, Fernwood Publishing, 2015.

Cooper, Afua. *The Hanging of Angélique: The Untold Story of Canadian Slavery and the Burning of Old Montréal.* Toronto & Moosic, HarperCollins, 2006.

Couch, Kenneth, and Robert Fairlie. "Last Hired, First Fired? Black-White Unemployment and the Business Cycle." *Demography*, vol. 47, no. 1, 2010, pp. 227-247.

Couture, Claude. "L'immigration et le malaise des sociétés dominantes au Canada." In Claude Couture, Josée Bergeron and Claude Denis (eds.). *L'Alberta et le multiculturalisme francophone: témoignages et problématiques.* Edmonton, Le Centre d'études canadiennes de la faculté Saint-Jean, 2002, pp. 145-158.

Creese, Gillian. *The New African Diaspora in Vancouver: Migration, Exclusion, and Belonging.* Vancouver, UBC Press, 2011.

Crenshaw, Kimberlé. "Twenty years of Critical Race Theory: Looking back to move forward." *Connecticut Law Review*, vol. 43, 2011, pp. 1253-1353.

———. "The first decade: Critical reflections, or 'a foot in the closing door'." *UCLA Law Review*, vol. 49, 2002, pp. 1343-1372.

Crocker, Diane, Alexandra Dobrowolsky, Edna Keeble, Catherine Moncayo, and Evangelia Tastsoglou. *Security and Immigration, Changes and Challenges: Immigrant and Ethnic Communities in Atlantic Canada, Presumed Guilty?* 2007, https://www. publicsafety.gc.ca/lbrr/archives/cn5191-eng.pdf.

CTV News Calgary. "Racism erupts at the Siksika First Nation Reserve," 28 August, 2008, http://calgary.ctv.ca/servlet/an/local/CTVNews/20080828/ CGY_siksika_racist_080828/20080828/?hub=CalgaryHome.

Dalley, Phyllis. "Définir l'accueil : enjeu pour l'immigration en milieu minoritaire francophone en Alberta." *Francophonies d'Amérique*, vol. 16, 2003, pp. 67-78.

Damas, Léon. *Pigments.* Paris, Guy Lévis Mano, 1937.

Danso, Ransford, and Miriam Grant. "Access to housing as an adaptive strategy for immigrant groups : Africans in Calgary." *Canadian Ethnic Studies*, vol. 32, no. 3, 2000, pp. 19-43.

Das Gupta, Tania. *Real Nurses and Others : Racism in Nursing.* Halifax, Fernwood Publishing, 2009.

———. "Anti-Black Racism in Nursing in Ontario." *Studies in Political Economy*, vol. 51, no. 1, 1996a, pp. 97-116.

———. *Racism and Paid Work.* Toronto, University of Toronto Press, 1996b.

De Gobineau, Arthur. *The Inequality of Human Races.* London, William Heinemann, 1915.

Dei, George. *Racists Beware : Uncovering Racial Politics in the Postmodern Society.* Rotterdam, Sense, 2008.

———. "Schooling and the dilemma of youth disengagement." *McGill Journal of Education*, vol. 38, no. 2, 2003, pp. 241-256.

———. "Critical Perspectives in Antiracism : An Introduction." *Canadian Review of Sociology*, vol. 33, no. 3, 1996, pp. 247-267.

Dei, George, and Mairi McDermott. "Introduction to the politics of anti-racism education : In search of strategies for transformative learning." In George Dei and Mairi McDermott (eds.). *Politics of anti-racism education*, Dordrecht, Spinger, 2014, pp. 1-11.

Delgado, Richard. *The Rodrigo Chronicles : Conversations About America and Race.* New York, New York University Press, 1995.

Delgado, Richard, and Jean Stefancic. *Critical Race Theory : An Introduction.* New York, New York University Press, 2017.

Denis, Wilfrid. "De minorité à citoyenneté : les défis de la diversité dans la communauté fransaskoise." *Thèmes canadiens*, Spring 2008, pp. 47-49.

Denzin, Norman, and Yvonna Lincoln. *The SAGE Handbook of Qualitative Research.* Thousand Oaks, Sage, 2011.

Diop, Cheikh Anta. *Antériorité des civilisations nègres : Mythe ou vérité historique?* Paris, Présence Africaine, 1967.

———. *L'Unité culturelle de l'Afrique noire.* Paris, Présence Africaine, 1963.

Dixon, Adrienne, and Celia Rousseau. "And We Are Still Not Saved : Critical Race Theory in Education Ten Years Later." *Race, Ethnicity and Education*, vol. 8, no. 1, 2005, pp. 7-27.

Du Bois, William Edward Burghardt. *The Souls of Black Folk.* Bantam, Fawcett, 1961.

Essed, Philomena. "Cloning cultural homogeneity while talking diversity: old wine in new bottles in Dutch organizations." *Transforming Anthropology*, vol. 11, no. 1, 2002, pp. 2-12.

Essed, Philomena, and Theo Goldberg (eds.). *Race Critical Theories: Text and Context.* Malden, Blackwell Publishers, 2001.

Ezekiel, Raphael. "An ethnographer looks at neo-nazi and klan groups: the racist mind revisited." *American Behavioral Scientist*, vol. 46, 2002, pp. 51-71.

Fairclough, Norman. *Language and Power.* London and New York, Routledge, 2014.

Fanjoy, Martha. "There's No Place Like Home(s): Southern Sudanese-Canadian Return Migration." In Amal Madibbo (ed.). *Canada in Sudan, Sudan in Canada: Immigration, Conflict and Reconstruction.* Montreal and Kingston, McGill-Queen's University Press, 2015, pp. 76-99.

Fanon, Frantz. *Black Skin, White Masks.* New York, Grove Press, 1967.

Fédération des commuautés francophones et acadiennes du Canada. *Francophone Community Profile of Alberta.* Ottawa, Government of Canada, 2009.

Femmes Africaines Horizon 2015. "Vers une société québécois juste et équitable. Sans racisme, ni discrimination." Brief presented as part of the consultation: Vers une politique gouvernementale de lutte contre le racisme et la discrimination. Montreal, FAH, 2006.

Fleras, Augie. *Racisms in a Multicultural Canada: Paradoxes, Politics, and Resistance.* Waterloo, WLU Press, 2014.

Fleras, Augie, and Jean Elliott. "The Quebec Question: A Canada quandary." In Augie Fleras and Jean Elliott (eds.). *Unequal Relations: An Introduction to Race, Ethnic and Aboriginal Dynamics in Canada.* Toronto, Prentice Hall, 2007a, pp. 208-225.

——. "Media and Minorities: A Contested site." In Augie Fleras and Jean Elliott (eds.). *Unequal Relations: An Introduction to Race, Ethnic and Aboriginal Dynamics in Canada.* Toronto, Prentice Hall, 2007b, pp. 315-23.

——. *Engaging Diversity: Multiculturalism in Canada.* Toronto, Nelson Thompson, 2002.

——. *Multiculturalism in Canada: The Challenge of Diversity.* Toronto, Nelson Canada, 1992.

Foggo, Cheryl. "Stalling Segregation." *Avenue Calgary*, 2015, http://www.avenue-calgary.com/City-Life/20-Decisions-That-Shaped-Calgary/.

——. *Pourin' Down Rain.* Calgary, Detselig Enterprises, 1990.

Foster, Cecil. *Blackness and Modernity: The Colour of Humanity and the Quest for Freedom,* Montreal and Kingston, McGill-Queen's University Press, 2007.

Friedman, Jonathan. "The Past in the Future: History and the Politics of Identity." *American Anthropologist*, vol. 94, no. 4, 1992, pp. 837-859.

Freire, Paulo. *Pedagogy of the Oppressed.* New York, Continuum, 2000.

Frye, Ann, and Hemmer Paul. "Program evaluation models and related theories: AMEE Guide no. 67." *Medical Teacher*, vol. 34, no. 5, 2012, pp. e288-e299.

Gabryś, Marcin, Sikora Tomasz, and Ewelina Bujnowska. *Towards Critical Multiculturalism: Dialogues Between / Among Canadian Diasporas.* Katowice, Agencja Artystyczna Para, 2011.

Gal, Susan. "Language and the 'Arts of Resistance.'", *Cultural Anthropology*, vol. 25, no. 4, 1995, pp. 407-424.

Galabuzi, Grace-Edward. *Canada's Economic Apartheid: The Social Exclusion of Racialized Groups in the New Century.* Toronto, Canadian Scholars Press, 2006.

Galarneau, Dianne, and René Morissette. *Immigrants' education and required job skills.* Ottawa, Statistics Canada, 2008.

Gallant, Nicole. "Les communautés francophones en milieu minoritaire et les immigrants: entre ouverture et inclusion." *Revue du Nouvel Ontario*, vol. 35, no. 36, 2011, pp. 69-105.

Garvey, Julius. "Julius Garvey: Pardon my father, Mr. President." *CNN*, 23 November, 2016, https://www.cnn.com/2016/11/22/opinions/marcus-garvey-should-have-a-presidential-pardon-garvey/index.html.

Garvey, Marcus. *Selected Writings and Speeches of Marcus Garvey.* Edited by Bob Blaisdell. Minesola, New York, Dover Thrift Editions, 2005.

Gillborn, David. "Education policy as an act of white supremacy: whiteness, critical race theory and education reform." *Journal of Education Policy*, vol. 20, no. 4, 2005, pp. 485-505.

———. "Critical race theory and education: Racism and anti-racism in educational theory and praxis." *Discourse: Studies in the Cultural Politics of Education*, vol. 27, 2006, pp. 11-32.

Gillborn, David, and Gloria Ladson-Billings. "Education and Critical Race Theory." In Michael Apple, Stephen Ball, and Luís Armando. *The Routledge International Handbook of the Sociology of Education.* London and New York, Routledge, 2010, pp. 37-47.

Girard, Magali, Michael Smith, and Jean Renaud. "Intégration économique des nouveaux immigrants: adéquation entre l'emploi occupé avant l'arrivée au Québec et les emplois occupés depuis l'immigration." *Canadian Journal of Sociology*, vol. 33, no. 4, 2008, pp. 791-814.

Goodman, Elizabeth, Bin Huang, Tara Schafer-Kalkhoff, and Nancy Adler. "Perceived socioeconomic status: a new type of identity that influences adolescents' self-rated health." *Epub*, vol. 41, no. 5, 2007, pp. 479-487.

Government of Canada. "Constitution Act, 1982, Part I, the Canadian Charter of Rights and Freedoms," 2016, https://laws-lois.justice.gc.ca/eng/Const/page-15.html.

———. "Official Languages Act," 1985a, http://laws-lois.justice.gc.ca/eng/acts/o-3.01/FullText.html.

———. "Canadian Multiculturalism Act", 1985b, http://laws-lois.justice.gc.ca/eng/acts/C-18.7/page-1.html#docCont.

———. "Multiculturalism", n.d., http://option.canada.pagesperso-orange.fr/multiculturalism.htm.

Gouvernement du Québec. "Communauté haïtienne du Québec. Profils des communautés culturelles du Québec." In *Québec, Les publications du Québec*, 2005, pp. 249-262, https://www.erudit.org/fr/revues/du/2012-v12-n2-du01192/1022852ar.pdf.

Govia, Francine. *Blacks in Canada: in search of the promise: a bibliographic guide to the history of Blacks in Canada.* Edmonton, Harambee Centres Canada, 1988.

Gutstein, Eric. "Critical Multicultural Approaches to Mathematics Education in Urban, K-12, Classrooms." In Stephen May and Christine Sleeter (eds.). *Critical Multiculturalism: Theory and Praxis.* London and New York, Routledge, 2010, pp. 127-137.

Habashi, Janette. "Language of political socialization: language of resistance." *Children's Geographies*, vol. 6, no. 3, 2008, pp. 269-280.

Hage, Ghassan. *White Nation: Fantasies of White Supremacy in a Multicultural Society.* London and New York, Routledge, 2012.

Hall, Stuart. "Who needs 'identity'?" In Paul Du Gay, Jessica Evans, and Peter Redman (eds.). *Identity: A Reader*, London, SAGE, 2000, pp. 15-30.

Haque, Eve. *Multiculturalism Within a Bilingual Framework: Language, Race, and Belonging in Canada.* Toronto, University of Toronto Press, 2012.

Harewood, Adrian (host). *Multiculturalism in Canada debated.* Ottawa, CBC, 2004, https://www.cbc.ca/player/play/1848926159.

Hébert, Yvonne (ed.). *Citizenship in Transformation in Canada.* Toronto, University of Toronto Press, 2003.

Henry, Frances, and Carol Tator. *The Colour of Democracy: Racism in Canadian Society.* Toronto, Nelson Thomson, 2009.

———. *Racial Profiling in Canada: Challenging the Myth of a "Few Bad Apples".* Toronto, University of Toronto Press, 2006.

———. *Discourses of Domination: Racial Bias in the Canadian English-Language Press.* Toronto, University of Toronto Press, 2002.

Hooker, Juliet. *Race and the Politics of Solidarity.* New York, Oxford University Press, 2009.

hooks, bell. *Teaching to transgress: Education as the Practice of Freedom*, New York and London, Routledge, 1994.

——. *Talking back: thinking feminist, Thinking black.* Boston, South End Press, 1989.

Hooks, Gwen. *The Keystone Legacy: Recollections of a Black Pioneer.* Edmonton, Brightest Pebble, 1997.Huffpost. "Jason Devine: White Supremacists Likely Behind Latest Attack Against His Home," 2013, https://www.huffingtonpost. ca/2013/10/11/jason-devine-blood-honour-attack-home_n_4086353.html.

Hunter, Margaret. "Color and the Changing Racial Landscape." In Tanya Das Gupta, Carl James, Roger Maaka, Grace-Edward Galabuzi, and ChrisAnderson (eds.). *Race and Racialization, Essential Readings.* Toronto, Canadian Scholars Press, 2007, pp. 309-315.

Huot, Suzanne. "'Doing' capital: examining the relationship between immigrants' occupational engagement and symbolic capital." *Migration Studies*, vol. 5, no. 1, 2017, pp. 29-48.

Immigration.ca. "Canada's Premiers: Give Us the Same Immigration Powers as Quebec," 2020, https://www.immigration.ca/canadas-premiers-give-us-immigration-powers-quebec#:~:text=The%20premiers%20of%20 Canada%27s%209,minimal%20input%20at%20federal%20level.

Ingram, David. *Rights, Democracy, and Fulfillment in the Era of Identity Politics: Principled Compromises in a Compromised World.* Lanham, Rowman and Littlefield, 2004.

Isajiw, Wsevolod. "Definition and Dimensions of Ethnicity: A theoretical Framework." In *Challenges of Measuring an Ethnic World: Science, politics and reality.* Ottawa and Washington, Statistics Canada and U.S. Bureau of the Census, 1993, pp. 407-427.

Jacquet, Marianne, Danielle Moore, Cécile Sabatier, and Mambo Masinda. *L'intégration des jeunes immigrants francophones africains dans les écoles francophones en Colombie Britannique.* Vancouver, Vancouver Research on Immigration and Integration in the Metropolis RIIM Working Paper Series, 2008.

Jahoda, Gustav. "Towards Scientific Racism." In Tanya Das Gupta, Carl James, Roger Maaka, Grace-Edward Galabuzi, and ChrisAnderson (eds.). *Race and Racialization, Essential Readings.* Toronto, Canadian Scholars Press, 2007, pp. 24-30.

James, Carl. *Seeing Ourselves: Exploring Race, Ethnicity, and Culture.* Toronto, Thompson Educational, 2010.

Jensen, Robert. *The Heart of Whiteness: Confronting Race, Racism and White Privilege.* San Francisco, City Lights Publishing, 2005.

Jiménez, Marina. "Immigrants face growing economic mobility gap," *Globe and Mail*, 14 September, 2008, https://www.theglobeandmail.com/news/national/ immigrants-face-growing-economic-mobility-gap/article1063 144/.

Joppke, Christian. "War of words: interculturalism v. multiculturalism." *Comparative Migration Studies*, vol. 6, no. 11, 2018, pp. 1-10.

Kelly, Jenny. *Borrowed identities.* New York, Peter Lang Publishing, 2001.

Kenny, Michael. *The Politics of Identity: Liberal Political Theory and the Dilemmas of Difference.* Malden, Polity Press, 2004.

Kinsella, Warren. *Web of Hate: Inside Canada's Far Right Network.* Scarborough, HarperCollins, 2001.

Knefelkamp, Lee. "Civic Identity: Locating Self in Community." *Diversity & Democracy*, vol. 11, no. 2, 2008, pp. 1-3.

Knight, Mélanie. *The Negotiation of identities: narratives of mixed-race individuals in Canada.* MA thesis, Toronto, University of Toronto, 2001.

Korostelina, Karina. *Social Identity and Conflict: Structures, Dynamics and Implications.* New York, Palgrave MacMillan, 2007.

Kubota, Ryuko. "Critical Multiculturalism Education and Second/Foreign Language Teaching." In Stephen May and Christine Sleeter (eds.). *Critical Multiculturalism: Theory and Praxis.* London and New York, Routledge, 2010, pp. 99-111.

——. "Critical Multiculturalism and Second Language Education." In Bonny Norton and Kelleen Toohey (eds.). *Critical Pedagogies and Language Learning.* Cambridge, Cambridge University Press, 2004, pp. 30-52.

Kymlicka, Will. "Testing the liberal hypothesis: normative theories and social science evidence." *Canadian Journal of Political Science*, vol. 43, no. 2, 2011, pp. 257-271.

——. *Multicultural Citizenship: A Liberal Theory of Minority Rights.* Oxford, Clarendon Press, 1995.

Labelle, Micheline. *Racisme et antiracisme au Québec: Discours et déclinaisons.* Laval, Presses de l'Université du Québec, 2011.

Ladson-Billings, Gloria. "From the achievement gap to the educational debt: Understanding achievement in US schools." *Educational Researcher*, vol. 35, 2006, pp. 3-12.

Ladson-Billings, Gloria, and William Tate. "Toward a critical race theory of education." *Teachers College Record*, vol. 97, no. 1, 1995, pp. 47-68.

Laing, Gregory, and Céline Cooper. "Royal Commission on Bilingualism and Biculturalism." *The Canadian Encyclopedia*, 2019, https://www.thecanadianencyclopedia.ca/en/article/royal-commission-on-bilingualism-and-biculturalism.

Lapshina, Natalia. *Canadians' Attitudes Toward Immigrants who Claim Employment Discrimination*, PhD thesis, London, University of Western Ontario, 2015.

Le Monde. "L'Assemblée supprime de la Constitution le mot 'race' et interdit la 'distinction de sexe,'" 2018, https://www.lemonde.fr/politique/article/2018/07/12/l-assemblee-supprime-dans-la-constitution-le-mot-race-et-interdit-la-distinction-de-sexe_5330615_823448.html.

Lewis, Stephan. *African and Caribbean Immigrant Youth Integration Practices: The Role of Hip-Hop.* MA thesis, Calgary, University of Calgary, 2017.

Lloyd, Cathie. "Anti-racism, social movements and civil society." In Floya Anthias and Cathie Lloyd (eds.). *Rethinking Anti-Racisms: From Theory to Practice.* Oxon, Routledge, 2001, pp. 60-77.

Lugones, Maria. "Radical Multiculturalism and Women of Color Feminisms." *Journal for Cultural and Religious Theory*, vol. 13, no. 1, 2014, pp. 68-80.

Madibbo, Amal. "The Way Forward: African Francophone immigrants negotiate their multiple minority identities." *Journal of International Migration and Integration*, vol. 17, no. 3, 2016, pp. 853-866.

———. "L'état de la reconnaissance et la non-reconnaissance des acquis des immigrants africains francophones en Alberta." *Francophonies d'Amérique*, vol. 37, 2014, pp. 155-171.

———. "Pratiques identitaires et racialisation des immigrants africains francophones en Alberta." *Canadian Ethnic Studies*, vol. 41-42, no. 3-1, 2012a, pp. 175-189.

———. "L'immigration francophone noire et le multiculturalisme." In Ewin Geoffery and Colin Coates (eds.). *Introduction aux Études Canadiennes: Histoires, identités, cultures.* Ottawa, Ottawa University Press, 2012b, pp. 121-136.

———. "Race, Gender, Language and Power Relations: Blacks within Francophone Communities in Ontario, Canada." *Race, Gender and Class*, vol. 14, no. 1-2, 2007, pp. 213-226.

———. *Minority Within a Minority: Black Francophone Immigrants and the Dynamics of Power and Resistance.* London and New York, Routledge, 2006.

Madibbo, Amal, and John Maury. "L'immigration et la communauté franco-torontoise : le cas des jeunes." *Francophonies d'Amérique*, vol. 12, 2002, pp. 113-122.

Madison, Soyini. *Critical Ethnography: Method, Ethics, and Performance.* Los Angeles, London, New Delhi, Singapore, Washington, Sage, 2012.

Maillé, Chantal. "De l'articulation entre race, classe et genre : éléments pour une analyse féministe intersectionnelle au Québec." In Naïma Hamrouni and Chantal Maillé (eds.). *Le sujet du féminisme est-il blanc? Femmes racisées et recherche féministe.* Montreal, Éditions du remue ménage, 2015, pp. 155-174.

Mark, Christian. "Marcus Garvey and African Unity: Lessons for the Future From the Past." *Journal of Black Studies*, vol. 39, no. 2, 2008, pp. 316-331.

Martin, Kevin. "Calgary white supremacist Kyle McKee denies assault, says the first time he saw alleged victim was in court." *Calgary Sun*, 16 June, 2015, http://anti-racistcanada.blogspot.com/2015/06/kyle-mckee-on-trial-for-assault-again.html.

Martinez, Aja. "Critical Race Theory: Its Origins, History, and Importance to the Discourses and Rhetorics of Race." *Frame*, vol. 27, no. 2, 2014, pp. 9-27.

Massaquoi, Notisha, and Njoki Wane (eds.). *Theorizing Empowerment: Canadian Perspectives on Black Feminist Thought.* Toronto, Inanna Publications and Education Inc., 2007.

Massinon, Stephane. "As Calgary's white supremacist groups fade, expectations for peaceful anti-racism rally rise." *Calgary Herald*, 22 March, 2013, http://www.calgaryherald.com/life/Calgary+white+supremacist+groups+fade+expectations+peaceful+anti+racism+rally+rise/8140273/story.html.

May, Stephen (ed.). *Critical Multiculturalism: Thinking multicultural and antiracist education.* London, Falmer, 1999.

May, Stephen, and Christine Sleeter (eds.). *Critical Multiculturalism: Theory and Praxis.* London and New York, Routledge, 2010.

Mayo, Chris. "Certain privilege: Rethinking white agency." *Philosophy of Education*, 2004, pp. 308-316.

Mazrui, Ali. *Black Reparations in the Era of Globalization.* Binghamton, The Institute of Global Cultural Studies, 2002.

McDonald, Jean. "Migrant Illegality, Nation Building, and the Politics of Regularization in Canada." *Refuge*, vol. 26, no. 2, 2009, pp. 65-77.

McLaren, Peter. *Revolutionary Multiculturalism: pedagogies of Dissent for the new millennium.* Boulder, Westview Press, 1997.

Mensah, Joseph. *Black Canadians: History, Experiences, Social Conditions.* Halifax and Winnipeg, Fernwood Publishing, 2010.

Mensah, Joseph, and Christopher Williams. "Seeing/being double: how African immigrants in Canada balance their ethno-racial and national identities." *African and Black Diaspora: An International Journal*, vol. 8, no. 1, 2015, pp. 39-54.

Merin, Oleschuk. "Engendering Transnational Foodways: A Case Study of Southern Sudanese Women in Brooks, Alberta." *Anthropologica*, vol. 54, no. 1, 2012, pp. 119-131.

Metapedia. "National Socialist Party of Canada," 2015, http://en.metapedia.org/wiki/National_Socialist_Party_of_Canada.

Mianda, Gertrude. "Francophone Sub-Saharan African Immigrants Organizing Tontines in Toronto: A Basis for Solidarity and Integration." *Canadian Ethnic Studies*, vol. 52, no. 3, 2020, pp. 7-26.

——. "Reading Awa Thiam's La parole aux Négresses through the Lens of Feminisms and English Language Hegemony." *Atlantis*, vol. 36, no. 2, 2014, pp. 8-19.

Milan, Anne, and Kelly Tran. "Blacks in Canada: A long history." *Canadian Social Trends*, vol. 72, Spring 2004, Catalogue no. 11-008.

Miles, Robert, and Rudy Torres. "Does "race" matter? Transatlantic Perspectives on Racism after "race Relations." In Tanya Das Gupta, Carl James, Roger Maaka, Grace-Edward Galabuzi, and Chris Anderson (eds.). *Race and Racialization, Essential Readings*. Toronto, Canadian Scholars Press, 2007, pp. 65-73.

Milton, Jon, Shannon Carranco, and Christopher Curtis. "Exclusive: Major neo-Nazi figure recruiting in Montreal." *Montreal Gazette*, 12 May, 2018, https://montrealgazette.com/news/local-news/major-neo-nazi-figure-recruiting-in-montreal.

Minsky, Amy. "Hate crimes against Muslims in Canada increase 253% over four years." *Global News*, 13 June, 2017, https://globalnews.ca/news/3523535/hate-crimes-canada-muslim/.

Moke Ngala, Victor. *L'intégration des jeunes des familles immigrantes francophones d'origine africaine à la vie scolaire dans les écoles secondaires francophones dans un milieu urbain en Alberta: conditions et incidences*. MA thesis, Edmonton, University of Alberta, 2005.

Montague, Dena. "Communitarianism, discourse and political opportunity in Republican France." *French Cultural Studies*, vol. 24, no. 2, 2013, pp. 219-230.

Morrison, Toni. *Playing in the Dark: Whiteness and the Literary Imagination*. Cambridge, Harvard University Press, 1992.

M'Pindou, Luketa. "La jeunesse Congolaise dans la société canadienne." In Claude Couture and Josée Bergeron (eds.). *L'Alberta et le multiculturalisme francophone*. Edmonton, Le Centre d'études canadiennes de la Faculté Saint-Jean, 2002, pp. 33-36.

Mulumba, Emmanuel. "Mot du Président." In *AJFAS, AGA 2012-2013*. Edmonton, AJFAS, 2013, p. 3.

Mwaniki, Munene. *Anti-black Racism and the Foreign Black Other: Constructing Blackness and the Sporting Migrant*. PhD thesis, Urbana, University of Illinois at Urbana-Champaign, 2014.

Nabors, Nina. "The Social Psychology of Stigma." In Reginald Nettles and Rochelle Balter (eds.). *Multiple Minority Identities: Application for Practice, Research, and Training* New York, Springer, 2012, pp. 13-34. Ndagije, Jidiri. "Bonne rentrée scolaire 2012 en Alberta!" *L'Écho de la Caravane*, no. 4, 2012a, p. 1.

——. "Activités estivales de la Caravane au nord de l'Alberta." *L'Écho de la Caravane*, no. 4, 2012b, p. 2.

Nussbaum, Martha. "Kant and Stoic Cosmopolitanism." *The Journal of Political Philosophy*, vol. 5, no. 1, 1997, pp. 1-25.

Office of the Commissioner of Official Languages. "Decades 1990," n.d., https://www.clo-ocol.gc.ca/en/timeline-event/the-supreme-court-of-canada-ruling-in-the-mahe-case-recognizes-the-right-of-parents.

OIF (Organisation internationale de la Francophonie). "Qui sommes-nous?" n.d., https://www.francophonie.org/qui-sommes-nous-5.

O'Keefe, Brendan. "5 Steps to Better School/Community Collaboration: Simple ideas for creating a stronger network." *Edutopia*, 2011, https://www.edutopia.org/blog/school-community-collaboration-brendan-okeefe.

Olaoye, Elaine. "Increasing Resilience in Multiple Minority Clients Using Positive Psychology." In Reginald Nettles and Rochelle Balter (eds.). *Multiple Minority Identities: Application for Practice, Research, and Training.* New York, Springer, 2012, pp. 141-162.

Omi, Michael, and Howard Winant. *Racial Formation in the United States.* London and New York, Routledge, 2014.

———. "On the theoretical concept of race." In Cameron McCarthy and Warren Crichlow (eds.). London and New York, Routledge, 1993, pp. 3-10.

Ontario Human Rights Commission. *Paying the price: The human cost of racial profiling*, 2003, http://www.ohrc.on.ca/en/paying-price-human-cost-racial-profiling.

Pabu, Justin. "Une Caravane sans-frontières au Sud de l'Alberta." *L'Écho de la Caravane*, no. 2, 2012, p. 3.

Palmer, Howard. *Patterns of Prejudice: A History of Nativism in Alberta.* Toronto, McClelland and Stewart Limited, 1982.

Palmer, Howard, and Tamara Palmer. "The Black Experience in Alberta." In Howard Palmer and Tamara Palmer (eds.). *Peoples of Alberta: Portraits of Cultural Diversity.* Saskatoon, Western Producer Prairie Books, 1985, pp. 365-393.

Perry, Barbara, and Ryan Scrivens. *Right-Wing Extremism in Canada.* Cham, Palgrave, 2019.

Phillipson, Robert. *Linguistic Imperialism.* Oxford: Oxford University Press, 1992.

Porter, John. *The Vertical Mosaic: An Analysis of Social Class and Power in Canada.* Toronto, University of Toronto Press, 1965.

Potvin, Maryse. "Blackness, haïtianité et québécitude: modalités de participation et d'appartenance chez la deuxième génération d'origine haïtienne au Québec." In Maryse Potvin, Paul Eid, and Nancy Venel (eds.). *L'expérience sociale des jeunes de « deuxième génération »: Une comparison France-Québec.* Paris, Presses du CRNS, 2006, pp. 137-170.

Razack, Sherene. "When Place becomes Race." In Tanya Das Gupta, Carl James, Roger Maaka, Grace-Edward Galabuzi, and Chris Anderson (eds.). *Race and*

Racialization, Essential Readings. Toronto, Canadian Scholars Press, 2007, pp. 74-82.

Reinharz, Shulamit, and Lynn Davidman. *Feminist Methods in Social Research.* New York, Oxford University Press, 1992.

Reitz, Jeffrey. "Closing the gaps between skilled immigration and Canadian labour markets." In Phil Triadafilopoulos (ed.). *Wanted and Welcome?: Policies for Highly Skilled Immigrants in Comparative Perspective.* New York, Springer, 2013, pp. 147-163.

Reitz, Jeffrey, and Rupa Banerjee. "Race, Religion, and the Social Integration of New Immigrant Minorities in Canada." *International Migration Review*, vol. 43, no. 24, 2009, pp. 695-726.

Ryan, Phil. *Multicultiphobia.* Toronto, University of Toronto Press, 2010.

Rummens, Joanna. "Conceptualising Identity and Diversity: Overlaps, Intersections, and Processes." *Canadian Ethnic Studies*, vol. 3, 2003, pp. 10-25.

Sall, Leyla. *L'Acadie du Nouveau-Brunswick et "ces" immigrants francophones. Entre incomplétude institutionnelle et accueil symbolique.* Laval, Presses de l'Université Laval, 2021.

Satzewich, Vic. "The Political Economy of Race and Ethnicity." In Peter Li (ed.). *Race and Ethnic Relations in Canada.* Don Mills, Oxford University Press, 1999, pp. 311-346.

Satzewich, Vic, and Nicolaos Liodakis. *"Race" and Ethnicity in Canada: A Critical Introduction.* Don Mills, Oxford University Press, 2013.

Sénat du Canada. "Comité permanent, Langues officielles," n.d., https://sen-canada.ca/fr/comites/OLLO/Contact/42-1.

Senghor, Léopold Sédar. *Négritude et humanisme.* Paris, Seuil, 1964.

———. "Le français, langue de culture." *Esprit*, vol. 311, no. 11, 1962, pp. 837-844.

———. *Chants d'ombre. Suivi de Hosties noires.* Paris, Seuil, 1945.

Shahsiah, Sara. *Identity, Identification and Racialization: Immigrant Youth in the Canadian Context.* CERIS Working Papers no. 49, Toronto, The Joint Centre of Excellence for Research on Immigration and Settlement, 2006.

Sharma, Sanjay. "Critical Multiculturalism and Cultural and Media Studies." In Stephen May and Christine Sleeter (eds.). *Critical Multiculturalism: Theory and Praxis.* London and New York, Routledge, 2010, pp. 113-123.

Sher, Julian. *White hoods: Canada's Ku Klux Klan.* Vancouver, New Star Books, 1983.

Shepard, Bruce. "Diplomatic Racism: The Canadian Government and Black Migration from Oklahoma, 1905-1912." *Great Plains Quarterly*, vol. 3, no. 1, 1983, pp. 5-16.

——. *Deemed unsuitable: Blacks from Oklahoma move to the Canadian prairies in search of equality in the early 20th century, only to find racism in their new home.* Toronto, Umbrella Press, 1997.

Shishehgar, Sara, Mahrokh Dotation, Alavi Hamid, and Maryam Bakhtiary. "Socioeconomic Status and Stress Rate During Pregnancy in Iran." *Global Journal of Health Science*, vol. 6, no. 4, 2014, pp. 54-60.

Shohat, Ella, and Robert Stam. *Unthinking Eurocentrism: Multiculturalism and the Media.* New York and London, Routledge, 2013.

Siekierska, Alicja. "Signs in Toronto urge white people to join 'alt-right'." *The Star*, 14 November, 2016, https://www.thestar.com/news/gta/2016/11/14/signs-in-toronto-urge-white-people-to-join-alt-right.html.

SLMC. "Northwest Territories Act (1877)", n.d., http://www.slmc.uottawa.ca/?q=leg_northwest_territories_act.

Stapleton, John, Brian Murphy, and Yue Xing. "The 'Working Poor' in the Toronto Region: Who they are, where they live, and how trends are changing." Toronto: Metcalf Foundation, 2012, http://metcalffoundation.com/stories/publications/the-working-poor-in-the-toronto-region-who-they-are-where-they-live-and-how-trends-are-changing/.

Statistics Canada. "French and the *francophonie* in Canada." 2018, https://www12.statcan.gc.ca/census-recensement/2011/as-sa/98-314-x/98-314-x2011003_1-eng.cfm.

——. "Census Profile, 2016 Census," 2017, d/prof/details/page.cfm?Lang=E&Geo1=PR&Code1=01&Geo2=PR&Code2=01&Data=Count&SearchText=Canada&SearchType=Begins&SearchPR=01&B1=Visible%20minority&TABID=1.

——. "Black population in Canada: A portrait," 2004, http://www.statcan.gc.ca/pub/11-002-x/2004/03/07604/4072459-eng.htm.

Storr, Juliette. "Décalage: A thematic interpretation of cultural differences in the African Diaspora." *Journal of Black Studies*, vol. 39, no. 5, 2009, pp. 665-688.

Strauss, Anselm, and Juliet Corbin. *Basics of Qualitative Research: Techniques and Procedures for Developing Grounded Theory.* Thousand Oaks, Sage Publications, 1990.

Sundstrom, William. "Last Hired, First Fired? Unemployment and Urban Black Workers During the Great Depression." *The Journal of Economic History*, vol. 52, no. 2, 1992, pp. 415-429.

Swain, Carol, and Russell Nieli. *Contemporary Voices of White Nationalism in America.* Cambridge, Cambridge University, 2003.

Talbani, Abdulaziz. "Intercultural Education and Minorities: Policy initiatives in Quebec." *McGill Journal of Education*, vol. 28, no. 3, 1993, pp. 407-419.

Taylor, Charles. *Multiculturalism: Examining the Politics of Recognition.* Princeton, Princeton University Press, 1994.

Tettey, Wisdom, and Korbla Puplampu (eds.). *The African diaspora in Canada: Negotiating Identity and Belonging.* Calgary, University of Calgary Press, 2005.

Thériault, Joseph, Anne Gilbert, and Linda Cardinal (eds.). *L'espace francophone en milieu minoritaire au Canada. Nouveaux enjeux, nouvelles mobilisations.* Montreal, Fides, 2008.

Thomas, Jim. *Doing Critical Ethnography.* Newbury Park, SAGE Publications, 1993.

Tomlinson, Carol Ann. "The Goals of Differentiation." *Educational leadership: Journal of the Department of Supervision and Curriculum Development*, vol. 66, no. 3, 2008, pp. 26-30.

Troper, Harold. *Only Farmers Need Apply: Official Canadian Government Encouragement of Immigration from the United States, 1896-1911.* Toronto, Griffin Press, 1972.

Tundula, Éric. "Éditorial." *L'Écho de la Caravane*, no. 1, 2012, p. 1.

Tuohy, Dympna, Adeline Cooney, A. M. Dowling, K. Murphy, and Jane Sixmith. "An overview of interpretive phenomenology as a research methodology." *Nurse Researcher*, vol. 20, no. 6, 2013, pp. 17-20.

Valli, Linda, Amanda Stefanski, and Reuben Jacobson. "School-community partnership models: implications for leadership." *International Journal of Leadership in Education*, vol. 21, no. 1, 2018, pp. 31-49.

Van den Hoonaard, Deborah. *Qualitative Research in Action: A Canadian Primer.* Don Mills, Oxford University Press, 2015.

Van Dijk, Teun. "Discourse and the denial of racism." *Discourse & Society*, vol. 3, 1992, p. 87-118.

Van McVey, Sarah. "Race, Gender, and the Contemporary White Supremacy Movement: The Intersection of 'isms' and Organized Racist Groups." *ProQuest*, 2008.

Vavrus, Michael. "Critical Multiculturalism and Higher Education: Resistance and Possibilities within Teacher Education." In Stephen May and Christine Sleeter (eds.). *Critical Multiculturalism: Theory and Praxis.* London and New York, Routledge, 2010, pp. 19-32.

Veronis, Luisa. "The Role of Nonprofit Sector Networks as Mechanisms for Immigrant Political Participation." *Studies in Social Justice*, vol. 7, no. 1, 2012, pp. 27-46.

Wane, Njoki. "African Canadian Women and the Criminal Justice System." In Njoki Wane, Jennifer Jagire, and Zahra Murad (eds.). *Ruptures: Anti-colonial & Anti-racist Feminist Theorizing.* Berlin, Springer Science & Business Media, 2013, pp. 107-125.

Washington, Jesse. "'Fruitvale Station' Shows Black Male Humanity." In *America's Black Holocaust Museum*, 2013, http://abhmuseum.org/fruitvale-station-shows-black-male-humanity/.

Welch, David. "Early Franco-Ontarian Schooling as a Reflection and Creator of Community." *Ontario History*, vol. 85, no. 4, 1993, pp. 321-347.

West, Cornel. *Race Matters.* New York, Vintage Books, 1994.

Wingrove, Josh. "Calgary's in-your-face neo-Nazis take to the streets." *The Globe and Mail*, 18 March, 2011, https://beta.theglobeandmail.com/news/national/calgarys-in-your-face-neo-nazis-take-to-the-streets/article573162/?ref=http://www.theglobeandmail.com&.

———. "Calgary anti-racism activist beaten, blames neo-Nazis for 'targeted' attack." *The Globe and Mail*, 8 November, 2010, https://www.theglobeandmail.com/news/national/calgary-anti-racism-activist-beaten-blames-neo-nazis-for-targeted-attack/article1241591/.

Winks, Robin. *The Blacks in Canada: a History*. New Haven, Yale University Press, 1971.

Wood, Damien. "Alleged white supremacist shot by cops after disturbing peace rally: Witnesses," *Toronto Sun*, 21 March, 2015, https://torontosun.com/2015/03/21/cops-shoot-man-at-calgary-peace-rally.

Woolfrey, Cathy. "Legislative Reports." *Canadian Parliamentary Review*, vol. 10, no. 2, 1987, http://www.revparl.ca/english/issue.asp?param=121&art=732.

Wright, Handel. "Between Global Demise and National Complacent Hegemony: Multiculturalism and Multicultural Education in a Moment of Danger." In Handel Wright, Michael Singh, and Richard Race (eds.). *Precarious International Multicultural Education: Hegemony, Dissent and Rising Alternatives*. Rotterdam, Sense, 2012, pp. 3-13.

Wright, Stephen, and Donald Taylor. "The social psychology of cultural diversity: Social prejudice, stereotyping and discrimination." In Michael Hogg and Joel Cooper (eds.). *The SAGE Handbook of Social Psychology, Concise Student Edition*. Los Angeles, Sage, 2009, pp. 361-87.

Younglai, Rachelle. "Alberta job woes deepen in largest loss for province since global economic crisis." *The Globe and Mail*, 25 March, 2015, https://www.theglobeandmail.com/report-on-business/economy/jobs/alberta-loses-63500-jobs-in-first-eight-months-of-2015/article27037057/.

Zaami, Mariama. *Experiences of Social Exclusion and Inclusion among Black African Immigrant Youth in Calgary, Alberta*. PhD thesis, Calgary, University of Calgary, 2017.

Zine, Jasmin. *Canadian Islamic Schools: Unravelling the Politics of Faith, Gender, Knowledge, and Identity*. Toronto, University of Toronto Press, 2008.

APPENDICES

APPENDIX A

The Research Participants[1]

Partici-pants	Education	Employment before immigration to Canada	Employment in Alberta at the time of the interviews	Employment in 2016
1	-BA, MA, PhD in sending country -Graduate degree[2] in Canada	A good job[3] in sending country	With a Black Francophone[4] organization	Underemployed[5]
2	-BA in sending country -BA in Canada	Business owner in sending country	Underemployed	Unemployed
3	-BA, MA, PhD in sending country -College diploma in Canada	A good job in sending country	With a Black Francophone organization	Underemployed
4	BA in sending country 1	A good job in sending country	With a Black Francophone organization	Unemployed
5	-BA in sending country -BA & Graduate degree in Canada	A good job in sending country	2 part-time jobs	Unemployed

1. I did not divulge the participants' gender and exact employment to protect their anonymity.
2. Participants obtained MA and/or PhD degrees in Canada, but I do not specify the exact degree to protect their anonymity.
3. A "good job" means well-paying employment commensurate with qualifications. Examples are work with international organizations, as professionals, or business owners.
4. These organizations are created and led by Black Francophones. They receive little funding, are not well paid, and their future is uncertain.
5. "Underemployed" means they were over-qualified for the work they were doing. Examples of such jobs are taxi drivers, factory workers, maids, and security guards.

Partici-pants	Education	Employment before immigration to Canada	Employment in Alberta at the time of the interviews	Employment in 2016
6	-BA, MA in sending country -Graduate degree in Canada	A good job in sending country	Owned a business	Unemployed
7	-BA, MA in sending country -Graduate degree in Canada	A good job in sending country	With a Black Francophone organization	Underemployed
8	-BA in sending country -BA, graduate degree in Canada	A good job in sending country	Underemployed	Returned to sending country
9	BA, MA in sending country	N/A	With a mainstream organization[6]	Underemployed
10	-BA in sending country -College diploma in Canada	A good job in sending country	A good contract job	With a Black Francophone organization
11	-BA in sending country -BA, graduate degree in Canada	A good job in sending country	Underemployed	Underemployed
12	-BA, MA in sending country -BA, graduate degree in Canada	Underemployed	A good contract job	Underemployed
13	-BA in sending country -College diploma in Canada	A good job in sending country	Underemployed	Returned to sending country
14	-BA in sending country -BA, graduate degree in Canada	A good job in sending country	A good contract job	Unemployed
15	-BA, graduate degree in sending country -BA in Canada	A good job in sending country	With a mainstream organization	Unemployed
16	-BA in sending country -College diploma in Canada	-A good job in sending country -A good job in Africa[7]	A good job	With a Black Francophone organization

6.   These are mainstream Francophone organizations and institutions.
7.   In an African country other than their sending country.

Partici-pants	Education	Employment before immigration to Canada	Employment in Alberta at the time of the interviews	Employment in 2016
17	-BA in sending country -Graduate degree in Canada	A good job in Africa	Underemployed	Same job
18	-BA in Africa -BA in Canada	A good job in Africa	With a Black Francophone organization	Underemployed, part-time job
19	-BA, graduate degree in Africa -College diploma in Canada	Business owner in Africa	With a Black Francophone organization	Unemployed
20	BA, graduate degree in France	A good contract job in France	A good contract job	Underemployed
21	-BA in sending country -BA in Canada	-A good job in sending country -Unemployed in France	Underemployed	Same job
22	-BA in sending country -BA in Canada	-A good job in sending country -Underemployed in France	With a Black Francophone organization	Underemployed, part-time job
23	-BA in Africa -BA in France -Graduate degree in Canada	-A good job in sending country -Underemployed in France	Underemployed	Same job
24	-BA, graduate degree in France -Graduate degree in Canada	Underemployed in France	Owned a business	Returned to sending country
25	-BA in sending country -MA in France -Graduate degree in Canada	-A good job in sending country -Underemployed in France	With a Black Francophone organization	Underemployed
26	-BA in sending country -BA in France -BA in Canada	-A good job in sending country -Underemployed in France	With a Black Francophone organization	Underemployed, part time job
27	-BA in sending country -BA in France	Underemployed in France	Underemployed	Unemployed

Partici-pants	Education	Employment before immigration to Canada	Employment in Alberta at the time of the interviews	Employment in 2016
28	-BA in Africa -Graduate degree in Canada	-A good job in sending country -Unemployed in France	Underemployed	Same job
29	-BA in sending country -Graduate degree in Africa -Graduate degree in France -College diploma in Canada	Unemployed in France	With a Black Francophone organization	Unemployed
30	BA in France	Underemployed in France	Underemployed	Unemployed
31	-BA in France -College diploma in Canada	Underemployed in France	A good job	Underemployed
32	-BA, graduate degree in Europe[8] -College diploma in Canada	Unemployed in Europe	Underemployed	Unemployed
33	-BA, graduate degree in Asia -College diploma in Canada	Unemployed in Asia	With a Black Francophone organization	Unemployed
34	BA, graduate degree in Canada (IS)[9]	N/A	With a Black Francophone organization	N/A[10]
35	BA in Canada (IS)	N/A	Underemployed	Underemployed
36	BA in Canada (GUSC)[11]	N/A	With a Black Francophone organization	Unemployed
37	Dropped out of high school (GUSC)	Underemployed in Asia	Underemployed	Underemployed
38	BA in Canada (GUSC)	N/A	Underemployed	Underemployed

8.   In a European country other than France.
9.   They came to Canada as an international student.
10. I was not able to reach the participant.
11. They came to Canada at a young age, grew up and were schooled in Canada.

Partici-pants	Education	Employment before immigration to Canada	Employment in Alberta at the time of the interviews	Employment in 2016
39	BA in Canada (GUSC)	N/A	Underemployed	Underemployed
40	BA, graduate degree in Canada (GUSC)	N/A	-With a Black Francophone organization -Part-time student	With the same organization
41	2 BAs in Canada (GUSC)	N/A	Underemployed	Retuned to a province in Canada
42	College diploma in Canada (GUSC)	N/A	Underemployed	Underemployed

Printed by Imprimerie Gauvin
Gatineau, Québec